Coffeehouse Fo

Peter Clark

Suzanne
To you
from me !

Peter Clark
France
2010

Twopenny Press
2010

First published in the UK in 2010 by:

Twopenny Press
www.twopennypress.co.uk

ISBN 978-0-9561703-2-3

Illustrations by Owen Robertson

Typeset in Adobe Garamond, designed and produced by
Gilmour Print, www.gilmourprint.co.uk

Contents

Introduction   1

Middle East
    Letter from Tel Aviv   5
    Palestinians and Israelis   9
    Israeli Diversity   13
    Christians and Jews under Islam   17
    Despair of the Heart   19
    Rentier Kingdom   21
    Food in Jordan   24
    The Future of Freya Stark   26
    Syrians in Two Worlds   32
    Ottoman Aleppo   36
    Three Views of Damascus   38
    The Shahrur Phenomenon   42
    Syria Seen by Outsiders   50
    A Turk from the North   53
    Cilician Armenia   55
    Kuwait and Iraq 1971   68

Sudan
    The Hicks Pasha Expedition   77
    The Battle of Omdurman   90
    'Dervish Wars'   105
    The Scars of Culture   107
    Greenlaw's Suakin   109
    Mohamed Omer Beshir   111

Arabia
    Tim Mackintosh-Smith   117
    The United Arab Emirates   121
    The Peacemaker   123

Muslims in Britain

The Background of British Muslims 129
Islamic Influence on Architecture in Britain 1800-2000 131

People

Edward Gibbon 141
Violet Gordon 144
Farid Hanania 146
Ulfat Idilbi 148
Peter Shinnie 150
Lord Henniker 154
Abd al-Salam al-Ujaili 157
Nazik al-Mala'ika 159
Fatma Moussa Mahmoud 161
Nizar Kabbani 163
Paul Bergne 166
Faris Glubb 168
Sa'dallah Wannus 170
Mahmoud Darwish 172
Mamdouh Udwan 177
Sargon Boulus 179

Literature

Marmaduke Pickthall and *Said the Fisherman* 183
Marmaduke Pickthall and his Yemen Novel 190
Pickthall's Busy Year 1931-32 200
Marginal Literatures of the Middle East 203
Agatha Christie and the Arab World 214
Translation and Responsibility 227

Index

Index 239

For Theresa, my best friend

Introduction

For over forty years I have been involved in cultural relations in the Middle East, thirty plus years as an employee of the British Council and ten as an independent consultant. I spent the great majority of my years with the British Council in seven different Arab countries – Jordan, Lebanon, Sudan, Yemen, Tunisia, the United Arab Emirates and Syria. Since retiring from the British Council in 1999 I have paid frequent trips to the region. As tourist or on assignments I have visited all Arab countries as well as Turkey, Israel and Iran.

An academic training (as a historian) made me intensely curious about the people and places I got to know. From 1970 to 1971 I studied Arabic at the Middle East Centre for Arab Studies in Lebanon. In each of the countries I worked I read whatever I could in the languages to which I had access – English, French and Arabic. In the 1970s I started an alternative career as writer, lecturer and translator. As well as translating from Arabic six works of fiction and two of history, I have written and edited several books. I have also produced articles for newspapers and journals, reviewed books and given talks about corners of Middle Eastern matters that have interested me. In the 1970s I started to write obituaries first for *The Times* and then later for *The Guardian*. There were people – often Arab writers – whose lives and work I felt were of significance, and should be known beyond their particular artistic and professional circles. All this part-time writing has occupied a territory between journalism and scholarship.

The present collection, I think, sheds light on aspects of the Middle East. The trivial can often cast light on issues that may preoccupy the headlines. In the Middle East there are many narratives. Some of them have become dehumanising ideologies. The only line I wish to promote is that the region is made up of a third of a billion individuals, each one with his or her own story, often mundane, but punctuated by joys and tragedies. Individual families have transmitted memories of the past. Personal experience and the historic past are interwoven in a way that defies those strident certainties that idealise, marginalise or demonise people.

This collection has no central theme. The pieces are roughly grouped according to a general subject. I have prefaced each piece with a note about the circumstances of its composition. My hope is that any reader will have their understanding, appreciation and enjoyment of a complex region deepened, and will pause and reflect before making assertions about people or places.

Every effort has been made to secure copyright permission. Any earlier publication is acknowledged in the introduction to each piece.

Peter Clark
Frome, Somerset, England
2010

Middle East

I owe my interest in the Middle East to Sir Anthony Eden, not because he had been an outstanding Arabic scholar when he was at university, but because of the Suez War of October 1956. I was at school at the time and became involved in angry discussions with fellow seventeen year olds. I was in a small minority in finding the whole venture wrong, but I also started to read about the background of modern Egypt and what was known as the Arab-Israeli dispute.

At university I became a friend of Ahmad al-Duaij, a Kuwaiti, from whom I learnt much about the attitudes of his generation. I was a student of nineteenth century history and did a special subject on the career of the nineteenth century Prime Minister, W E Gladstone. I became totally absorbed in writing a paper on the Egyptian background of Urabi Pasha, whose revolt led to the British occupation of Egypt in 1882 during Gladstone's government.

It was my intention after graduating in History and Politics from the University of Keele in 1962 to spend a year in either Paris or Vienna and learn a language thoroughly. I chanced to hear about some earlier Keele graduates who had gone to Ankara College in Turkey to teach. The more I thought about it, the more I was interested. I was recruited as a mathematics teacher and spent a year based in the Turkish capital. During that year I travelled extensively around Turkey and also to Syria, Lebanon, Jordan (which then included Jerusalem) and Egypt. I was fascinated by everything. Half a century later the fascination persists.

Letter from Tel Aviv

This appeared in *The Times Literary Supplement* of 1 September 2000.

I was apprehensive when the Israeli official stamped my passport, stuffed with visas from Arab countries and with evidence of five years' residence in Syria.

'Why have you been in Israel?'

'I was invited to give lectures at Beit Berl College.'

'Do you have the letter of introduction?'

Fortunately I had. The official was satisfied and I was permitted to check in for departure.

In 1997, sponsored by the British Council, I had made a lecture tour of the Palestinian territories. I talked about translation in Gaza, Nablus, Hebron and Ramallah. After that trip, an Israeli friend, Dr Hannah Amit-Kochavi, told me I should also visit Israel. I said that, if invited, I would happily accept. I was, I did, and here I find myself in the departure lounge after an intensive week.

As well as lecturing, I have met writers of Arabic, both Palestinians in Israel and Jews who have migrated from Arab countries. The most interesting of the last group is Samir Naqqash, who has persisted in writing in Arabic and sees himself as part of a wider Arab culture. I had lunch with Samir at his flat in Petah Tikvah. He has lived in Iran and India, as well as Iraq and Israel, and has written novels, short stories and plays. Some of his work has been published by the Association of Jewish Academics from Iraq. His writing is not easy, and very little has been translated into English; he uses the Baghdad Jewish dialect of his childhood, and much of the action takes place within the Iraqi Jewish community. His works are psychological, intense and innovative. He is held in higher regard in Arab countries than in Israel and has been the subject of Arab theses. Naguib Mahfouz has described him as 'one of the greatest living artists writing in Arabic today.'

Samir feels at home in Arab countries, and has made many visits to Egypt. He has refused to write in Hebrew or to take a less Arab-sounding name, and has been saddened by his student daughter, whose political sympathies are more with the right-wing settlers of the West Bank. I asked him about contemporary Palestinian literature. He reads the literary journal, *al-Karmel*, but feels that much Palestinian literature is preoccupied with the experience of dispossession.

'Much is committed to time and place. Take that commitment away and not a lot is left. Literature should be either personal or universal.'

'Is there not a built-in difficulty in writing in a Baghdad Jewish dialect?' I asked. 'The potential readership must be constantly diminishing.'

Samir pointed out that he provides a glossary; indeed, each page of his Baghdad novels has twenty or so footnotes. He thinks a universal message can emerge from the crucible of particularism – a message of the individual confronting the system, any system, physical or psychological.

Nazareth is the principal city of one of the main Arab areas of Israel and the one with the highest proportion of Christians. Pilgrimage centres dominate the old city. I had lunch with Salem Jubran, a poet in his fifties who has repeatedly been in prison or under house arrest for political activity. I asked him what the limits of freedom of expression were today. 'Things have improved,' he said. 'Before 1966 when the Arab parts of the country were under military rule, a love poem was interpreted as code for Palestinian patriotism and the poet liable to arrest. Even prison food got better over the years. Today the Israeli authorities are watchful and are sensitive to what they interpret as "incitement".'

Carmela Shehada collected me the next day. She is from Shafa Amr, a Galilean town with a mixed population of Christian, Muslims and Druze. She took me to her home town to meet her family, and we were joined by Yoram Mirun, an Israeli Jew, who has been a teacher most of his life, and his wife. Carmela and Yoram have together produced a volume of popular Palestinian stories.

After lunch we drove into the countryside. Many Palestinian villages have been uprooted and demolished. I wanted to see the site of Birwa, the village where Mahmoud Darwish was born. Much of his poetry invokes the local landscape, with its stones and plants, above all *za'tar*, thyme, which has become as symbolic of Palestinian identity as the head-dress. I wanted to see the source of his inspiration. It was Salem Jubran who wrote, in the translation of Lina Jayyusi and Naomi Shihab Nye:

> You can uproot the trees
>   from my village mountain
>   which embraces the moon.
> You can plough my village houses under
>   leaving no traces of their walls.

You can confiscate the rebec,
	rip away the chords and burn the wood
but you cannot suffocate my tunes –
for I am the lover of this land
and the singer of wind and rain.

This could be a description of the site of Birwa. Rocks and undergrowth cover a hill. We walked through the scrubland. There was no trace of any buildings, but we did come across the remains of an oil-press amid the undergrowth – too big either to destroy or remove. I gazed at it and saw the whole village coming to life in my mind's eye. I could feel the resigned pain of Palestinians who had been ethnically cleansed. 'If you see Mahmoud Darwish,' said Yoram, 'tell him a Jew showed you the way to Birwa.'

In Jerusalem, I had an introduction to Betsy Rosenberg. I turned up at her flat at Rehavia. Betsy is originally from Philadelphia and has lived in Jerusalem for thirty years. She has translated novels by David Grossman, but is also a poet and has been a professional musician. She exudes enthusiasm and excitement about literature, her work, the arts and Jerusalem. She had nothing to do with politics, but we talked about Syria. 'You must meet Mrs Bakhshi,' she said. 'She was born in Aleppo nearly ninety years ago, and is always talking about the beauty of her birthplace. She hopes there will be peace with Syria so she can go back.'

Betsy made a quick phone call, and we walked the couple of hundred yards to a modest flat where Mrs Bakhshi received us. Over Turkish coffee we talked in Arabic. Aleppo has lost none of its charm, I assured her. She talked of the *hara*, the Jewish quarter, and we worked out places we both loved and families we both knew. She last saw Aleppo in 1943.

I was at Baqa al-Gharbiyeh last night, the guest of Jamil al-Ghana'im. We spent the evening on a rooftop, drinking coffee and eating sweets and fruit and talking with local writers and translators. Among them was Muhammad Hamza Ghana'im, a younger relative and former pupil of Jamil. Muhammad translates between Arabic and Hebrew, composes poetry in Arabic and writes for the Haifa Arabic newspaper, *al-Ittihad*. He interviewed me for this paper with an Israeli efficiency – with brisk, direct and searching questions. Muhammad has translated some poems of Mahmoud Darwish into Hebrew for a new publisher in Tel Aviv, the Andalus Press, which aims to bring the best of contemporary Arabic literature to Hebrew readers. The volume of Darwish is the first in the series.

Palestinians in Israel, I learned, feel isolated from the rest of the Arab world. It is easier to maintain contact with Palestinians and Arabs in Europe and America, or with sympathetic Jewish Israelis. 'Yet we are nearly a million and a half people, more than the numbers of Kuwaitis or Omanis,' Muhammad said. 'We are highly educated and have undergone unique experiences. Partly as a result of our isolation we have been affected by Israeli and Hebrew culture. We have learnt Hebrew at school and all our dealings with Israeli officialdom are in Hebrew. Yes, we have become fluent in the language, indeed we have internalised Hebrew. We can read Hebrew literature with no less appreciation than an Israeli Jew. Samih al-Qasim, after Mahmoud, our leading poet, who has been a member of the Communist Party, has translated modern Hebrew poetry into Arabic. Nor is it surprising that Palestinians like Anton Shammas have won literary prizes for Hebrew work. Hebrew is part of our cultural environment – rather as North Africans may write in Arabic, but also operate successfully in a French-language environment. Their Arab identity has not thereby been challenged.'

The airport lounge is more European or American than Middle Eastern. The bookshop has plenty of Israeli and Jewish literature, but no Palestinian literature. Yet at least one sixth of the population has a culture and a memory that is quite distinctive. They share with other Palestinians a sense of loss and dispossession. But they have had lives of adjustment and accommodation, rather than of slogans and confrontation. Moreover, their presence is an embarrassment to many Israelis, an awkward challenge to their legitimacy.

A call for the London flight breaks up my thoughts. I must fly.

When I was speaking with Mrs Bakhshi, she suddenly turned to me and said I was not very good at Arabic. It was true that I could not follow all she was saying. Afterwards I learned why. Betsy told me she was switching from Arabic to Hebrew, probably unconsciously. Betsy could understand the Hebrew bits but not the Arabic, an exact reversal of what I was getting from the conversation.

I was in Aleppo the following year. I bought some old postcards of the city and arranged for Betsy to pass them on to Mrs Bakhshi.

Palestinians and Israelis

This was an article reviewing two books: *Israeli and Palestinian Identities in History and Literature*, edited by Kamal Abdel-Malek and David C Jacobsen, published by Macmillan, Basingstoke and London, 1999, and *Modern Palestinian Literature and Culture* by Ami Elad-Bouskila, published by Frank Cass, London, 1999. The review appeared in *The Times Literary Supplement*, 16 February 2001.

Emile Habiby was a Palestinian novelist who lived and died in Haifa, promoting the rights of Palestinians in Israel as journalist, politician and novelist. In his novel translated into English as *The Secret Life of Saeed the Pessoptimist*, the narrator, Saeed, tells how, during the June 1967 war, the Arabic language service of Radio Israel called on defeated Arabs to raise white flags on their homes. Saeed decided that he was a 'defeated Arab' and put a white flag on a broomstick on his house in Haifa. For this 'extravagant symbol of my loyalty to the state', Saeed was taken off to prison.

Habiby's joke represents the humour of the repressed, the cornered. It is akin to classical Yiddish humour. Both *Israeli and Palestinian Identities in History and Literature* and *Modern Palestinian Literature and Culture* draw attention to other parallels between Jewish culture and its successor, Israeli literature, on the one hand, and Palestinian literature on the other. Victimhood is a common theme. Both literatures are implicitly political. Both deal with stereotypes of the Other. These two books look at the paradoxes and dilemmas of Saeed's cultural world. Both were prepared well before the recent intensification of the crisis between Palestinians and Israelis, during which a large number of Palestinian Israelis have been killed by Israeli security forces. Both books examine the cultural consequences of Jewish and Palestinian Israelis living together and interacting with each other.

Israeli and Palestinian Identities in History and Literature is a collection of papers given at a 1997 Conference at Brown University, where, during the 1990s, the editors, Kamal Abdel-Malek and David C Jacobsen, devised an undergraduate course on 'Arabs and Jews: Their encounters in contemporary and Arabic literature'. Most of the papers cover aspects of contemporary Israeli culture – the cinema, the fiction of the 1948 and 1967 wars, and the psychological obstacles to Israeli reconciliation with Palestinians. *Modern Palestinian Literature and Culture* includes one paper from the other book, rewritten and updated. The title of the latter book is misleading. It is not a

9

comprehensive account of Palestinian literature. Poets like Fadwa Tuqan and Mahmoud Darwish and novelists such as Liyana Badr and Yahya Yahklif receive just a mention. In seven perceptive chapters the author concentrates on writers based inside Israel, especially on those Palestinians who write in Hebrew and on polemical literature inspired by the intifada.

In the Brown University collection of essays, Sammy Smooha examines opinion polls since 1976 and argues from them that Palestinians have become reconciled to life in Israel: in 1995 82.7 per cent 'preferred life in Israel to any other country', and 95.8 per cent would not consider moving to a Palestinian state. This conclusion can be interpreted in a way not intended by Professor Smooha. It does not mean Palestinians are attached to being second-class citizens in a Jewish state. For Palestinians, Israel is a geographical reality rather than a political ideal. They certainly do not wish to leave Nazareth, the villages of Galilee, or Beersheba, or even Haifa and other mixed cities. All evidence points to an intense Palestinian attachment to their villages and homelands. Palestinians in Israel have no wish to migrate to Gaza or Jericho. Those cities are already full of people who 'would prefer' to live in geographic Israel but have been denied their right of return.

But there has been a cultural 'Israelisation' of the Palestinians inside Israel. This should come as no surprise. Israel has impinged heavily on the lives of all Palestinians. Palestinians – like Israelis and Arabs throughout the region – have enjoyed the benefits of an expanded education system. They have learned Hebrew from primary school. All their dealings with authority have been conducted in Hebrew. All have access to the Hebrew media. Just as local Arabic has affected modern Hebrew, so code-switching in Palestinian Arabic is common. Palestinians have benefited from a society that, with major qualifications, is relatively open. Palestinians write for the Hebrew press. An Arab press expresses a diversity of opinions. The daily Communist newspaper, *al-Ittihad*, is comprehensive and lively in its coverage. Israel has much in common with many European countries – a rational infrastructure, a work ethic, a belief in the rule of law. Palestinians are subject to discrimination socially, economically and politically. However, means for redress – in theory at least – exist, and Palestinians in Israel have many Jewish allies. Politically, Palestinians in Israel aspire to equal rights. They have had no choice but to accept Israel as a reality. Over two generations they have acquired strategies for survival. These have included a fluency in the Hebrew language. It is not surprising that the language has been internalised for many Palestinians to the extent that it has become a vehicle for self-expression and imaginative writings.

Ami Elad-Bouskila looks at the language choices Palestinians have in writing novels and poetry. In the past twenty years, Hebrew became a literary language. Some writers, born after the birth of the State of Israel – Na'im Araydi, Anton Shammas, Siham Dawud, Salman Masalha – write extensively, poetry and fiction, in Hebrew. Others, such as the older Emile Habiby and Samih al-Qasim, write novels and poetry in Arabic, but non-literary work in Hebrew. Most of the Palestinians who write in Hebrew are Christian or Druze. The latter are more integrated into Israeli society, not least because they are subject to compulsory military service.

The phenomenon of Palestinians writing in Hebrew has caused unease among both Arabs and Israeli Jews. For some Arabs it is seen as a betrayal of Arab culture. Thirty years ago, one of the first historians of modern Palestinian literature, Ghasan Kanafani, wrote of the 'literature of resistance'. To write in the language of the enemy was an abandonment of resistance, a surrender, a betrayal. Zionist Israelis see the revival of Hebrew, not unreasonably, as an extraordinary linguistic miracle of modern Jewry. For Palestinians to adopt Hebrew for literary purposes undermines that notion of exclusive possession of the language.

Motivations for writing in Hebrew vary. In 1962 an Arabic novel by Atallah Mansur was published by Histadrut, the Israeli Jewish trade union movement. This was harshly condemned by the Hebrew press for being anti-Israeli. Mansur then chose to get his own back with a novel in Hebrew. His novel was a scathing attack on the central Zionist institution of the kibbutz. To his bewildered embarrassment, this Hebrew novel had praise heaped on it by Israeli critics. One explanation is that by using Hebrew, a writer in Israel has greater freedom. Mansur's first book 'was reviewed by the so-called experts on Arab affairs, who saw their role as censors of the enemy'. His second novel was reviewed by liberal literary critics, practising the norms of a Western open society.

A generation later, the novel translated into English as *Arabesques*, by Anton Shammas, was written in Hebrew partly because, Shammas himself argues, he was inhibited about writing about village life in Arabic. 'I certainly would have been more cautious', he said in an interview (in Hebrew) in 1988, 'had I written in Arabic about the village. The Hebrew language paradoxically seems to give me security. I would not have had this freedom had I written in Arabic, because

11

what would my aunt and uncle have said?' Now, his aunt and uncle would have been of a generation that had not been schooled in Hebrew. His nephew and niece, on the other hand, would have no such difficulty in reading the novel in Hebrew: evidence of a hebraisation of Palestinian society.

Dr Elad-Bouskila has many interesting insights and observations. He argues that there are three Palestinian literatures, produced by people in Israel itself, in the Occupied Territories, and in the greater Palestinian Diaspora. The social, political and cultural circumstances of each have been distinctive. He might have divided the Palestinians of the Diaspora into those in the Arab world and those outside. Palestinians outside the Arab world enjoy far greater cultural freedom. And some – like the Palestinian American poets Suheir Hammad and Naomi Shihab Nye – write in English.

In discussing the bilingualism of Palestinian writers, Elad-Bouskila talks of the significance of translation. Anton Shammas and Salman Masalha have translated Hebrew poetry into English; Samih al-Qasim has translated Hebrew poetry into Arabic. An area of intimate cultural overlap of interests and activity exists in Israel and is one of the few gleams of encouragement in an otherwise grim situation. Awareness of Hebrew culture among Palestinians is more widespread than that of Palestinian culture among Israeli Jews. It is possible for Jews to live and work in Tel Aviv and not to meet or be aware of Palestinians.

Ami Elad-Bouskila teaches Arabic at Beit Berl College. His appreciation of trends and nuances in Palestinian literature and culture within Israel is profound and generally sympathetic. A Palestinian might, however, object to his use of 'Temple Mount' for al-Haram al-Sharif. The Palestinian would also wonder why he does not mention that the assassination of the second-in-command of the PLO, Abu Jihad, in Tunis in 1988, was carried out by Israeli agents. This was, after all, a major factor in his 'being raised to a level of a military, political and national myth, who continues to act after death as a symbol and model for Palestinians fighting in Jerusalem for independence.'

Israeli Diversity

This reviewed two more books on aspects of Israeli identity. One was called *Israeli Identity: In Search of a Successor to the Pioneer, Tsabar and Settler* by Lilly Weissbrod, published by Frank Cass, London, 2002. The other was *The Other Israel: Voices of Refusal and Dissent*, edited by Roane Carey and Jonathan Shainin, published by the New Press, New York, 2002. The review article was published in *The Times Literary Supplement*, 18 July 2003.

Committed opponents of Zionism often fall into the trap of seeing Israel and the Zionist movement as both monolithic and unchanging. The Israeli narrative similarly imposes a continuity, if not to a biblical existence, at least to the pioneers of modern Zionist settlement in the 1880s. Opposition to this narrative is often ascribed to anti-Semitism, but in fact there has been a continuous counter-narrative of victimhood: Zionism always aiming at the displacement of the Palestinian Arab population. The process, it is feared, is not over and statements made by members of the current Sharon government of 'transfer' add to the anxiety that the Zionist project aims at control of all the land of Palestine without the burden of a Palestinian population. The two books under review show that there is a more nuanced reality.

Lilly Weissbrod is an Israeli who has spent many years outside Israel and is able to see the changing self-perceptions of Israelis with some detachment. In *Israeli Identity*, she traces a century of Zionist thought, the different strands and also the responses to events – two World Wars, the Holocaust, Independence, immigration from Islamic countries, the wars of 1956, 1967 and 1973, changing Palestinian policies, the two intifadas, the peace process, the murder of Yitzak Rabin and the disillusion of the present day. She brings the story up to the election of Ariel Sharon in early 2001. It is clear that the story is ongoing, and an ideological alliance between the neoconservatives of the Bush administration and the Likud Party brings a new identity to Israel as a bastion and ally against international terrorism. A new identity, and a new response: this is also the theme of *The Other Israel*, a collection of dissident voices from historians, journalists and peacenik activists. It underlines the diversity of Israeli political thought.

Modern Zionism has its roots in Judaism but grew out of European nationalism. Its emergence in the nineteenth and twentieth centuries owes a debt to post-Enlightenment ideas of creating the ideal society. Israel is a supreme example of social engineering, with even a newly fashioned language.

But there are also many parallels with Islamic ideas, not least the notion of the good community upheld by law. The Zionist intellectual debate was self-contained and inward looking. Although there was a Christian and humanitarian (but not a Muslim) Zionism, there was rarely dialogue between non-Jewish and Jewish Zionists. Rather there were tactical alliances, with first British and later American supporters.

Dr Weissbrod examines much of the internal Zionist debate with clarity and insight. She sees three successive waves, reflected in the subtitle of her book, that have dominated the sense of Israeli self-identity. First were the pioneers who settled from the 1880s with little idea that they would form the acorn of a modern state. There had, of course, been Jewish migrants into Palestine for centuries, from Andalusia and Morocco, from Yemen and from Europe, but they came as networking individuals rather than as a movement. The second generation, the *tsabar* – more familiarly the sabras – became the prototype of the Zionist from the 1930s to the 1960s. He (usually a he) was self-contained, a would-be reluctant soldier, secular and socialist, a child of the kibbutz, linked culturally and politically with progressives in Europe. The sabra was well represented in the senior ranks of the defence forces who, with their 'purity of arms', replaced the pioneer as the symbol of national regeneration. The Israeli Labor Party was their political vehicle. They aspired to build the ideal just society. The partition in 1947-48 came as a boon. They accepted this and did not demand the whole of Palestine: 'agreement to partition was interpreted as a supreme ethical act, a gesture of magnanimity in line with the Messianic principle of perfect justice. Thereupon, it absolved the State of Israel of any further moral obligation towards Palestinian Arabs'.

A third trend asserted itself after the 1967 war: the settlers. It is sometimes forgotten today that the conquest of the whole of Palestine with another million Palestinian Arab subjects after the June 1967 war took many Israelis by surprise. There was a conflict between those who believed in the inalienable God-given Jewish legacy of the whole of Palestine, and those who upheld progressive ideas of democracy. To the latter, Eretz Israel could be either Jewish or democratic, but not both. The settler movement was not encouraged by the post-1967 Labor governments. But their move to centre stage occurred with the rise of Likud, the 1977 election of Menachim Begin as Prime Minister and the consolidation of his authority in 1981. Most of the arguments about Israeli self-identity took place among Jews of European origin. The 'orientals' (as Dr Weissbrod calls them) had their own histories, of upheaval and displacement

14

rather than of European persecution. But Begin in 1981 brought them over permanently to Likud. Jews from Muslim countries were more punctilious in their religious obligations than the generality of western secular Jews who formed the backbone of the Labor Party. Begin was able to exploit a religiosity that converged with his forward policy of settlements.

There was even less debate with the people of the country, the Palestinian Arabs. In the early years, most Zionists either ignored them or saw them as an obstacle. It was only in 1930 that the case for a Jewish presence in Palestine was argued on the grounds that Arabs had a large homeland in neighbouring countries. Thereafter Palestinians were outmanoeuvred, marginalised, won over, patronised, or demonised and conquered. There has been an enduring school of thought, represented in the present Israeli cabinet, that has wanted to expel them. But the Palestinians have not been without their Zionist friends. From the beginning one school of thought has envisaged a bi-national state. This school has never been near the mainstream of Zionist thought, though, paradoxically, the modern State of Israel is in actual fact a bi-national state albeit with an overwhelming bias to one nation. Even so, the Sharon cabinet is the first in Israel's history to include a Palestinian Arab.

The heirs of the believers in bi-nationalism are represented in *The Other Israel*, edited by Roane Carey and Jonathan Shainin, a collection of nearly forty short essays, some of which have been published elsewhere. They are an angry repudiation of current neo-Zionist ideology and practice. With a foreword by Tom Segev, the contributors include the historians Avi Shlaim and Ilan Pappé, the journalist Amira Hass, the novelist David Grossman and several soldiers who have refused to serve in occupied Palestine. These essays are expressed in a context of both Jewish history and universal values. 'I was raised on two value systems', says Assaf Oren. 'One was the ethical code and the other tribal code, and I naively believed that the two could coexist.'

A constant theme is how the debate on Israel has changed since 1967. In spite of the huge asymmetry of power between Israel and the Palestinians, the Israeli establishment argues that the threats from Palestinian terrorism are a real threat to the state, and that a massive military response is the only course of action that can avert the state's extinction. 'I cannot be convinced,' writes Shamai Leibowitz, 'that the existence of the state of Israel hangs on the killing of children in refugee camps.'

The collection was prepared after the Jenin campaign of April 2002. Amira Hass gives an unemotional description of her visit to the camp after the Israeli army's invasion. Other essays record the daily humiliations and suffering, direct and indirect, of Palestinians under occupation. Activists document campaigns of Israelis working with Palestinians in their unequal struggle against the demolition of houses and orchards. Several record conscientious resistance to military service in the Occupied Territories.

The Other Israel offers no solutions, no 'road map'. It challenges the received notion of Ehud Barak's 'generosity' at Camp David in 2000, and is full of despair at the prevailing climate of Likud negativism. But perhaps through the anger of the contributors we can see hope. Ariel Sharon, on his election, promised security. Palestinian resistance, 'terrorism', has increased in proportion to the aggressive responses of the present Israeli government. Jews possibly feel more at risk in Israel than anywhere else in the world. Sharon's policies have destroyed one of the fundamental pillars on which the State of Israel was founded: the provision of a safe haven for Jews. There must be another way, and contributors to *The Other Israel* show that there are plenty of Israelis who wish to live in peace and harmony with Palestinians. Though currently unfashionable, they also – as can be seen from Lilly Weissbrod's book – are the heirs of an important strain of Jewish Zionist ideology.

Christians and Jews under Islam

This review of *Christians and Jews under Islam* by Youssef Courbage and Philippe Fargues, translated by Judy Mabro, published by I B Tauris, London, 1997, appeared in *Asian Affairs* in 1998.

This study, originally published in French, consists of a series of interrelated essays on aspects of the demography of the Arab world and Turkey. The title is thus a bit of a misnomer. However, by examining the scanty demographic evidence, of variable reliability, the writers come forward with several hypotheses that modify some political interpretations of the last thousand years or so.

Available demographic data suggest that Islamic society, both of the Levantine Arab world until the time of the Crusades, and of the Ottoman Empire until the end of the nineteenth century, was multicultural. The Arab conquests of Syria guaranteed the rights of Christians and Jews. Over the centuries, conversions to Islam took place for reasons of convenience, conviction or opportunism, rarely by compulsion. The Crusaders' confrontational intolerance took no account of the fact that many Syrians had converted to Islam only in the previous century. Whereas the Fatimids and the Ayubids were tolerant towards minorities, the successful Mamluk reaction to the Crusaders was repressive and exclusive. Moreover, in North Africa, the authors observe, 'official history hides, as though it were shameful, the thousand years during which Berbers were Christian.'

Ottoman history has, for most of the twentieth century, been seen in a negative light. The Ottoman Empire was a loser in the First World War. Successor states in the Balkans, in the Arab world and in Anatolia itself, owed their legitimacy to a repudiation of the Ottomans. But this book adds to the revisionist view of the Ottoman Empire, which was one of the most successful Islamic political institutions ever.

For Christians and Jews, the Ottoman centuries were an era of prosperity. 'The Jewish population doubled and the Christian tripled.' The minorities, who were generally urban-dwelling, enjoyed the greater prosperity of the towns. The Ottoman rulers involved the minorities in power, political and economic, and welcomed minorities persecuted elsewhere. Cults were shared. But the composition of migration changed from the nineteenth century.

Christians were among the out-migrants. The newcomers from the Balkans or the Caucasus were Muslim.

The First World War was a multicultural disaster for the Ottoman Empire. Three million Christians were massacred or displaced. The exchange of population after the Greek-Turkish war of 1921-22 was of Greek Muslims and Anatolian Christians. The Republic of Turkey, in spite of its laicism, has been culturally Islamic, and Christian minorities have continued to emigrate.

Courbage and Fargues also examine the demography of Palestine/Israel and make fascinating contrasts with other imposed states – the Crusader Kingdoms and French Algeria. In each case the new politics relied on immigration and a sense of exclusiveness. The ideology of each state was based on confrontation, to the extent that opportunities for cooperation have been lost. Each time the response from the indigenous marginalised people has been violent. For Israelis the long-term demographic prospects are not encouraging. If current trends persist, Arabs will outnumber Jews in Eretz Israel by the year 2010.

There is in this book much food for reflection. But some of the academic infrastructure is inadequate. Notes refer to books without page references. The translator should also have referred to English publications, rather than French, where they exist. Some of the statistical data are confusing and, I am sure, in places (as in table 4.7 on page 87) arithmetically incorrect. And more careful proofreading would have averted the bizarre statement that 'between 1906 and 1914, the population of the province of Edirne fell from 1,334 million to 631,000 as a result of territorial losses.'

Despair of the Heart

This review of *I Saw Ramallah* by Mourid Barghouti, translated by Ahdaf Soueif, and published by the American University in Cairo Press in 2000, appeared in *The Times Literary Supplement* on 19 April 2002. The book was later published – with a much larger print-run - by Bloomsbury of London. Their edition has a quote from this review on the cover.

Mourid Barghouti is a Palestinian poet from near Ramallah. At the time of the June 1967 war, he was a student at the University of Cairo. His village was part of the West Bank occupied by Israel, and Barghouti was not permitted to return. He married the Egyptian novelist Radwa Ashour and settled in Cairo. In 1977, when President Sadat visited Israel, Palestinian activists and alleged activists in Egypt were deported. Among the latter was Mourid Barghouti. Ashour was pregnant with their only child, and for the next fifteen years or so the family was able to be together only in those foreign capitals where Barghouti could get work. In 1996 he was permitted to return to the place of his birth, and *I Saw Ramallah* is the account of that return. It has been superbly and sensitively translated by Ahdaf Soueif, and is the most eloquent statement in English of what it is like to be a Palestinian today.

As he crosses the River Jordan, he wonders what his status is: 'A visitor? A refugee? A citizen? A guest? I do not know.' Before June 1967, no one had disputed his right to Ramallah, but 'now I pass from my exile to their … homeland? My homeland? The West Bank and Gaza? The Occupied Territories? The Areas? Judea and Samaria? The Autonomous Government? Israel? Palestine? Is there any other country in the world that so perplexes you with its names? Last time I was clear and things were clear. Now I am ambiguous and vague. Everything is ambiguous and vague.'

Barghouti describes the daily reality of the military occupation of the West Bank. It has meant the destruction of a community, a deliberate and sustained psychological humiliation of a people:

Occupation prevents you from managing your affairs in your own way. It interferes in every aspect of life and of death; it interferes with longing and anger and desire and walking in the street. It interferes with going anywhere and coming back, with going to market, the emergency hospital, the beach, the bedroom, or a distant capital.

Families are broken up, so that reunions take place not at home but in a foreign hotel. Roads to towns under the Palestinian Authority from Jordan are designed to prevent visiting Palestinians even having a glimpse of Jerusalem.

Security is given as the reason for forbidding Palestinians to build. Land is taken for security reasons, and illegal Israeli settlements are constructed, thereby extending security needs. Israel controls water supply, and the needs of the settlements are adequately met. There is less green in the areas under Palestinian control.

Barghouti's account is controlled, reflective, factual, unemotional, eloquent. He explains Palestinian bitterness, but shows little himself. The Arabic original (published in 1997) won the prestigious Naguib Mahfouz Prize. The gap between public rhetoric and Barghouti's personal restraint was noteworthy in Arabic; translation cannot transfer the political and cultural context of the book's initial reception. No other book so well explains the background to recent events in Palestine/Israel.

Rentier Kingdom

This was a review of two books: *Jordan in Transition 1990-2000*, edited by George Joffe, published by C Hurst, London, 2001, and *Leap of Faith: Memoirs of an Unexpected Life* by Queen Noor, published by Weidenfeld and Nicolson, London, 2003. The review appeared in *The Times Literary Supplement*, 12 September 2003.

The Hashemite Kingdom of Jordan is under sixty years old. But for over three quarters of that time it was ruled in a distinctly personal way by one man, the late King Hussein. He became King at the age of eighteen, following his grandfather who was murdered and his father who, of unsound mind, was shuffled off to one of the Princes' Islands off Istanbul for the rest of his life. Jordan came to a full stop at his death in February 1999 but rapidly picked itself up and has adapted to the reign of Hussein's eldest son, the equally personable Abdullah.

The two books under review explain much of the personality of Hussein and the remarkable politics of a country that has defied many rules of logic and history. The essays in *Jordan in Transition* vary in readability, but in all a number of themes emerge. Jordan during the 1990s was under pressure – from the United Nations and the World Bank – to 'liberalise' its economy. A majority of the population of Jordan is Palestinian, but the King's basic support has come from Transjordanians. The private sector has largely been Palestinian. Although both kings have favoured liberalisation and have been keen to respond to American pressures, economic changes have potentially threatened their power base.

Several essays refer to the 'rentier' nature of the regime; that is to say, the political system has relied on funding from outside: from international aid, income derived from transit goods, from financial support from other richer Arab states and from remittances from Jordanians and Palestinians working overseas. This 'rent' has allowed the government to be less responsive to pressures from taxpayers or domestic stakeholders. Consequently, in spite of transformations and upheavals in the region, the balance of power has not changed at all.

Luck has played its part. Hussein's apparent neutrality in the war for the liberation of Kuwait led to the repatriation of hundreds of thousands of Jordanians and Palestinians in the Gulf with their savings; this gave a boost to the Jordanian economy. The peace with Israel in 1994 was not popular with domestic Palestinians and failed to produce the prosperous 'new Middle East' of Shimon Peres's dreams. But it did lead to the cancellation of a US$900 million debt, and an increase in foreign aid. Riots in the south of the country allowed Hussein to sack a Prime Minister, thereby appearing to have no direct responsibility for the economic and political consequences of his government's decisions.

Three essays examine the development of tourism in the country. After the peace with Israel, heady ambitions led to an overproduction of hotels and facilities. One hundred thousand Israelis came to Jordan as tourists, but Jordan gained little economically. They came on day trips, even bringing their own water and sandwiches. To compensate, the fee for visiting Petra soared.

None of the essays mention Queen Noor, King Hussein's fourth wife. But her beautifully written memoirs, *Leap of Faith*, cover the same years. Her Majesty was born Lisa Halaby, the privileged daughter of a successful and driven Christian Arab American and his Scandinavian wife. She met King Hussein by chance when she accompanied her father on a business trip to Jordan. Hussein already had eight children from three previous wives, was sixteen years older and two inches shorter than Miss Halaby. But in spite of these unpromising prospects love prevailed, four more children appeared and they shared a happy, Western, married life.

Queen Noor threw herself with enthusiasm into her new role. She embraced Islam, took on the name, Noor al-Hussein ('light of Hussein'), worried about children's adenoids and whether to pack a tiara on state visits, and undertook vigorous activities involved with children's and women's rights, education and the environment. She lectured in the United States about Palestine's and Jordan's needs. She has turned herself into an international celebrity, promoting issues of human rights and landmine awareness.

Noor writes with affecting frankness about her love for King Hussein. The final chapters about the King's last months and the quiet courage with which he endured his illness are moving. Photographs show a happy, mutually supportive family. And the Hashemites are a remarkable family, quite apart from their skills in survival. King Hussein saw himself as the patriarch of his nation. He encouraged members of his family to take up social issues such as campaigning against honour killings or for abused children. Many have seriously pursued higher education in Britain and the United States.

The Queen's book adds personal detail to the essays in *Jordan in Transition*.

Common themes are there but are difficult to tease out. She does not use the language of political science to illustrate the workings of the rentier state. Instead, she has an unwittingly revealing paragraph about Hussein's finances:

Hussein personally supported the expenses of our home and of the extended royal family through financial resources he was given from within the Arab and Muslim world. He had a basic allowance from the government that had not changed in all his years as King, and neither of us took any personal money from the Jordanian government.

This support ensured the financial and political security of the large royal family. But what compromises had to be made? What payback was expected? Would things have been different if the Hashemites had had a civil list paid by the Jordanian taxpayer?

Queen Noor was still in her forties when King Hussein died. She ends her book with an assertion of her Islamic faith, and a pledge to uphold throughout her life his legacy of love, tolerance and peace. Affecting words, but from the evidence of this book, she has a lot to offer on her own account rather than as the widow of an admittedly remarkable man.

Food in Jordan

This review of *Jordan, The Land and the Table* by Cecil Hourani, published by Elliott and Thompson, London, 2006, appeared in *Asian Affairs* in 2007.

Jordan is not the first country that springs to mind when one thinks of Middle East cooking. Cecil Hourani, who is now in his late eighties, has changed our perceptions with this fascinating volume. In it he displays his passion for food and for cooking and curiosity about the social and environmental context of food.

Cecil is no theoretical cook. A few years ago I was wandering around southern Lebanon with a Tunisian friend whose uncle had known Cecil when he was Director of the Hammamet Cultural Centre. Cecil invited us both to lunch and at short notice cooked a splendid meal in his family home at Marjayoun.

The first half of the book is a description of the traditional ingredients of the Jordanian diet, a mixture of Bedu and village. Over the last century or so the country has been enriched by refugees and migrants – Armenians from Turkey, Palestinians, Syrians and Circassians. Each group has added to what is available in the country, so 'there is indeed a Jordanian cuisine which mirrors a society composed of several ethnic and cultural communities which form a distinct national entity'.

Cecil Hourani writes of *jameed*, a Bedu method of conserving the abundant milk of springtime for use in the drier months later in the year. Made from buttermilk, it is dried in the sun and formed into pyramid shapes. The sour and pungent taste has become an integral component of the cultural identity. One Jordanian visiting compatriots in Chile was pleasantly surprised to be provided with the Jordanian national dish – *mansaf* – cooked with jameed. Was it on sale in Chile? No, he was told. The Jordanian community made their own jameed in their washing-machines, imitating the revolving mechanism of their ancestors.

Cecil also tells of his curiosity about omelettes made from ostrich eggs. Doughty had seen ostrich eggs being eaten with herbs like an omelette, and H B Tristram in the 1870s found ostrich eggs 'excellent eating'. Ostriches are preserved only in a few farms, but their eggs are – apparently – still available in specialist London food shops. Alan Davidson, in his *Dictionary of Food*, said ostrich eggs cannot easily be made into omelettes. Cecil decided to test this hypothesis. He 'invited eight neighbours and friends to dinner. I bought the egg at a farmers' market for £7.50. It weighed almost a kilo, and its shell was so thick that I had to ask a neighbour to drill a hole at both ends with his electric drill and to blow the egg out through the smaller hole … The omelette was made with herbs, butter and a cup of milk. There was sufficient omelette for us, with some left over, and by general agreement Tristram's description was declared accurate.'

Cecil Hourani claims that the book is not aiming to instruct the reader how to cook, but is rather 'a book about food, with some recipes to illustrate the text.' (How to make an ostrich omelette is on page 93.) The second half of the book consists of recipes. They make mouth-watering reading but are not always helpful to any but an instinctive cook. It is not easy to work out how long the preparation or the cooking – at what heat or in what kind of vessel – will take. For this we need to turn to Claudia Roden and others. But few writers on food write with such informed and infectious enthusiasm as Cecil Hourani.

The Future of Freya Stark:
The View from Damascus

In 1992 I reopened the British Council in Damascus. I decided to inaugurate the return of British cultural activities with an exhibition of the photographs of Freya Stark. I looked at the collections at St Antony's College Oxford and selected pictures she had taken during the 1920s and 1930s. I made postcard size prints of these, and spent an agreeable summer tracing some of the individuals who appeared in them. One lead led to another. One of the most interesting led to the Azem family. They illuminated aspects of Freya Stark's first visit to the Arab world. After she died, *Asian Affairs* invited me to write about her. The following article appeared in that journal in October 1994.

Dame Freya Stark died in May 1993 at the age of one hundred. The obituaries have been written and assessments made; and one carping biography was published on her hundredth birthday just four months before she died. The record of her travels is clear. Her memory is held dear by many friends who, because of her longevity, are decades younger than her. But how much of her reputation will stand fifty years from now?

Freya Stark was much concerned with her own posthumous reputation. Her faithful publisher, John Murray, brought out four volumes of her autobiography but baulked at a separate edition of her letters. They were, however, published at her own expense by Michael Russell in eight volumes between 1974 and 1982. A project is under way for a series of volumes of her photographs. There will be ample time to assess and reassess the work of an extraordinary woman. As time goes by the memories of her extensive network of friends will fade unless they too are recorded. A remarkable personality shines through all she wrote and is cherished by many she met. Although happiest in the study or in the saddle, she played a small part in public affairs during the Second World War. She left an impact that is less documented on the people among whom she travelled. And her skills as a photographer are being more and more recognised.

Both her friends and detractors are agreed on many aspects of her personality. She was flamboyant, vain and manipulative. She had a reverence for the British Empire and combined a belief in its benevolence with disrespect for many of its servants. She was able to communicate directly with those she was interested in and to share in their lives, their joys and their sorrows. But her detractors do not stress what her friends savoured. Whenever Freya Stark was around life seemed more fun and horizons were extended. Such an enrichment – personal, intellectual and spiritual – secured a fierce loyalty from her allies that allowed them to overlook her foibles, her obsession with clothes, and her habit of getting other people to run around on her behalf.

Her travels were primarily in the Islamic lands of Asia. The first of these countries she visited were Lebanon and Syria in 1927 and 1928. At the age of thirty-four she went to Broumana in Lebanon to improve her Arabic and spent the winter months in Damascus. The letters she wrote during these travels are full of girlish enthusiasm. They were not published until fifteen years later by which time she had received fame from her travels and praise for her books about Iraq, Persia and the Hadramaut. Yet in her *Letters from Syria* the mature Freya can be recognised: an unhurriedness, a readiness to involve herself in the lives of all she met, a steely individualism, along with meditations on life, history and contemporary affairs, an endurance of hardship but also an honest appreciation of comfort. Whenever she travelled she prepared herself with intensive reading in several languages. She was widely read in history and in the Greek and Latin classics, but also in Arabic and medieval European literature. She travelled with a sensitivity for the centuries of the past and a kindly curiosity about all those she met.

Syria was also one of the last of the countries of Islamic Asia she returned to. John Julius Norwich, in his obituary of her published in *The Independent*, recalled how in 1982, at the age of eighty-nine, she 'climbed unaided to the topmost tower of Krak des Chevaliers, talking to village children in her careful, courteous Arabic as she went.'

Her standing as a traveller and explorer rests on those pre-war books. That reputation opened up for her the drawing rooms of London and the Home Counties and gave her a wide acquaintance with that world of social, literary and political England which has all but disappeared but which she has described in her letters. It gave her access during the war to the makers of policy and the men of action in the Middle East, such as 'Jumbo' Wilson and to Lord Wavell.

Her own contribution to the war effort was not insignificant. She spent time in Iraq and Egypt identifying friends of the Allies through her network – Brotherhood of Freedom. Institutionally her efforts came to nought. Yet she identified a generation of Arabs that few of her contemporary compatriots sympathised with – the young *effendi* class of journalists, civil servants and professionals. Imperial experience in India had made colonial servants suspicious and contemptuous of the *babu* class, young men who were the first of their race to be educated on western lines and were stirred by western liberal ideas. Disappointment in the westerners whom they encountered in their daily lives and who did not practise these liberal values led to disillusion and political activism.

Indirect authority in the Middle East and the efforts of British and American missionaries had produced a small Anglophone class that overlapped with the earnest public-spirited young men of Freya Stark's brotherhood. Many had attended English medium schools such as Victoria College Alexandria, St George's Jerusalem, or Broumana High School, or had gone on to further education at the American Universities of Beirut and Cairo. They came from the more prosperous but also more far-sighted families throughout the Middle East. They were equally at home in different capitals of the region and were imbued with a vague Edwardian liberalism. They had a sense of mission, a desire for progress and a belief in democracy – in spirit if not in detail. The Allied war aims matched well with their attitudes. Freya Stark identified them, sought them out and helped to mobilise them. This class after the war produced Ministers and public servants as well as scholars and businessmen. Humiliated by the reverses over Palestine, they were in general swept from power by the harsher populist ideologies of the Arab nationalism of Abdul Nasser. Yet throughout public, professional and academic life in the last half-century their influence has been considerable, a humane and gentle leaven to the froth and violence of public life. Freya Stark writes sympathetically of this class in her own war memoirs, *East is West*.

When she dealt with this class she wrote with authority and deep personal knowledge, having got to know on her first visit to Damascus one family that epitomised that class. In *Letters from Syria* Freya Stark refers to her meeting with 'the Sheikh' and his sister, 'Handmaid of Allah'. The almost chance encounter led to a friendship that lasted for over half a century. It also brought her into contact with one of the leading political families of Syria.

The Azems had been the most prominent land-owning and office-holding family for two centuries. They had provided Governors of Hama and Damascus. Two of the finest monuments from the Ottoman period in old Damascus were built by the family – their splendid town house, the Azem Palace in the shadow of the Umayyad Mosque, and the Khan of As'ad Pasha, the cathedral-like caravanserai a hundred yards to the south.

The Azems were a large family, public spirited and able to move with the times. Freya Stark's 'sheikh', far from being a grey-bearded man of religion, was in 1928 a sprightly young bachelor in his late twenties. Dr Yasir Mu'ayyid al-Azem was a graduate in medicine from the American University of Beirut and had already served for two years as a doctor in the Anglo-Egyptian Condominium of the Sudan. He had returned to Damascus where he set up a practice as one of the first two radiologists in the city. He was out of the country at the time of the national revolt against the French mandate authorities. But his family were closely involved. One sister, Sara, was the wife of Dr Abdul Rahman Shahbandar, the leader of Syrian nationalism between the wars. Dr Shahbandar was imprisoned and exiled, and on his release shortly before the Second World War it was at the house of his brother-in-law that he received congratulations and greetings from his supporters. Sara herself was known as Umm al-Suriyyin, 'Mother of the Syrians'. Dr Yasir died in 1991.

The 'Handmaid of Allah' was Amat al-Latif al-Azem, a year or two older than her brother. She lived to the age of ninety-six and died in March 1994, having been bedridden for the previous six years. She never married but was active in the promotion of girls' education.

One brother of Dr Yasir and Amat al-Latif was Nazih (whose widow also died in 1994). Nazih was ten years older than Dr Yasir and was also a graduate of the American University of Beirut. He had got to know Charles Crane during the latter's extended visit to Syria in 1919, when, with Dr Henry King, he investigated the views of the people of Syria and Palestine about their political future. Charles Crane was a Chicago businessman who had been an enthusiastic private traveller in the Near East since 1878 when he was twenty years old. Later in the 1920s Crane visited Yemen and called on the Imam Yahya in San'a, taking Nazih al-Azem with him as interpreter. Nazih wrote an account of the Yemen at the time (in Arabic), still a valuable work of reference.

In 1993 I organised an exhibition of the photographs Freya Stark had taken of Syria in the 1920s and 1930s for the British Council in Damascus. I got to know the Azems in my researches into the Syrian background of Freya Stark's travels. Freya Stark used to stay with the family right up to the 1970s. Dr Yasir had married relatively late in life and had a family of lively daughters and one son. One of his daughters recalls how the two old friends would embrace on meeting, cooing to each other, '*Ya Faraia*', '*Ya Shaikh*'. The daughters all have fond memories of the kindly old lady who took a warm interest in their concerns.

I also met Amat al-Latif, physically frail but with clear and detailed recollections of Freya Stark's first visits to Damascus sixty-five years earlier. 'She borrowed from my brother Nazih a map of routes to Ma'rib in the Yemen. She promised to return it but never did. Can you get it back?'

Although her strongest friendship was with the Azem family she was in touch in the 1940s with other political families of the region – the Khalidis in Jerusalem, Shukri al-Quwwatli in Damascus as well as the wartime Prime Ministers of Egypt. These friendships add an important dimension to our understanding of her. She had a serious and well-informed awareness of the issues of contemporary Arab politics.

At the same time Freya Stark shared with many other travellers a romantic affection for the desert. (Indeed in Syria she was acquainted for over fifty years with the Nuri Sha'lan family, leaders of the Ruala tribe.) For many Europeans this affection for the desert was an escapism, a flight from the twentieth century, a kind of technophobia. But this was not the case with Freya Stark. She welcomed innovations that would bring a better (albeit transformed) life in the future. Her sense of history was not restricted to contemplation of the past. When in 1977 she set eyes on the Euphrates dam in north east Syria she was thrilled, saying that she had 'a marvellous look-out to the future.'

In Britain she appeared very much at home although she always spoke with distinctive north Italian vowels. She wrote for posterity, and like other travellers of her own and preceding generations she did not write for those among whom she travelled. Many travellers record with pen and camera images that are already in their minds. Indeed the camera has mechanised the nineteenth century orientalist tradition of painting. Freya Stark was not free of this habit. Her photographs of women and children are sometimes romanticised but always have humour and humanity.

Her photographs of landscapes and buildings are a contrast to her portraits of people. Sometimes she preferred to have no people in pictures, which consequently convey an austere geometric coldness. But when landscape and artefact mingle – as with castles of Syria and Iran or the architecture of Yemen or Turkey – there is a fastidious composition of form and line. And occasionally the introduction of a man or a woman or a group fills up a space and gives perspective to the composition and makes the viewer want to know more. Who is that? Where is he going? As Freya Stark wrote in 1939 from the Assassin castle of Khawabi in central Syria, 'It is not *what* one sees, but *how* one sees it that counts.'

Freya Stark's earlier books – *The Valley of the Assassins* (1934) and *The*

Southern Gates of Arabia (1936) – and the four volumes of autobiography are likely to remain classics of travel writing. But the painstaking craftsmanship in her later books, her limning of a word-picture as if she is working on a huge canvas, are an inadequate compensation for the happy spontaneity of her letters and photographs, recorded on the spot and in the heat of the moment. It is these that will preserve for us and for the generations to come the warm personality and acute perceptions of a great lady.

Syrians in Two Worlds

The following first appeared in *Syria Through Writers' Eyes*, edited by Marius Kociejowski, published by Eland Publishing, London, in 2006.

On my first visit to Syria, in 1962, I travelled by bus from Homs to Palmyra and sat next to the headmaster of the secondary school in Tadmor, the modern town to the east of the classical site. (Until the French Mandate between the wars the whole town was settled in the enclosure around the Temple of Bel. From the air the geometric grid plan of the town is clear.) The headmaster invited me to visit the school. I took up the invitation and the next morning he put me in the hands of the teacher of English, Ibrahim Abd al-Nur, a bachelor of thirty, a few years older than myself. We spent the evening together visiting friends, and playing table tennis and chess. After a brief correspondence we lost touch.

Thirty years later I was back in Syria, reopening the British Council. I had fond memories of that first visit and of my evening in Tadmor, and wanted to find Ibrahim. I made enquiries wherever I went, and a senior army officer friend suggested we get the security services to trace him, I resisted the idea, imagining the alarm of an elderly teacher suddenly being interrogated about conversations he had had with some foreigner a generation earlier.

The Principal of the University in Homs helped me to track Ibrahim down. One of the students at the university – studying English – was called Abeer Ibrahim Abd al-Nur. To her consternation she found herself summoned to the Principal's office. We met and I asked her whether her father had taught English in Palmyra in the early 1960s. She thought so. She told me her father was retired and living in his home village, a Christian village, Fairouza, a few miles east of Homs. Abeer's initial alarm and wariness of me melted, and later in the day we went in my car to the village and called on her father. On the way Abeer puzzled me by talking of diamonds growing in the fields. It was only later that she corrected herself – 'Almonds, not diamonds.'

Ibrahim was shorter and stouter than my memory of him, but there was the same rubicund face and we greeted each other with a spontaneous bear hug. His English was precise with strange nineteenth century turns of phrase, the result of the reading of much Thackeray and Dickens. His memory of that evening in Palmyra was as clear as mine. Ibrahim was now married with four children – three sons and a daughter, more or less the same family set-up as my own. The eldest son was in the United States, and Abeer was engaged to an American, called George.

Over the next few months I got to know the family and the village better. Abeer's fiancé, George, did have American citizenship but he had actually been born in Fairouza. Abeer, on graduation, would be joining him in the United States, in Burbank California, on the northern outskirts of Los Angeles, where George ran a liquor store. The eldest brother was also in Burbank. Indeed I gradually learned that there were *hundreds* of people from Fairouza who had migrated in the last decade or so to Burbank, creating an informal twinning arrangement. 'People from the next village, Zaidan,' Ibrahim informed me, 'go to Jacksonville Florida, but we go to Burbank California.'

The next summer George came over and I met him in Fairouza. George had a cheery Californian accent and a big grin. He and Abeer married in the village and went off to Burbank. The following year Ibrahim died but I continued to call on the family in Fairouza. I also exchanged Christmas greetings with George and Abeer.

I left Syria in 1997 and in the summer of 2000 I was in Los Angeles and phoned George's liquor store. My wife and I were invited to spend a day with Abeer and George, and their two young children, Linda and Ibrahim. I took for Abeer a packet of almonds and for both of them a copy of Brigid Keenan's book on Damascus. They lived in a house, one of six, around a shared courtyard. Three of the houses were occupied by people originally from Fairouza, one by Abeer's closest friend from their primary school days.

We ate a mezze and a Syrian stew followed by sweetmeats from Damascus. A video was playing all the time, the record of their recent summer trip to Fairouza. They had taken the children back to be baptised by the village priest. The video included scenes of a late night party in the Fairouza community centre. People were dancing into the night. The women looked exhausted. Had they been up from dawn, chopping tomatoes and parsley for the tabbuleh?

'Every night there is a party,' said George. 'People go back there from Burbank looking for brides and bridegrooms for the young men and women.'

'But how many people from Fairouza are there here in Burbank?' I asked.

'About two thousand.'

'And what work do people from Fairouza do?'

'Mostly the liquor trade. The first migrant in the early 1960s became involved in selling liquor. There are now about two hundred liquor stores in the northern Los Angeles area, either owned or managed by people from Fairouza. We sell everything, including araq produced in Fairouza and exported here.'

We talked on. The children spoke Arabic, but they would quickly learn English at school. Abeer and George saw themselves as having come to live in Burbank for good, although they did maintain links with the home village.

'I have some land in Fairouza,' said George.

'Who looks after that?'

'My mother and sister.'

The Syrian President, Hafez al-Assad, had died earlier that year, and George and Abeer had been to the Syrian Consulate General in Los Angeles to cast their vote in the Syrian presidential election, voting for Bashar, the late President's son. Taking advantage of their US citizenship, they were also preparing in the autumn to vote for George W Bush, another son of another former President. Until the second Bush, most Arab Americans voted Republican. The Republican Party was more representative of non-European, and especially Arab, immigrant cultural values – suspicion of and distance from federal government authority, shared family values, and a belief in and practice of private enterprise.

The Lebanese in the World: A Century of Emigration, edited by Albert Hourani and Nadim Shehadi, published by the Centre for Lebanese Studies in association with I B Tauris of London in 1992, deals primarily with Lebanese migration. But the reader is able to place the Fairouza/Burbank phenomenon into a broader context. Migration from greater Syria to Europe and the Americas and elsewhere has persisted since the early nineteenth century. It was not – as local myth maintains – the consequence of Ottoman oppression. Life steadily improved for Syrians in the latter years of the Ottoman Empire. The explanation can rather be found in rising expectations following faster and cheaper steam-driven shipping. Often the pioneer from one village would settle in one place in the new country, and others from the village or area would follow. Druze and Syrians from the south of the country migrated to Venezuela. People from the small town of Yabrud, eighty kilometres south west of Fairouza, migrated to Argentina. Among the latter were the parents of former President Carlos Menem, who exchanged their Islam for Christianity and modified their family name of Abd al-Munim. Southern Lebanese went to

West Africa and people from Homs went to Sao Paolo. Occasionally one village may buck the trend. People from Bishmizzin in northern Lebanon migrated in all directions.

The pattern of Syrian/Lebanese migration is similar to other waves – organised by no government and the result of individual initiative on a huge scale – such as Poles, Greeks and Italians to the United States in the nineteenth and twentieth centuries, and from South Asia to western Europe in the late twentieth. The migrants become citizens of the adopted countries and, to a greater or lesser extent, become assimilated in the new country. The first generation are traders and the second generation become professionals. But contacts are maintained with their places of origin, in the form of marriage patterns, language, food and values. A minority return to their home country. Many Syrians returned from South America to the region south and west of Homs, and brought back some customs, such as mate tea, sucked through a metal filter.

Syria now has a Ministry for Expatriates, headed by Dr Bouthaina Shaaban, who has a PhD from the University of Warwick for a thesis on Chartist poetry. She has taught at university level in the United States. The establishment of the Ministry follows the example of Lebanon. Some expatriates have become extremely rich – in Latin America, but also in Europe and, to a lesser extent, in the United States. The new Ministry is keen to attract investment from those who still feel Syrian. The communities of expatriates are also seen as possible allies in presenting Syria in a favourable light.

My accidental but cherished friendship, now well over forty years old, with Ibrahim and his family reveals on an individual scale something that has been happening to Syrians (and others) on a massive scale, to the enrichment of the societies of both worlds.

Ottoman Aleppo

This review of *The Image of an Ottoman City: Imperial Architecture and Urban Experience in the Sixteenth and Seventeenth Centuries* by Heghnar Zeitlian Watenpaugh, published by Brill of Leiden in 2004, appeared in *Asian Affairs* in 2005.

A learned tome on the history and urban development of Aleppo in the sixteenth and seventeenth centuries may seem of limited interest. But far from being a provincial history, this volume enlightens us enormously on the dynamics of the Ottoman Empire.

When Aleppo became part of the Ottoman Empire after the collapse of Mamluk rule in Syria in the early sixteenth century, the new imperial overlords set about Ottomanising the city through architecture and the use of urban space. They had carried out similar policies in Europe, and in Istanbul after 1453, but Aleppo (and Damascus and Cairo) were different. The Ottoman Empire was, from first to last, an Islamic polity. Istanbul and the European cities were turned into Islamic cities – with the construction of mosques and major public buildings with an Islamic function, and the transformation of churches into mosques. But Aleppo, which was now the third largest city of the Empire, already had an Islamic heritage – with shrines, holy places and a principal mosque to which succeeding dynasties had added their own architectural signatures. The transformation of Aleppo was to bring out the unique qualities of Ottoman political culture.

New buildings were sponsored by new imperial governors and officials, with local craftsmen. Extensive use was made of the *waqf* (religious endowments), especially in the walled city. Mosques, *khans* (caravanserais), *madrasas* (religious schools), shops, baths and even coffeehouses became *waqf* endowments and so, in theory and also in practice, continued to be so in perpetuity. This explains why the souks of Aleppo have hardly changed over five hundred years. A distinctive visual Ottoman touch was the building of mosques with domes and slender minarets. But the Ottomans also saw Aleppo's commercial potential, as a staging post in the trade route from Europe to the Euphrates valley, Basra and so on to India and the Far East.

Istanbul had its large complexes – around the Fatih and Süleymaniye mosques, for example – that were cities within cities, with schools, mosques, baths, hospitals and soup kitchens. These were, in a similar way, replicated in

Aleppo under the patronage of individual imperial servants whose power base was Istanbul, allied with their own ability. They had been recruited as children into service – often from the Balkans – and so were not part of a network of powerful families, locally based. But they did represent the Empire and had a succession of postings that might take them to Belgrade, Cairo, the Hijaz or the imperial capital. The document establishing the *waqf* endowment, the *waqfiya*, would ensure a distribution of revenue throughout the Ottoman lands.

The nature of the Ottoman state also determined the flow of profits to and from these endowments. The size of the empire allowed patrons to assign the revenue from a shop in Sivas to support a Koranic school in Aleppo. Income from disparate regions of what we call today the Middle East, Eastern Europe and North Africa could be combined in one endowment. Conversely, sections of the usufruct of foundations in Aleppo could be dedicated to support structures in Mecca, Medina or anywhere else in the empire. Thus the wealth in certain parts of the empire could be redistributed to others. Imperial realities dictated the convergence of large amounts of wealth on Istanbul and the Two Noble Sanctuaries, Medina and Mecca. Aleppo, and other 'provincial' cities, thus contributed to and benefited from the prosperity of the Ottoman Empire as a whole.

Dr Watenbaugh's book also tells us much about the social history of early Ottoman Syria. Aleppo was built as a commercial city in contrast to Damascus where the Ottomans focused on developing its religious character, with the construction of complexes by the tomb of the sufi, Ibn Arabi, and the Selimiya mosque, which sustained the annual pilgrimage. In these centuries Aleppo flourished not only commercially but also intellectually. Scholars and local men of religion were integrated into the imperial system, occupying posts with approval from Istanbul. The seventeenth century saw a flourishing of letters, biographies, dictionaries and topographical histories.

The book is excellently produced, as one would expect from Brill, with photographs and prints including a delightfully stylised view of Aleppo drawn by an Ottoman official in 1537-38, taken from a manuscript in the University of Istanbul library. This book should be widely read. But the price is prohibitive for all but specialist libraries.

Three Views of Damascus

These are reviews of three books and were written for *Asian Affairs*. The first review is of *The Gates of Damascus* by Lieve Joris, published by Lonely Planet Publications, Hawthorn Victoria, Australia, in 1996. The second is of *Cleopatra's Wedding Present: Travels Through Syria by Robert Tewdwr Moss*, published by Duckworth, London, in 1997. The third is of *Damascus Hidden Treasures of the Old City* by Brigid Keenan, published by Thames and Hudson, London, in 2000. The reviews were published, respectively, in 1997, 1998 and 2001.

For many young backpackers from Australia, Britain, Europe and America their first introduction to Asia has been with the help of the Lonely Planet Guides – practical, readable, idiosyncratic. Lonely Planet has now started a series, '*Journeys*', volumes of travellers' tales, aimed to 'catch the spirit of a place, illuminate a culture, recount a crazy adventure, or introduce a fascinating way of life.'

One of the first titles is this account of a few months in Damascus in 1991, written by a Dutch travel writer, Lieve Joris, and translated by Sam Garrett. Joris stayed with a young university lecturer, Hala, whose husband had been a political prisoner for over ten years. Life in Damascus revolves around the family of Hala, her struggle for professional survival and personal dignity. In the background are the ubiquitous *mukhabarat*, the secret (or not so secret) police upholding a political system that seems to have lost any other function but its own survival. We see very much the viewpoint of the Damascus Sunni Muslim professional class, the class that has lost most in the social revolution that has transformed Syria under President Hafez al-Assad. From the point of view of that class the country is an Alawite dictatorship, the Alawites being the Muslim group from which the Assads spring.

Lieve Joris describes a sombre pattern of life with the captive husband, still pathetically trying to assert a patriarchal authority over the family from behind bars. Her descriptions of domesticity in adversity are painfully convincing. But it is a different story when she gets out of Damascus into other communities. There, things are seen in a far more positive way. They fear a 'fundamentalist' Syria, and see Assad as having averted that fate. And in Aleppo there is prosperity, and people upholding different traditions.

Throughout Syria Lieve Joris meets courtesy and kindness. She is excellent in noting the detail of local oppressiveness: the family visits to the prison outside Damascus, the prisoners' handicrafts, the sense of being watched all the time. A generation of Syrians has learnt not to be involved in politics, save through prescribed channels. Those Syrians who have eschewed politics can still live a varied and creative life. Although social patriarchy prevails, Syria's civil code is more liberal in terms of women's rights than that of any other in the Arab Islamic world. And Christians and other minorities (who make up forty per cent of the population) see the oppressive features of the regime as an acceptable price to be paid for 'stability' and avoiding the bloody sectarianism of Lebanon.

The Gates of Damascus certainly catches part of the spirit of Damascus, and it illuminates a culture. But the backpacker would be well advised not to take the book into Syria. The mukhabarat do not always have a sense of irony.

Robert Tewdwr Moss was a gifted journalist who was brutally murdered at his Little Venice flat in August 1996 when only in his mid-thirties. In 1994 he visited Syria and wandered around, making friends with a great variety of people. *Cleopatra's Wedding Present* is a record of those journeys. He completed the book on the day of his death.

Its beautiful English and sardonic detachment will make it a classic of camp, gay travel writing. It will not feature on the list of books recommended by the official Syrian tourist authorities of today. The shadow of the secret police hangs over most of his encounters. He is mockingly savage about the rhetoric of the regime's propaganda and unsparing in his descriptions of the constraints on personal freedoms. But on his travels he was playing with fire, having homosexual liaisons with young Syrians and Palestinians with such predatory abandon that Arab accusations of the corrupting nature of Western tourists could be justified.

A guileless good humour and irresponsibility pervade the book. Moss has an intellectual curiosity and an eager appreciation of Syria's multifaceted cultural mix. He meets the head of Damascus's small Jewish community. He wanders in search of the Roman bridge over the Tigris where Turkey, Iraq and Syria meet. He makes friends with a prematurely aging Palestinian commando who has nowhere to go in life, nothing to hope for. He locates the Damascus house of Lady Jane Digby and inspects many of the justly famed tourist sites, as well as others less known, such as the cave not far from Deir ez-Zor where Armenians were massacred during the First World War. He describes the physical attractions of every young man he meets.

He also has some magnificent pen portraits, including one of an overweight, seldom sober Daniel Farson, who would stagger around the bar of the Hotel Baron, Aleppo. 'He took a few uncertain steps towards the bar, like a toddler in nappies, one arm raised, trying to catch the eye of the barman.' He tells some nice stories, such as one related by Sally Mazloumian of that same famed Aleppo hotel. Agatha Christie often stayed there with her archaeologist husband, Max Mallowan, en route for the site of Tell Barak in eastern Syria. Agatha Christie liked anonymity, but in moderation. She disliked being on display but was dismayed if she did not receive the recognition she felt was her due.

Robert Tewdwr Moss lived near the edge. Indeed, he could be accused of sexual tourism. But he was sensitive to the dangers of physical violence – whether falling horribly ill, or being beaten up by one of his louche acquaintances, or electrocuted by spectacularly dangerous wiring in the squalid flat of one of his friends. These passages read almost like a grim premonition of his own violent and untimely end.

The first mosque visited by a Pope in office, in May 2001, was the Umayyad Mosque in Damascus. This is appropriate. The mosque developed from a Christian church and still houses the head of St John the Baptist. It was also the first 'cathedral mosque' outside the homeland of Islam. Syria, in spite of political repression, is a country with traditions and habits of religious openness and tolerance. The Pope's visit drew attention to the contemporary global importance of the city of Damascus.

The old city of Damascus is an amazing treasure store of two thousand years and more of architectural history. It is also a living and working metropolis. Patterns of life, the distinct quarters, the blend of sacred and secular, all have adjusted to modern times. Changes are, however, superficial and visitors from previous centuries would not take long to be able easily to pick their way around the city.

Brigid Keenan celebrates the durability of the features of Damascus. For example, Damascus has for centuries attracted Muslim pilgrims from Anatolia, the Balkans and the Caucasian mountains, on their way to Mecca. With official Ottoman support a caravan would set off from the south of the city on the two month overland trek to the Hijaz. The transport and economics of the pilgrimage have been transformed, but Brigid Keenan notes the Daghestanis of today who come overland in battered buses for the season of the pilgrimage and sell carpets south of the old city.

She also records the procession of visitors, and honours the craftsmen who have contributed to the city's domestic architecture. Her enthusiastic writing is matched by Tim Beddow's superb photography. Those who have had the good fortune to have been born into middle-class Damascus families cherish for the rest of their lives the memories of the courtyards, the jasmine blossom, the fountains and the scents of coffee and cardamom. Wafic Rida Said has written a nostalgic introduction on this theme, and Brigid Keenan quotes the poetry of Nizar Kabbani recording how such memories 'linger with fragrance in our midst.' Foreign visitors have tried to recreate such paradises. The Burtons in their brief sojourn assumed the lives of Damascus notables. Lady Jane Digby built a house outside the walls. Today it is divided into the homes of thirty families, but it is still possible to see her imported wallpaper peeling on the stucco walls. Lord Leighton's celebrated painting of a Damascus house courtyard is identified as Bait Farhi in the Jewish quarter, now also occupied by several families. Leighton brought back artefacts from the Near East and designed his own Damascus home, now Leighton House in Kensington.

Many of the older houses today are expensive to maintain; they are homes for rats and scorpions. Family life has changed. Access for cars is limited, and many households have moved out to the hillside suburbs of Salihiya and Abu Rumaneh. Brigid Keenan's epilogue is a plea to maintain the life of the old city. There are hopeful signs. In the 1990s the Christian quarter to the east has seen the opening of restaurants and bars that have drawn in the prosperous from all over the city. Some individuals – Shaikha Hassa Al Sabah of Kuwait, Mrs Nora Jumblatt – have invested in properties that have been sensitively restored. The German Embassy and the Danish Institute have rented old houses and injected contemporary life into them. The craftsmen of Damascus are as skilled as ever. The old city has been spared high-rise apartment blocks, multi-storey car parks and supermarkets, but vigilance and determination are still needed to sustain the life and relevance of the city.

Brigid Keenan and Tim Beddow have given us a magnificent record of Damascus. Thames and Hudson have excelled themselves in producing a book that is reasonably priced.

The Shahrur Phenomenon: A Liberal Islamic Voice from Syria

In 1993 there was a brief article about Shahrur in *The Economist*. I was living in Damascus at the time, read his work and sought out the man. This consequent article appeared in *Islam and Christian-Muslim Relations* in 1996.

In the early 1990s the Arab world witnessed an extraordinary publishing phenomenon. An 800-page book on Islam, *Al-kitāb wa'l-qur'ān: qirā'a mu'āsira* (The Book and the Koran: a Contemporary Reading), was first published by the Ahali Publishing House Damascus in 1990. The book challenges a millennium of Islamic tradition. It is highly critical of the social, political and intellectual state of contemporary Arab countries. The author has been denounced as 'an enemy of Islam' and as 'a western and Zionist agent'. To date eleven other books have been written attacking his theses. Yet the book has been repeatedly reprinted and has sold 20,000 copies in Syria alone. And despite bans, tens of thousands of further copies, as well as pirated, faxed and photocopied versions, have circulated in Lebanon, Jordan, Egypt and the Arabian Peninsula.

The author, Professor Muhammad Shahrur, is a mild-mannered professor of Civil Engineering who was born in Damascus in 1938. After secondary school in Damascus, Muhammad went to the Soviet Union to study Engineering in Moscow. He was not a Marxist though he was challenged by the Marxist dialectic. He owed far more, he has told me, to Hegel and to Alfred North Whitehead. He returned to Syria in 1964 to teach at the University and was due to do research at Imperial College London in 1967. The June war with Israel that year and the consequent break in diplomatic relations between Britain and Syria put an end to that. Instead he went to Dublin and completed a Master's degree, and a PhD for a thesis on soil mechanics and foundation engineering. For the last twenty years he has been teaching at the University of Damascus. He is also a partner in an engineering consultancy.

He has followed up the first book with a sequel, *Dirāsāt islāmiya mu'āsira fi'l-dawla wa'l-mujtama'* (Contemporary Islamic Studies on State and Society), under four hundred pages long, published also by Ahali of Damascus in 1994, which elaborates and extends some points made in the earlier book. A third volume is promised at the end of 1996.

Shahrur is stating the secular liberal case for Islam. He 'deconstructs' the Koran and is highly critical of the tradition of *fiqh* (jurisprudence) that has distorted the message of Islam, and had a stifling effect on Arab Islamic society. Throughout the two books he affirms his own faith as an Arab Muslim. He follows all references to the Prophet Muhammad with the letter *sad*, for the formalistic invocation, *salla allāhu 'alayhi wa sallam*. Similarly he always refers to Allah with the extolment *subhānahu wa ta'ālā*.

His methodology, the use he makes of that methodology, his historical interpretations and his own positive view of Islam are very different from conventional received traditions of the faith.

I propose to outline Shahrur's methods and arguments and to assess the impact of his work. I am not an expert in *fiqh* or *tafsīr* (Koranic exegesis). Nor is it possible to discuss all Shahrur's ideas. He may disagree with aspects of my presentation. This is unavoidable when considering over a thousand pages of closely argued theology.

References henceforth will be to the texts of his two books. *KQ* refers to *Al-Kitāb wa'l-qur'ān*, *DIM* to the *Dirāsāt islāmiya mu'āsira*. Translations from the Koran are from *The Meaning of the Glorious Koran*, the version of Mohammad Marmaduke Pickthall, of which there have been many editions.

Shahrur asserts the timelessness of the Koran. It is the word of Allah as interpreted by the Prophet Muhammad, his contemporaries and immediate successors (*KQ*, 36). However there is a direct dialogue between the reader and the text and today's Muslims must concentrate on that text and by-pass the intermediary of the traditions of tafsīr. The Koran should be read as if the Prophet Muhammad had only recently died (*KQ*, 41). Just as the Prophet, his contemporaries and immediate successors understood the text of the Koran in the light of their intellectual capacities and of their perception of the world, so we should read and understand it in the light of ours. A key concept of Shahrur's is *ardiya 'ilmiya* or *ardiya ma'ārifiya* which might be translated as 'scientific premises'. (Shahrur himself prefers the rendering 'scientific background'.) Seventh century Arabia had a limited concept of the principles determining the natural world, but the history of scientific discovery has been one of continuous expansion of what was known and the diminishing of what was unknown (*KQ*, 43). These subsequent scientific discoveries and new hypotheses give us a greater understanding of particular passages in the Koran. For example, modern theories of the creation of the world and of the existence of hydrogen are anticipated in the first three verses of *sūrat al-fajr* (*KQ*, 235);

Darwinism in *sūrat al-zumar* (*KQ*, 280). Thus the Koran needs to be read and re-read in the light of developing and changing premises. Koranic studies are dynamic. The Koran itself appeals to those who are *rāsikhūn fī 'l'ilm* (those who are of sound instruction) or *ūlū al-albāb* (men of understanding) (*sūrat al-imrān*). The relationship between reader and text is bound to change over the centuries. It will continue to change to the end of time (*KQ*, 192).

In order to understand the text of the Koran each word has to be analysed in the light of what we know, not as has been told us by the traditions of fiqh (*KQ*, 182)

Shahrur looks hard at the meaning and possible variant meanings of most of the key words of the Koran. In this analysis he relies largely on standard classical dictionaries. His analyses enlighten and explain some points anew. I will give a few examples.

The Koran was revealed by a process that is described sometimes as *inzāl*, sometimes as *tanzīl* (*KQ*, 147-51). Translations do not always make a distinction between the two verbal nouns. Shahrur does, looking at all the references to both words in the Koran, and comparing the usual nature of the difference between the second and the fourth form of the verb. *Tanzīl* has a general sense; *inzāl* is more specific. The latter form of the word is always used when the Koran refers to the revelation being in the Arabic language and directed at a particular group of people – the Arabs. Shahrur uses the (contemporary) analogy of the recording of a message or a video cassette (*tanzīl*), with the act of switching it on to hear or to watch (*inzāl*). This distinction has only become clear to us, he argues, in the light of recent developments in communications.

Secondly he examines the word, *ummī,* often interpreted as 'illiterate', describing the Prophet Muhammad (*KQ*, 139-40). *Ummī* was applied by Jews and Christians before Islam to those who were outside the faith. They were ignorant of the faith. 'Illiterate' was a logical but misleading extension of that meaning. With the inherited pre-Islamic meaning, however, the Prophet Muhammad was *ummī*, insofar as he was outside the faiths of Islam and Christianity. It does not mean that he was unable to read or write.

Thirdly he looks at the word *banīn* in *sūrat al-shu'arā*, 133: *amaddakum bi-an'ām wa-banīn*, which Pickthall translates as '[Allah] hath aided you with cattle and sons'. Shahrur (*KQ*, 644) analyses the verse in the context of a long argument against patriarchal interpretations of Islam. *Banīn* is from the root meaning 'to build' and is used here, in contrast to *an'ām*, and means 'buildings' or 'fixed assets', as opposed to livestock or moveable assets.

Another example of his methodology seems on a first reading to be taking that methodology to extremes. He analyses (*KQ*, 206-07) *sūrat al-qadr*, 3: *laylat al-qadr khayrun min alf shahr*, translated by Pickthall as 'the Night of Power is better than a thousand months'. The Night of Power was the night in the month of Ramadan when the Prophet Muhammad received his Call and the first verses of the Koran were revealed to him. Shahrur puts the last two words under his etymological microscope. *Alf* means 'a thousand', yes, but also has the idea of creation, the bringing of things together (as in *mu'allif*, a writer). And *shahr* is connected with the root meaning 'to unsheathe (a sword), to proclaim, to make public or famous'. In other words, the meaning of the verse is that the occasion of the revelation of the Koran is of greater value than of any other kind of fame that can be devised. On a second reading, this may not seem such a fantastic interpretation. After all a thousand months is only eighty or so years, a lifetime. The message of the Koran is eternal and of far greater duration than a lifetime.

Shahrur also deconstructs the concepts of *risāla* and *nubūwa*, the abstract nouns relating to *rasūl* and *nabī*, which are both usually translated as 'prophet', though the former also has the idea of 'messenger'. The declaration of faith is that Muhammad is the *rasūl* of Allah, not the *nabī*. Shahrur states (*KQ*, 37) that all parts of the Koran can be classified as either as either *nubūwa* or *risāla* or an explanation. In the *nubūwa* parts of the Koran we find statements that cannot be challenged – the Oneness of Allah, the *firqān* (based on the Ten Commandments), the natural laws, the history of previous prophets, though these parts may be reinterpreted in the light of new knowledge. *Risāla*, on the other hand, contains ethics and rules of conduct. Some parts are absolutely fixed, like rules of worship and morals, but others such as prescribed legislation and punishment, can be subject to *ijtihād*, independent individual judgment. They can even be dropped, as the Khalifa Umar al-Khattab did with *sūrat al-anfāl*, 41 (*KQ*, 38).

One area where Shahrur applies his own ijtihād relates to the question of alcohol (*KQ*, 477). He looks at all the verses in the Koran that refer to wine. Attitudes are not consistent and there is even some ambivalence. In *sūrat al-nisā*, 43, believers are enjoined not to come to prayer in a state of intoxication, with the implication that it is not impermissible to be intoxicated at other times. In *sūrat al-baqara*, 219, the sinfulness of strong drink is compared with its usefulness. And in *sūrat al-mā'ida*, 90-91, believers are told to turn aside from, to avoid, strong drink: there is no denunciation of the practice. And in one of the descriptions of Paradise in *sūrat Muhammad*, 15, there flow rivers of wine. Condemnation is not absolute. This is in contrast to the injunctions about eating pigflesh where the ban is absolute and unequivocal: *hurimat alaykum al-mayyita wa'l-dam wa-lahm al-khanzīr* (*sūrat al-mā'ida*, 3). 'Forbidden unto you (for food) are carrion and blood and swineflesh.' There are no pigs in Paradise.

In Shahrur's view Islam is a dynamic and revolutionary faith, relevant for all time and all places (*KQ*, 555). The dynamism started from the revelation of the Koran itself. The Prophet Muhammad himself was the first to practise tafsīr (*KQ*, 60).He made a distinction between the authority of the Koran and his own commentaries, the *hadīth*. The Prophet Muhammad did not give instructions for his commentaries to be collected as he did for the Koran (*KQ*, 546). The Prophet Muhammad was a fallible human being. His tafsīr was as subject to revision as that of anybody else.

But in the century following the death of the Prophet Muhammad the Islamic Empire became a major power under the Umayyads, and a religious class emerged that was separate from the wielders of political authority. This class upheld political authority and was uncritical of those possessing it. The people wielding power were content that the religious establishment invoked Allah only for things that did not challenge their power. Fiqh and authority became twins (*KQ*, 569, 622). The interpretation and development of Islam in the next few centuries became fossilised. Fresh interpretation was not permitted. The 'Gate of Ijtihād' was closed. But, says Shahrur, the gate of ijtihād was never closed (*DIM*, 218). The authority of the religious classes and the fossilisation has had a harmful effect on all subsequent Islamic Arab history. The character of fiqh-dominated Islam has been conservative, formalistic, obsessed with rules, out of touch with contemporary thought and concerned with the minutiae of human relations rather than with wider political and social morality (*KQ*, 579, 586-88; *DIM*, 24, 41, 160). The *faqīh*s were ignorant. Great medieval Arab Islamic scholars such as Ibn Sina and Ibn Rushd were condemned in the Islamic world but were studied and respected in Europe. In contrast, those such as al-Shafi'i, revered by the Islamic religious establishment, had no impact on the rest of the world (*DIM*, 228). The faqīhs and *ulamā* were concerned with what was or was not permissible, not what was or was not reasonable. They were unaware of their own ignorance (*DIM*, 225). The progressive can understand the reactionary, but the reactionary cannot understand the progressive, nor does he – and it is usually a he – want to (*DIM*, 239). Their deleterious influence has prevailed to the present day. Contemporary Islamic philosophy goes round in circles (*KQ*, 30). Shahrur's purpose in his writings is to call for a new fiqh, not a new Islam (*DIM*, 235).

Shahrur's strictures, never *ad hominem*, on practices and beliefs of today's fundamentalists are equally vigorous. To imagine that the practices of seventh century Arabia are of relevance today is ahistorical (*DIM*, 42). The Prophet Muhammad cleaned his teeth with a stick. The lesson to be drawn is that it is meritorious to clean your teeth, not that you use a stick for the purpose (*KQ*, 580).

He is similarly fierce about the fundamentalists' attitude to women's dress. The status of women greatly improved at the birth of Islam. The liberation of women started with the Prophet, but should not end then (*KQ*, 564, 595). The Koran addresses men and women equally. But fiqh has imposed a patriarchal view on society. Women came to be seen as possessions to be cherished as if they were camels or cars (*DIM*, 326). The Koran stressed the voluntary nature of belief (*DIM*, 143): *la ikrāh fi'l-dīn* (*sūrat al-baqara*, 256) ('There is no compulsion in religion.'). *Fa-man shā'a fa-liyu'min wa-man shā'a fa-liyakfur* (*sūrat al-kahf*, 29) ('Then whosoever will, let him believe, and whosoever will, let him disbelieve.')

If such an essential aspect of Islam as belief is voluntary, then what is the basis for thinking that dress is anything but voluntary and optional? (*DIM*, 329, 351) The custom in Syria today of having a party to celebrate 'the return to religion' of a girl who takes to wearing a headscarf is offensive to Islam (*DIM*, 327). Religion is far more than a piece of cloth. Fundamentalists and the religious establishment do not campaign with the same energy against bribery, fraud, irresponsibility, incompetence or political immorality (*DIM*, 175).

One concept that Shahrur develops in his second book is that of *istibdād* (absolutism, arbitrariness), which he sees as of three kinds, all described in the Koran and symbolised respectively by Far'ūn (Pharaoh), Hamān and Qarūn (*DIM*, 241, 246). The first is political absolutism, the second religious, the third economic. Each Arab and Islamic country has had its Pharaoh and its Qarūn legitimised by its Hamān (*DIM*, 259). The religious establishment has legitimised political absolutism and economic oppression. The challenge of contemporary Islam is to liberate people from these absolutisms.

There are positive concepts that Shahrur sees at the centre of Islam, above all *shūrā* (taking counsel) and *ibāha* (freedom and openness) (*DIM*, 142). Just as fiqh and authority are one pair of twins, so freedom and science are another (*DIM*, 220, 299). *Sīrū fil-ard fa'nzur kayfa bada'a al-khalq* (*sūrat al-ankabūt*, 20). ('Travel in the land and see how he originated creation.') Open enquiry and research should be the basis of legislation. There are always alternative points of view and these should not be silenced (*DIM*, 145). Allied to this scientific approach is the need to promote an educated social conscience (*DIM*, 145). An Islamic state should be pluralistic. The way to resolve consequent tensions is through consultation (*DIM*, 193) in a democratic environment. We are beholden to use Allah's gifts of reflection (*fikr*) and power of reasoning (*aql*) (*DIM*, 330). These gifts should be given total freedom to analyse rather than to memorise (*DIM*, 319).

Shahrur's Islamic society has more in common with European and American countries than any in the Arab or Islamic world today. He has, not surprisingly, been the subject of criticism.

But the popularity of Shahrur's work indicates that he is saying something that has hit a chord in contemporary Arab and Islamic thought. Shahrur has not been personally threatened, and in 1995 was an honoured participant in public debates on Islam in Lebanon and Morocco. He receives correspondence from readers all over the world. Most Muslims are conscientious believers who, like the rest of us, try to make sense of the world. Shahrur's work resembles that of other contemporary Arab writers on Islam – Farah Fuda and Nasr Hamid Abu Zayd of Egypt, and Muhammad Abd al-Jabiri of Morocco – who are articulating an Islamic intellectual system that repudiates that of Sayyid Qutb and his successors.

In many ways Shahrur's work goes beyond religious debate. He is identifying flaws in contemporary society – social and intellectual. People are reading his work not purely as religious commentary or an updated tafsīr. They are reading a social and political analysis of closed Arab Islamic societies.

The 1970s and 1980s witnessed a great Arab migration: an expansion of Arabs studying in Europe and America, a recruitment of labour and skills to Arabia and the Gulf and among Arab countries, an emigration of hundreds of thousands of Lebanese. Arabs have been able to see the strengths and limitations of their own heritage and society and compare them with others. The monopoly of information claimed by individual governments has broken down. The information technology revolution of the 1990s has accelerated these changes to the intellectual environment. Arab Muslims have the opportunity to think for themselves in a way that was discouraged a generation ago.

Shahrur's message is a contemporary message, a reassurance to the perplexed, a reassertion of the liberal tradition of Islam and an affirmation of the relevance of the faith to the pluralistic global village of the twentieth and twenty-first centuries. Hence the importance of his work.

Syria Seen by Outsiders

This was a review of three books published in *Asian Affairs* in June 2000, the month that Hafez al-Assad died. The three books were *Modern Syria: From Ottoman Rule to Pivotal Role in the Middle East*, edited by Moshe Ma'oz, Joseph Ginat and Onn Winckler, published by Sussex Academic Press, Brighton, 1999, *Demographic Developments and Population Policies in Ba'thist Syria* by Onn Winckler, published by Sussex Academic Press, Brighton, 1999, and *Syria and the New World Order* by Neil Quilliam, published by Ithaca Press, Reading, 1999.

We can expect a shelf of books in the next decade on Syria. The thirty-year regime of the old and ailing President Assad must be approaching its end though both his parents lived into their nineties. The possibilities of a peace settlement seem as good as they have ever been, with points of convergence of interests on the part of both the Israeli and Syrian governments. Peace – or its failure – will surely generate a literature.

Two of these books are the products of Israeli scholarship. For years Syria has been the demon of Israeli public opinion. For this reason the country has been watched closely by Israeli scholars who have used every resource available. Perhaps familiarity with an old enemy has led to a grudging appreciation or even affection. Both the collection of studies edited by Moshe Ma'oz, Joseph Ginat and Onn Winckler and the single volume by Onn Winckler have many positive points to make about Assad's Syria. In the former volume David W Lasch acknowledges the constraints on the liberalisation of the economy, but also understands the Syrian caution in its approach to the peace process. Assad, he writes, is well aware that 'Israel has benefited much more than its peace partners'. Eyal Zisser writes with authority on the likely scenario after President Assad goes. 'The 'Alawi coalition is not as cohesive as is generally believed,' he notes, 'and its ability to group together behind a single candidate should not be taken for granted.'

The case against Assad is assumed by Daniel Pipes who argues that Assad has fooled most people into thinking that he is a man of integrity: even Benjamin Netanyahu was taken in. But Pipes's case is flawed. Most leaders might keep their options open by giving out diverse signals, but when Assad does this it is duplicitous. Many of the instances cited of Assad's bad faith do not add up. A concurrence (p 275), an unwritten agreement (p 276), a reported agreement (p 276), an agreement with a third party about action by a fourth (p 277), an understanding (p 278) are built up into solemn commitments.

Assad's duplicity, Pipes argues, goes back to his Alawi origins. Alawis live 'double lives'. No Alawite can be trusted. The final proof of Assad's double game is his policy of 'simultaneously negotiating with Israel and building up his military machine against it', a policy based on precedents that go back at least two thousand years. *Qui desirat pacem, praeparet bellum.*

Moshe Ma'oz's essay provides us with a more balanced and reasoned assessment of Syria's role in the peace process.

Although most essays in *Modern Syria* are concerned with Syria as Israel's neighbour, two or three essays are thrown in that give perspective and an added value to the book. Yoram Shalit writes of the full social life of the English in nineteenth century Aleppo:

In the winter and spring they went on rabbit and wild goose hunts twice a week, while in the searing summer heat they went horseback riding at sunset. To this end, the traders kept their own horses and hunting dogs. They also played cricket, went on nature trips and held picnics at which they ate, drank wine and played games.

Neil Quilliam's book is the rewriting of a PhD thesis. He examines Syria's role in foreign affairs over the last thirty years and sees a consistency in objective. Syria's foreign policy has been determined not by internal affairs or opportunism, but by adapting to external circumstances. In particular, the collapse of the Soviet Union obliged Syria 'to leave the eclipsing shadow of the Soviet Union, and seek shelter on the periphery of US influence.' There was no surprise in Syria allying itself with the United States against Iraq in the war over Kuwait.

Quilliam's book is meticulously researched and clearly presented. He has a political scientist's approach to the distribution of power, the cascading of authority from the President through either the party or the security apparatus. A surprising omission from his excellent bibliography (albeit only of works in English) is *The Ba'th and the Creation of Modern Syria* by David Roberts (1987).

Onn Winckler's book is also rigorously researched. He places Syria's population policies within the broader regional context. He too is full of positive things to say about the policies of the Syrian government over the last thirty years. There has been a distinctive improvement in the quality of life as measured in life expectancy, infant and child mortality, and access to social services. 'According to UN data, by the late 1980s, ninety-nine per cent of the Syrian rural population had access to health services, compared with eighty per cent in Tunisia and only thirty per cent in Morocco.' Governments have reversed the previous hostility to contraception. Emphasis on women's rights to education and to outside work has also checked population growth. In contrast to most Middle Eastern countries the urban drift has been to most provincial centres and not to the one or two major cities.

The Syrian government does not encourage research in Syrian studies. There is no department of Political Science at any Syrian university. The books under review have all been written by outsiders. There is consequently in all of them a detachment and a clinical remoteness. They join other authoritative works by Patrick Seale, Volker Perthes, Nicolaos van Dam and Raymond Hinnebusch. But all would be enriched by the insights of a Syrian scholar. For this we will have to wait patiently.

A Turk from the North

This is a review of *Between Two Empires: Ahmet Ağaoğlu and the New Turkey* by A Holly Shissler, published by I B Tauris, London, 2003. The review appeared in *Asian Affairs* in 2005.

Ahmet Ağaoğlu (1869-1939) was from a prosperous Shi'ite family, living in the Armenian dominated part of Azerbaijan in the Russian Empire. He identified himself, initially, as a Muslim, but in the course of his life he was defined as a Persian, a Russian Muslim, an Azerbaijani, an Ottoman Turk and finally as a citizen of the Turkish Republic. He was educated in St Petersburg and in Paris and returned to Azerbaijan with the epithet 'Frank' Ahmet. This was not because of any fickleness on his part. The times and places in which he grew up were for most of his life in an extraordinary state of flux. This book, by an Assistant Professor of Near Eastern Languages and Civilizations at the University of Chicago, has told the story of his life and the times in which he lived, with scholarship and fascination. Chapters of biography alternate with assessments of Ağaoğlu's prolific writings.

Azerbaijan, at the end of the nineteenth century, had close cultural links with Persia. The majority of the population spoke a Turkic language. Armenians were a favoured Christian minority. Strengthening of Russian control coincided with a nascent nationalism. Ahmet went off to Paris as a young man and studied with Ernest Renan and James Darmesteter, and absorbed some of the positivist orientalism of the time. His first writings on contemporary Persian society appeared in the French journal edited by Juliette Adam. On his return to Azerbaijan, he worked as a lawyer and writer. But as Russian control tightened in the new century, Ahmet's Turkish identity asserted itself and he transferred to Istanbul. Ahmed Aghayev became Ahmet Ağaoğlu.

Although he was briefly in the parliament of the first Azerbaijani Republic after the First World War, it is as one who helped to define modern Turkishness that Ağaoğlu is perhaps best remembered. In the 1890s, he had been concerned about the future of Muslim peoples and argued that the Turkic languages were ill suited to the Arabic script and held back progress. He also argued for the full participation of women in public life. Thus he became a natural ally of Mustafa Kemal, later Atatürk, founder and first President of the Turkish Republic, especially as his arguments were based on wide Islamic scholarship. Ağaoğlu was one of a number of Turkish intellectuals in the generation before Mustafa Kemal's reforms of the 1920s who came from the Russian Empire. There, these men had been second-class citizens because they were Muslims. They were able to empathise not with the old Ottoman ruling class but with the marginalised small town Anatolian Muslims who were the core of Atatürk's support. Ağaoğlu worked as a Director-General of Press and Information and was a Professor of Law at the University of Istanbul. He was active in the Free Republican Party, the opposition party that flourished for a year and was suppressed in 1930. It may be that he never received the full recognition his talents and experience merited because of poor relations with Ismet Inönü.

Professor Shissler weaves her way through the maze of Russian, Persian and Turkish – and even French – cultural and political complexities with skill and readability. It is an absorbing story and raises questions of religious, ethnic and political identity that have echoes far beyond the Caucasus a century ago.

Cilician Armenia

I have been interested in Cilician Armenia since the 1960s. My interest was triggered by an essay in *Aspects of the Crusades* by the New Zealand historian, J J Saunders. I went to the castle of Sis (Kozan) in 1963, in which year I also read for the first time *Life in Asiatic Turkey* by E J Davis, who described his visit to Sis and other Cilician castles in 1876. In the 1990s I made visits to Cilicia from Damascus and became enchanted by the castles, their locations and their history. I have been taking tour groups to the castles since 2001. This was the text of a talk I gave to the Royal Society for Asian Affairs in January 2003. It has not been published before.

In Shakespeare's *King Henry the Fourth Part Two*, it will be recalled, the dying king says:

> It hath been prophesied to me many years
> I should not die but in Jerusalem,
> Which vainly I supposed the Holy Land.
> But bear me to that chamber; there I'll lie:
> In that Jerusalem shall Harry die.

Shakespeare is recording the unfulfilled allure of the crusade in the case of King Henry, who reigned over a century after the fall of Acre, the last Crusader mainland territory, in 1291. In King Henry's childhood, a visitor from the Near East came to England trying to revive interest in a crusade. He was the deposed King Leon V of Armenia whose reduced kingdom based in Cilicia in southern Turkey was finally crushed by the Egyptian Mamluks in 1375. Leon had been captured, was ransomed and settled in France. He came to England in 1385, offered to be a peace broker in the Hundred Years War, and celebrated Christmas with the court of King Richard II at Eltham Palace. Leon returned to France and died in 1393 and is buried among the French kings at the Cathedral of St Denis, north of Paris.

Midway between the reign of Henry IV and the writing of the play, London saw the publication of a book by another member of the royal family of Armenian Cilicia. This was *The Floure of Histories*, the translation of a chronicle that was also a call for a crusade. This work had been written (or dictated) in French by Prince Hetum of Korykus at Poitiers in 1307. There were two English editions of this chronicle, in 1515 and 1520. This work obviously had significance throughout western Europe in the sixteenth century for it was available also in Latin, German, Italian, Dutch and Spanish. Hetum's book,

La Fleur des Histoires de la Terre d'Orient, included a history of western Asia and of the Mongols.

What was this Armenian kingdom, representatives of which had fitful access to and influence with kings and popes and potentates in western Europe in the later Middle Ages? The Christian Cilician kingdom of Armenia lasted, as a kingdom, from 1199 to 1375, though Armenians had migrated to the area from the tenth century and there was a major Armenian presence in Cilicia and neighbouring areas until the early twentieth century.

In the next few pages I wish to draw attention to a remarkable political structure that defies normal categorisation. There is no adequate available history, partly because of the intimidating skills required in writing such a work. When the Greek American historian, Speros Vryonis, proposed writing of the transformation of Asia Minor from being Christian and Byzantine to being Muslim and Turkish, an older colleague told him 'simply and calmly, that it would be impossible'. A similar challenge faces the historian of Cilician Armenia. He or she would need to be familiar with chronicles written in medieval Armenian, Latin, Syriac, Arabic, Turkish and Byzantine Greek. Much has been written on aspects of the history of the period in many European languages, but mostly in French and Russian.

Cilician Armenia has been marginal to greater historical processes – to the history of Byzantium, to the rise and fall of the Eastern Mediterranean Crusader states, to Seljuk and Ottoman Turkey and even to the history of mainstream Armenia, based around Ani in far eastern Turkey and the modern Republic of Armenia. Cilician Armenia was a Christian state with a historical tradition that predated Byzantium. It was Christian on the frontier of Islamic lands but was made up of migrants and settlers not from Europe (like the Crusading states) but from further east. Its position was vulnerable with potential enemies on all sides, unlike the Christian kingdom of Georgia with securer natural geographical boundaries – the Caspian and Black Seas and the Caucasus mountains.

Yet the remains of Cilician Armenia on the ground are colossal. In the area north of Adana there are literally dozens of castles and fortifications that are as vast and as architecturally fascinating as any other castles in the world. But herein lies another problem. The area has always been a frontier between civilisations. It saw the battle of Issus between Alexander the Great and the Persians. It saw a shifting border over the course of hundreds of years between Byzantium and Arab Islam. Today it is the borderline between speakers of

Turkish and speakers of Arabic. These castles are often located in strategic sites and have been occupied by Greeks, Romans, Byzantines, Arabs, Crusaders, Mamluks and Turks as well as Armenians. It is sometimes difficult to identify who contributed what when. But recent scholars, most notably Robert W Edwards, have teased out the Armenian features.

Multiple occupancy of the region has led to a further challenge. Different people gave different names to the one site. The castle just north of Birecik on the Euphrates is known as Rum Kalesi in Turkish, Hromgla in Armenian and Ranculat in Crusader literature. There are linguistic similarities there. But the port of Ayas has also been known as Lajarro. Today it is known as Yumurtalık. We have names without identifiable places and places whose medieval name is not known for certain. One of the best known and most frequently visited castles in the area, forty kilometres east of Adana, is Yılan Kalesi, Snake Castle. It is a massive pile with distinctly Armenian features. It has obviously been of vital strategic importance but its medieval name is still disputed. Only in the last twenty years have serious attempts been made to reconcile names and sites.

My own fascination with Cilician Armenia has been fired by visits to the castles and other sites in the area over the last forty years. I approach the subject as a passionate amateur and have sought answers to questions I constantly ask myself. It has seemed to me that the kingdom has had an interest beyond a mere narrative of the events of two or three hundred years. But let me summarise those events and at the same time draw attention to some of the broader points of interest.

In the tenth century an Armenian kingdom stretching from Lake Van to the Caucasus saw a flowering of art and architecture based at their capital of Ani, east of Kars, on the present-day Turkish Armenian border. That kingdom traced its history back to the fourth century. Its Christian identity was based on a liturgy, a script and a language, and a frosty relationship with Byzantium. The Armenian Church accepted the first Councils of the Church but diverged from the defining Council of Chalcedon in 451, whose decrees were accepted by both Rome and Constantinople. The Armenians were monophysites, insisting on the single nature of Christ. Armenian liturgy and the alphabet were also established in the fifth century. In subsequent centuries individual Armenians served the Byzantine state up to the level of Emperor, such as Heraclius during whose reign Syria was lost to Arab Muslims in the seventh century. But during the tenth and eleventh centuries Turks were advancing west threatening both Armenia and the eastern realms of the Byzantine

Empire. Ani fell to the Byzantines in 1045. The Byzantines suffered a major defeat to the Seljuk Turks in 1071 at the Battle of Manzikert. Most of eastern Anatolia broke up into small Turkish statelets owing nominal allegiance to the Abbasid Caliphate in Baghdad, and small Armenian statelets that lived on their wits.

Armenians had for long had a delicate relationship with Constantinople, resisting attempts to assume or impose political or ecclesiastical authority. The Byzantine Empire awarded individual Armenians with castles and territories in Cilicia from the tenth century after those lands were recovered from the Abbasids.

Cilicia is cut off from the Anatolian plateau by the Taurus mountains that rise in places to 4,000 metres. From classical times and earlier the land of Cilicia had looked out to the Mediterranean rather than inland. Along the coast there were remains of Hellenistic and Roman sites that were developed and rebuilt under Byzantine auspices. Today the coast to the east of Silifke is richly scattered with masonry from Hellenistic, Roman and Byzantine times. In the years from 600 to 1100, Cilicia was successively under the control of Constantinople and Baghdad, and Constantinople again. The towns of Korykus, Tarsus, Adana and Mısıs were culturally mixed. Villages in the plains and on the mountain slopes were agriculturally rich, with wheat, cotton, grapes, olives and other fruit. Tiny coastal ports were ideal bases for piracy, the sea abundant with fish. The mountains in eastern Cilicia enclose a triangle of fertile, well-watered (and frequently malarial) land around the Pyramus (Ceylan) river and its tributaries, now the cotton-growing region of Çukurova.

The most prominent Armenian family that built up a base under Byzantine sponsorship was the Hetumids. Their base was at Lampron, in the present-day town of Çamlıyayla, sixty kilometres north-west of Tarsus. The Hetumids accepted Orthodox religious authority and were on the whole loyal to Constantinople.

In the late eleventh century a second family, the Rupenids, who had been closer to the Armenian establishment in the east, migrated south through the mountains south of present day Kayseri, and took possession of the castle of Vahka, perched on a crag in the heart of the thickly wooded Taurus mountains.

The story of Cilician Armenia revolves around these two families, and their relations, hot and cold, with Greek Byzantium, the Turkish Seljuks and the Latin northern Crusader state of Antioch. Each family and members of the families competed for the support of other notables. The detailed history is as bloody as any, marked particularly by fratricide and treachery. The Hetumids were for long sympathetic to Byzantium and tended to be scholarly and artistic. The Rupenids were tougher, more politically astute and flexible. Although loyal to the Armenian church, Rupenid leaders had a wider vision and were readier to make political, religious and cultural compromises with western Europe.

I will not stretch your patience with a detailed narrative. The whole history is concisely summarised in thirty pages by T S R Boase in the volume he edited, *The Cilician Kingdom of Armenia*, published in 1978. I will pause on two reigns: first, that of King Leon I, known as 'the Great' or 'the Magnificent' who introduced many western features and made Cilician Armenia a major minor regional power and then, that of the reign of King Hetum I in the middle of the thirteenth century, who was a pivot in east-west relations, being an active ally of the Mongols and remaining in touch with the Pope.

Throughout the twelfth century the Rupenids consolidated their authority based on the city-fortresses of Anavarza and Sis, above the modern town of Kozan. Their power was based on these and other mountain fortresses, frequently rebuilt on earlier sites. But they also expanded their authority down to the plains and the cities of Korykos (Kız Kalesi today), Tarsus, Mısıs (ancient Mopsuestria) and the port of Ayas (today's Yumurtalık). The Armenian state became an uneasy alliance of the mountains and the more cosmopolitan plain. The limits of power fluctuated, within the natural boundaries of the Mediterranean Sea to the south, the Taurus mountains to the north, the Amanus range of mountains to the east and the Seraph river (the Gök Su today) to the west. Byzantium made claims to the southern ports. Beyond the Amanus range from 1099 the Crusader Principality of Antioch lay to the east. To the north behind the Taurus mountains for most of the period lay the Seljuk Sultanate of Rum, based in Konya.

Towards the end of the twelfth century Leon the Magnificent introduced many remarkable features into Cilician Armenia. It will be recalled that in the 1180s the Crusader states were all but wiped out by Saladin's campaigns. The Armenians had negotiated relations of detached cordiality with the Kingdom of Jerusalem. It was a relationship. The Rupenid Armenians had assisted the First Crusade in their overland trek across Anatolia. During the century of the Kingdom of Jerusalem, Armenians strengthened their presence in Palestine and founded the cathedral of St James in Jerusalem. Crusaders and Armenians intermarried. When Jerusalem fell in 1187 the other major Crusader-held cities of Tyre, Tripoli and Antioch were under threat. Meanwhile confused rivalries in Constantinople were weakening the Byzantine state, making it an easy picking for the Venetian-led Fourth Crusade in 1204. The abdication of one of the most successful Seljuk sultans, Kilij Arslan II, in 1189, led to a struggle for succession in central Anatolia. In the 1190s the Armenian state in Cilicia under Leon was the only area of stability in a region of change and turmoil. Leon aspired to raise his state from the status of a nominal Byzantine vassaldom to that of an independent kingdom. He was in diplomatic touch with the Holy Roman Empire, first with the Emperor Frederick Barbarossa. That Emperor was drowned in Armenian-held territory north of Silifke en route for a Crusade, but ten years later his son, Henry, awarded Leon an independent kingship and on 6 January 1199 Leon was crowned king at the cathedral in Tarsus by the head of the Armenian church, the Catholicos, in the presence of representatives of the Pope, the Holy Roman Emperor, the Byzantine Emperor and of the Syrian Nestorian church. Bishops and barons and the leading men of the realm were witnesses.

Leon also worked to neutralise the Rupenid-Hetumid conflict. He besieged and seized the Hetumid base of Lampron, then married one of his nieces into the Hetumid family and installed his mother as chatelaine of the castle of Lampron. He also appointed Hetumids as his closest advisers. A united Armenia became politically internationalised.

And not only politically. Saladin's campaigns had checked the commercial activities of the Italian city states, Genoa, Venice and Pisa. The Armenians, having come from landlocked lands, had no naval tradition. Leon awarded the sea-faring merchant states privileges in the ports of Ayas and Korykos. The Genoese quarter of Korykos was around the church of St Laurence. A leading Genoese, Benotto Zakaria, was close to King Leon. The Pisans specialised as money-changers. Venetians had their own church, St Mark's. But also there were people from Montpellier and Barcelona and one of the gates was called Porte des Allemands, suggesting a German presence. The chief exports were slaves, timber, hides and wheat. Timber was particularly coveted by regimes in Egypt. Export dues built up an economy.

Further western interests were introduced by concessions to the Latin church. The Franciscans opened up houses, and renewed concessions were made to the Pope on matters of liturgy and ecclesiastical dress. Shortly before Leon's reign, one Armenian monk, Nerses, surnamed the Gracious and later canonised, had gone along with these reforms. He wrote a long poem on the

Fall of Edessa, described by Steven Runciman as 'somewhat lacking in both poetical and historical interest'. However he welcomed these changes, in words translated a century ago by Zabelle Boyajian:

> … I shall lift mine eyes above
> Beholding near me those I love.
> My arms about you I shall fold,
> Rejoicing with a joy untold;
> And my black robes aside will lay
> To dress in greens and crimsons gay.

In this sphere Leon took the biggest risks, encountering popular resistance from many in the church and his leading nobles. From 1147 the head of the Armenian Church, the Catholicos, was based outside the Cilician territory controlled by the kings. Hromgla on the Euphrates was awarded to the Armenian Church after the fall of the Crusader Principality of Edessa (today's Urfa or Şanlıurfa) in 1146: paradoxically a Christian centre in a Muslim state. It remained the base for the Armenian church, a famous centre for manuscript illumination, until it fell to the Mamluks in 1292 when the headquarters was transferred to the political capital of Sis.

The strength of Cilician Armenia was based on the elaborate castles in the mountains, but the castles away from the hilly homeland were expensive to keep in repair and Leon had no hesitation in handing over some castles to the military knights who were becoming a feature of the Crusading states. There too castles were too expensive for families to maintain. The orders of the military knights were like multinationals with enormous wealth throughout Europe. Only they with their gigantic resources were able to build and maintain the newer city-fortresses. The Knights Hospitallers received the castle of Silifke, at the western extremity of Armenian control and rebuilt it at the same time that they were recasting their masterpiece in Syria, Krak des Chevaliers. Leon diversified his European contacts by handing sites over to the Teutonic Knights who received the small castle of Amouda on the Pyramus river, and reconstructed the square keep in the 1220s.

Relations with the Templars were less happy. They had acted as a buffer statelet between the Principality of Antioch and Cilician Armenia. Leon's long-term aim was to unite Armenia and Antioch. With the Prince of Antioch he followed a policy like the one he successfully employed against the Hetumids. The Templar stronghold of Baghras, north of Antioch, was seized; the Prince of Antioch was captured. In exchange for his release Leon haggled for the castles between Antioch and the Mediterranean and the Prince's son received the hand of another of Leon's nieces. With this peace offensive the role of buffer state and the services of the Templars were no longer needed.

Perhaps the greatest innovations were cultural. Leon was impressed by the artificial feudalism of the Crusader states. There was a notion of what might be called 'line management' that would be an improvement on the chaotic anarchy that was the norm in Cilicia. He introduced Frankish titles for his officials: *maréchal, connetable, préfet.* Such titles coexisted with other titles such as *proximus* and *sebaste* derived from Latin and Greek, and *amīr* and *naqīb* derived from Arabic. Such cultural changes extended into private life. Men took to addressing each other as Sire. Personal names such as Geoffrey, Simon and Robert start to appear, in addition to Thoros and Oshin and Constantine.

By the time of Leon's death in 1219, Cilician Armenia was an independent state, the most substantial Christian state in the Eastern Mediterranean. The Crusader states never recovered from the campaigns of Saladin, and throughout the thirteenth century fought and negotiated survival from a position of weakness. Byzantium was shattered by the Fourth Crusade of 1204. Constantinople was occupied, and three successor states preserved an Orthodox identity in Trebizond, Nicaea and Epirus.

For fifty years after Leon's death Cilician Armenia played a role in the geopolitics of western Asia. Armenia was courted by the West and by Constantinople. In the words of the nineteenth century British historian, Bishop William Stubbs:

[There was a] skilful balancing of Greek and Roman influences; to obtain money from the West and arms from Constantinople, to obtain alternate alliances by royal marriages, and ecclesiastical freedom by regular variations between the two poles. For this latter policy the position of the Armenian Church was peculiarly fitted. It was so far schismatic as not to be integrally a portion of either Roman or Byzantine obedience, and so little heretical that its alliance was courted by both communions.

Leon had no sons but his only daughter, Zabel, married (as her third husband) Hetum from the rival family; he became King Hetum I. As in the Kingdom of Jerusalem heiresses could not rule themselves and an appropriate escort had to be found. In the case of Hetum this was a great success.

In the 1240s a new force burst on to the scene – the Mongols. Already Georgian Christians had allied themselves with the Mongols and both

Georgians and Armenians fought in 1243 on the Mongol side in a battle near Sivas that defeated the Seljuks. (The Seljuk army included 2,000 Franks) The Seljuk ruler was killed. His wife and daughter fled to Hetum who handed them over to the Mongols. Four years later Hetum sent his brother, the Constable Sempad, on an embassy to the Mongol capital, Karakorum, and secured concessions and protection for the Armenians. Sempad was a remarkable man – a translator from the French, a military leader, a diplomat, a lawyer and a poet. He corresponded in French with the Crusader noble, Jean d'Ibelin, and wrote an illuminating report on his far eastern travels. In return for protection from the Mongols – and bear in mind that they were to sack Baghdad in 1258 – the Armenians agreed to withhold the export of timber to Mamluk Egypt. The King himself then took the road to Karakorum in 1253. Hetum accompanied the Mongols on their occupation of Mamluk Aleppo and Damascus but in the 1260s the Mamluks fought back. After the Mongols were forced out of Syria the Mamluks levelled their sights on the Mongols' most visible allies, Cilician Armenia.

The beginning of the long drawn-out end for Cilician Armenia came with the Mamluk Baybars's raid on Armenia in 1266. The capital, Sis, was devastated, and castles to the east were taken. For the next century there were periodic raids on the kingdom. Armenia was on the defensive. Even so, the final collapse of the Crusader states in 1291 gave something of a new lease of life. Ayas became a major port for western traders. When Marco Polo came to Ayas to start his overland journey to the Far East at the end of the century he noted:

... [the] lord of Lesser Armenia is a king who maintains good and just government in his country . . .It is a land of many villages and towns, amply stocked with the means of life. It also affords good sport with all sorts of wild game, both beast and fowl. The climate, however, is far from healthy; it is, in fact, extremely enervating. Hence, the nobility of the country, who used to be men of valour and stalwart soldiers, are now craven and mean-spirited and excel in nothing but drinking.

On the sea coast lies the town of Ayas, a busy emporium. For you must know that all the spices and cloths from the interior are brought to this town, and all other goods of high value; and merchants of Venice and Genoa and everywhere else come here and buy them. And merchants and others who wish to penetrate the interior all make this town the starting-point of their journey.

Hetum's successors persisted in pinning their hopes on the Mongols. There were heady dreams of the Mongols embracing Christianity. One khan's wife was Christian and had her son baptised with the name Nicholas, but these hopes turned to dust and the Mongols seemed ultimately to be false allies. At the beginning of the fourteenth century, the Mongol khan, Ghazan, embraced Islam and his successors showed no sympathy for Christian Cilician Armenia. Meanwhile the kingdom was pressed on the east by regular raids from the Mamluks who allowed independence only on the condition of the payment of a huge annual tribute. The Mamluk base was Egypt. It is interesting to note that the final threats to Cilician Armenia came not from inland Anatolia – the Taurus provide adequate protection – but from the sea.

During the final decades, Cilician Armenia was constantly battered by Mamluk raids. Its ports and castles were periodically sacked. The Armenian barons gave little security to a succession of kings, none of whom had the strategic insight and determination of Leon I or Hetum I. The kings and his leading counsellors hoped for relief from the west. Successive synods accepted latinisation measures in liturgy. Such concessions led to riots in Adana and Sis. Appeals were made to western Europe. One such was the book I have already mentioned, *The Floure of Histories*, a call to arms that had an extensive appeal in western Europe, albeit a futile reminder of an obsolescent vogue. There were vain proposals of an alliance with the Mongols and the use of Armenia and Cyprus as bases for a new crusade.

An alliance with the Lusignan Christian kingdom of Cyprus was the only lifeline left. In 1342 Guy de Lusignan was invited to be king of Armenia. The Lusignans had several family ties with the two main Armenian families and for much of its last thirty-three years the kingdom was ruled by a family that was basically French. Three kings, all called Constantine, ruled defensively. The last was murdered in 1373 and a Lusignan, Leon, was called to the throne. He never had a chance. He and his wife, Margaret of Soissons, were crowned at Sis on 14 September 1374 to face an immediate siege from Mamluk Egyptians. The city fell and was sacked. Leon, his wife and daughter were captured and taken first to Aleppo, and then to Egypt. Leon declined an invitation to become a Muslim and an amir. Margaret and the daughter ended up in Jerusalem and are buried in the Armenian Cathedral there. Leon set off on his travels that ended up in a tomb a few metres from that of Louis XIV and other mighty kings of France.

So what has survived of the Cilician Armenian kingdom? Sis remained the base for the Catholicos until 1441 when it was transferred to Etchmiadzin in the Armenian heartlands just north-east of Mount Ararat. In and around the modern Turkish town of Kozan there were churches and monasteries until the beginning of the twentieth century, and ruins of religious buildings just about survive. The castles that were the strongholds of Armenian kings and barons survive, huge city-fortresses, with their rounded towers and their exploitation of physical environment. Today they are conscientiously protected and looked after by the Turkish government, but do not attract the visitors that they deserve.

Vahka is on a limestone spine of mountain several hundred metres above a valley on the road from Kozan to Kayseri. Originally Byzantine it was captured by the Armenians in the late 1090s and was of importance for most of the twelfth century, until the centre of political gravity under Leon I moved southwards.

Sis, above Kozan, is an eyrie-like citadel, commanding extensive views over the plain of Çukurova. It was developed by the Byzantines, and became a fortified site under the Abbasids in the ninth century. During the eleventh and twelfth centuries it changed hands between the Byzantines and the Rupenids. But the Armenians occupied and constructed the citadel in the years around 1172, and it became the principal residence of the king. Most probably Hetum I was responsible for the Armenian work in the mid-thirteenth century. It has many characteristic features of Armenian military architecture – the exploitation of the terrain and the use made of the irregular cliffs of the mountain. The total circuit walls measure almost three kilometres. It was occupied and used by the Mamluks who inserted an inscription into the main entrance.

Anavarza, on a mountain two hundred metres above the remains of a Roman city, had also been an Abbasid city. The entire outcrop is nearly five kilometres in length. The Crusaders occupied it briefly in 1097 on their way to Antioch and the keep shows the earliest Crusader architecture in the Middle East. During the twelfth century it was mainly, though not exclusively, in Armenian hands and became their capital and the site for burial of Armenian kings. A church still stands with frescos and Armenian inscriptions. Anavarza was subject to both Mamluk and Mongol raids in the thirteenth century and after the collapse of the Armenian kingdom the site was occupied by the Mamluks for a century. There is evidence for all periods of occupation.

Lampron, the Hetumid base in the wooded hills to the east of the Cilician Gates, the main route from the coast to the Anatolian plateau, is on a mound above a modern summer resort town. The construction is a mixture of

Byzantine and Armenian. Its impregnability allowed the Hetumids to retain a degree of independence in spite of attempts by the Rupenids to capture it. It was absorbed into the Rupenid kingdom by subterfuge.

Yılan Kalesi, Snake Castle, has a triple wall adding to the existing defences provided by the rugged mountain outcrop. Those who climb to the castle can see a relief of one of the Armenian kings. For long it was thought that the portrait was of Leon the Magnificent. But this portrait shows him wielding a sceptre and sitting on the ground. If we look at the coinage of Leon I he is always shown sitting on a chair or throne. Later coinage of Hetum I and his fourteenth century successors show the kings seated on the floor. It is suggested that nominal vassaldom to neighbouring Muslim states obliged the portrayal of the king to be in what was seen as sitting in an 'oriental' fashion.

Hromgla, Rum Kalesi, the religious centre, far from the commercial and political centres, is on a peninsula formed by the Euphrates and a tributary. T E Lawrence went there in 1911 and Freya Stark nearly fifty years later. But it does not receive many visitors and is today accessible only by boat.

These are only six castles, five of them in Cilicia. Robert W Edwards, who spent nearly twenty years researching Cilician Armenian fortifications, lists seventy-five Armenian fortifications in the area, some remote and accessible only by foot or by mule, others the re-working of earlier constructions. Most of the churches and religious buildings have been lost though Kilise Camii (Church mosque) in the centre of Tarsus was built as a church by an early fourteenth century king. The Armenians relied on their forts and have left little in their cities, Korykos, Tarsus, Mısıs or Ayas. Some of the earlier coins were based on the Arab dinar. In the otherwise excellent museum of Tarsus there is a collection of coins used in Cilicia from classical to Ottoman times but the Armenian centuries are ignored. The thirteenth and fourteenth centuries saw something of a flowering of Armenian literature, with chronicles and universal histories, at least one written in verse. The most impressive artistic remains however have been the illustrated manuscripts. At Hromgla, Rum Kalesi, Toros Roslin headed a scriptorium. He broke away from the more formulaic traditions and brought in elements of contemporary life with a dynamic realism. Some of these have survived and are in museums around the world – Yerevan, Washington, Jerusalem and St Petersburg.

I have called this paper 'medieval multiculturalism' because I think this state showed an extraordinary openness to cultural influences from all directions. Cilician Armenia was not a foreign Christian imposition as were the Crusader states. Though traditionally landlocked the people of Armenia quickly exploited their proximity to the Mediterranean. Maritime commerce was delegated to the Italians, though an Armenian diaspora from the western Mediterranean to China provided agents in ports and cities everywhere. Western dress, the French language, titles and feudal notions were adopted without the Armenians losing the essentials of their own culture – their religion, their language and script, and their distinctive architecture. Armenians often worked well with Muslim powers. Armenian soldiers served in Seljuk armies. Armenian craftsmen worked all over the Eastern Mediterranean.

Some of the linkages were the result of marriage policies. The Crusader migrants to the Eastern Mediterranean were mostly male. The first two kings of Jerusalem both took Armenian brides – not from Cilicia but from the statelets to the east. I have already mentioned Leon I's policy of working for long-term security with marriage alliances. Several Cilician Armenians married women from the Kingdom of Jerusalem. In the last century of the Armenian kingdom there were marriage alliances between the families of Cyprus and Armenia. There were, as far as I can gather, no marriages between Armenian men and Muslim women. By contrast Seljuk sultans married outside the faith with brides from Byzantium and Georgia – and very occasionally Armenia.

In many ways the geographical situation of Cilicia lent itself to this multiculturalism. Until a century ago many of the cities of the eastern Mediterranean were similarly cosmopolitan. We tend to see history in terms of modern nation states, and Cilicia is today part of Turkey and Turkish history. But Cilicia only became under the control of the Ottomans in the middle of the fifteenth century. The Ottomans occupied swathes of south eastern Europe before they occupied Adana. And until the early twentieth century Cilicia had mixed communities – Greeks, Italians, Persians and Arabs, as well as Armenians and Turks. Mersin, a nineteenth century city, was built up largely by Syrians. The cities, ruins and mountains of Cilicia are a palimpsest of the people who have made a home there over the last three millennia. Not least among these people have been the kings, barons, masons and artists of the kingdom of Cilician Armenia.

Kuwait and Iraq 1971

From September 1970 to July 1971 I studied Arabic at the Middle East Centre for Arab Studies (MECAS) at the village of Shemlan in Lebanon. For most of the time it was an intensive period of immersion in the language: five hours of tuition in small classes (no more than four) every day and homework due for the following day. In May, the teachers – all Palestinian or Lebanese – had a holiday and the students went off for a 'language break', living in another village or a monastery. The Centre closed down in 1977. Thirty years later a volume of memoirs of students was published, *The Arabists of Shemlan Volume 1 MECAS Memoirs 1944-1978*, published by Stacey International, London, 2006. A shorter version of this paper was published in that volume.

I kept a diary during my MECAS year, September 1970 to July 1971. For the most part, it makes pretty boring reading today. Little things, like a lost fountain pen, depressed me for days on end. I was intensely competitive about word tests. I record the behaviour of the cat, visits to restaurants and the weather. Why did I bother? Well, the memory is stimulated. Feelings, aspirations, disappointments are recalled. Scraps of reported dialogue bring to mind more of the conversation. Some people spring back to life. Other names I recorded mean nothing to me today. I have seen many of my fellow-students in later years. The MECAS Association and various official networks keep us briefed about what we are all up to. But as I look back on that year it was an intense experience that reflected previous events in my life and anticipated others. Outside the intellectual and aesthetic appreciation of the Middle East, the central theme has been the establishment, sustaining and renewal of friendships with individuals from the region.

I had first become interested in the Arab world at the time of Suez. In 1956 I was still at school and my parents dissuaded me from going to London and demonstrating against Anthony Eden's policy. Two years later I went to university and formed a close friendship with a Kuwaiti student, Ahmad al-Duaij. Ahmad brought an international sophistication and an air of affluence – *he had a motorcar* – to our small provincial university. We spent much time together. He cooked Arab meals. I learned about the importance of Gamal Abdul Nasser to his generation. Ahmad asked me to check the English of his dissertation on the history of Kuwait and invited me to the annual gathering of Kuwaiti students in the UK, held at a hotel in Weston-super-Mare. I learned a lot from Ahmad. My own special subject was Gladstone and I chose to write a long essay on the Egyptian background to Urabi Pasha – a less successful

Abdul Nasser – whose revolt led to Gladstone's government occupying that country.

Immediately after graduating, I went off to spend a year teaching mathematics (badly) in Turkey. I travelled around that country during long weekends and also Syria, Lebanon, Jordan and Egypt during the holidays that were generously provided. I returned to Britain to do research on Whiggism and to teach, but was restless about the Middle East and found easy distraction in books about the region. After getting Whiggism out of my system, I joined the British Council in 1967 and asked for a posting to the Arab world. The following spring I was told I was to go to Jordan.

In the month or two before setting off for Jordan, I was working in the Manchester office and started to take some Arabic lessons from an Iraqi student, Ilham Said, who was working for a PhD at the University of Manchester Institute for Science and Technology. Ilham taught me how to distinguish the letters and some basic conversation. We were together watching the television news on the evening of 14 July 1968 when the Ba'th Party came to power in Baghdad.

In Amman, I took Arabic lessons privately and asked my bosses to send me to MECAS. Undeterred by Jordan's descent into civil war – Black September – or the loss of my car taken at gunpoint by (I learned later) the Popular Front for the Liberation of Palestine, I arrived for lessons at Shemlan in late September 1970. The first week of studies was interrupted by the death of Nasser. Classes were cancelled and we were advised not to go down to Beirut.

Rereading my diary, I find life was pretty routine. Classes, heavy rain and consequent problems with plumbing, good food at cheap restaurants, lots of entertaining, meeting visitors to Shemlan and getting to know my fellow-students and their wives. Life, wives apart, was collegiate if not monastic. Thatcher's Bar, named after a nineteenth century author of an Arabic grammar, at lunchtime on Friday provided a release and weekends opportunities for exploration.

Throughout the first six months loomed the prospect of The Language Break – as if what we had been studying at MECAS was not The Language. We were expected to get away from the Centre and to cope alone in real life situations with real Arabs, not the kindly and indulgent teachers and villagers of Shemlan. People had various ideas – monasteries, remote villages in Jordan or Yemen. I had the offer of staying with some Bedu for a few days but my diary records an anxiety – 'two nights under canvas might be bearable'.

I decided to look up Ahmad in Kuwait and Ilham in Baghdad. So I drove to Damascus and took a plane to Kuwait. I booked myself into a cheap hotel, and wandered round the town, spending afternoons on the balcony of the oldest hotel in Kuwait, Funduk al-Jāzira al-ʿArabiya, built in 1946. I caught up with Ahmad, who was head of the Kuwait Planning Board. He was as bright as ever and asked about Beirut. 'People from the Gulf no longer go to Lebanon to enjoy themselves,' he told me. 'There are too many of our friends, family and neighbours there. We go to Athens instead.' He offered me a bottle of (forbidden) whisky. I declined: 'I never drink spirits and I am sure you can find someone who will really enjoy it. But thank you for the thought.'

Kuwait was far more interesting than I had anticipated. I talked to anyone and everyone, and met Syrians, Yemenis and Palestinians. I sailed on a dhow to the island of Failaka, the price of the ticket including a communal meal eaten off a reed mat on the deck of the boat. I enjoyed the variety of communities, Arab, Iranian and South Asian, who made up the working population. I was fascinated by the museum illustrating the life and work of the pearl fishers.

I moved on. I found my way to the bus station early one morning and took a shared taxi to the Iraqi border. Then another car took me on to Baghdad, at great speed through the Marshes, Amara and Kut and reached the capital in the middle of the afternoon. In Baghdad I stayed with Gail and David Wright. David had been Administrative Officer at MECAS and was now doing commercial work in the Embassy. Their house was my base for a few days.

I now set off in search of Ilham. I had a telephone number and an address. The former did not work and locating houses that matched addresses in the Najib Pasha quarter was not straightforward. I eventually found Ilham's mother who directed me to the Centre for Petroleum Studies, and there I met up with Ilham. I showed off my Arabic, which amused her greatly.

'What a cute Lebanese accent you've got. You say *quwais* and *muta'assif* and *min fadlak.*'

'That's what I've been taught. What am I supposed to say, then?'

'*Zain* and *aasif* and *rajaan.*'

'Well, I'll try while I'm here, but they'll laugh at me back in Lebanon if I use them there.'

'Come to a party on Sunday evening with some of my friends.'

And what a party that was. Just before sunset we boarded a boat and sailed down the Tigris to Jazīrat al-Khanāzīr, the Island of Pigs. There were twenty or

70

thirty of us, friendly sympathetic people. Among them were, I noted, men and women, Muslims, Christians and Jews; people whose first language was Arabic, Turkish or Kurdish. We landed after dark on the island that was unoccupied and uninhabited. By the river some of my new friends got a fire going. They circled the fire with sticks and a few plaice-like fish were skewered on to the sticks. *Mazgouf*. Food, conversation, laughter, games, music and dancing: this was not the grim Iraq I had been led to expect.

The following day I had to return westwards. I took the Nairn bus to Damascus. 'A long bus for passengers is attached to an articulated lorry. It is air-conditioned inside, with small windows, tunnel-like and resembles the inside of an aeroplane,' I noted in my diary. Then over the desert – Falluja, across the Euphrates at Habbaniyya, and on and on to Rutba. Leaving Rutba and Iraq was no trouble but the entry into Syria at Khan Abu Sham took three pitiless hours, between one and four in the morning. Damascus by mid-day.

I collected my car and decided to wander off north of Damascus, without any clear objective. There were always people hitching lifts. I picked people up, imposed my Arabic on them, remembering to drop *zain* and *aasif*, and to revert to *quwais* and *muta'assif*. I took people to Rankus and was invited in for lunch. I went on to Yabrud and was invited by a teacher to stay the night. Next morning the teacher, Abd al-Rahman, showed me round the village. It was a summer resort, two thirds Muslim, one third Christian. The hospital was provided by Yabrudis who had migrated to Brazil. A stream flowed through the courtyard of the mosque. Roman masonry formed part of the fabric of the church. Back at the house my hosts asked if I would take a startlingly attractive young relation, Bushra, back to Damascus. I agreed, surprised at the trust given to me.

'Bushra is 17 and Muslim. Her father is dead,' my 1971 diary records. 'She admires the easier relations between the sexes in the West and is impatient about many traditions. Her brother is a soldier and there is a plan to marry her off to a cousin. She would like to travel, and to study French at the university. She is very outspoken, relaxed and friendly. I enjoy talking to her immensely. It is very hard for the likes of me to get to know the likes of her.'

And this was the beginning of a beautiful friendship. I met her mother and her siblings and kept in touch with Bushra, who married the following year, but not her cousin. Nor did she go to the University and study French. Through the 1970s and 1980s I often visited Damascus and would always see her, her husband (who had a clothes store in Bab al-Barid near the Umayyad Mosque) and her growing family. When I went to live and work in Damascus twenty-one years after first meeting her, I became part of Bushra's extended family. And on the last night of my five years residence in Syria, I stayed with Bushra and her family. Bushra is now a grandmother and what started on the language break is one of my most cherished friendships.

I stayed on for a day or two in Damascus. Someone at MECAS had told me of an experimental play by an angry young Syrian playwright and I secured a ticket to see it at the Qabbani Theatre. The play was a Brechtian piece called *An Evening's Entertainment for the Sake of 5 June* and the author was Sa'dallah Wannus. The play started with the recorded intoning voice of Nasser after the 1967 war. The play was a challenge to the lies of official propaganda, statements that contradicted people's everyday experience.

That evening sowed the seed, though I knew it not at the time, of another friendship. When I reopened the British Council in Syria in 1992, I got to know Sa'dallah, read his plays – and translated one of them – and took every opportunity to see any performance of them. During the 1990s he was slowly dying from cancer. The illness turned an otherwise morose personality into a man who valued life and creativity. He was writing right up to the end, challenging the illiberalism, oppression and hypocrisy of the contemporary Arab world with savage humour. He died a few days before I left Syria in 1997 and I wrote his obituary for *The Guardian*.

But the Damascus leg of my language break also found me looking back. A Palestinian friend was the great niece of Izzat Darwaza, a writer and notable from Nablus, and she urged me to call on him in Damascus. He had been a member of al-Fatat, one of the Arab nationalist organisations before the First World War. He lived with his much younger wife in a flat near the Italian hospital in Damascus. Izzat Bey was well into his eighties, short and plump and with a twinkle in his eye. But he was somewhat deaf and I had to communicate with him by writing my questions in Arabic. He had been a post office worker in Beirut in 1914. Although he was a nationalist he told me that an Arab Muslim's primary loyalty before the war was to the *dawla*, the Ottoman state. That changed only with the hangings of nationalist young men in Beirut and Damascus in 1916. We drank mint tea together, the sun went down and I listened to memories and passions of a vanished world.

The last month or two of studies at Shemlan were an anticlimax. Routine: study, preparation for final exams and an adjustment to a posting to Sudan.

Ahmad al-Duaij became Director General of the Kuwait Real Estate Development Fund. I met him a few years later in the Sudan when he was trying to buy up chunks of Khartoum Zoo. And, in 1981, I attended an amazing party he hosted to mark the opening of the Sheraton Hotel, Sana'a. I was near him late that night and asked a waiter for some champagne.

'There is no more champagne,' the waiter told me.

Ahmad overheard and asked the waiter to fetch him some champagne.

'What kind of champagne would you like, Sir,' said the waiter.

Ahmad turned to me.

'You see,' he said, 'we Kuwaitis have become the new Americans. Our money gets us anywhere.'

Ahmad was killed in a car crash in Kuwait the following year.

I lost touch with Ilham, but heard that she rose in the ranks of the Iraqi oil industry and became the Iraqi expert on the corrosion of oil pipes. I would love to see her again.

Izzat Bey died in 1980 at the age of 92.

I anticipate being in Damascus next Christmas and expect to spend an evening with Bushra and her family.

Sudan

I spent six years in the Sudan, from 1971 to 1977. I had the opportunity to travel extensively around the country. In my first two years I was the 'overseas arm' for Voluntary Service Overseas, which sent thirty young British graduates to teach English at provincial secondary schools throughout the country. My job included pastoral visits, and I influenced the decisions to provide particular schools with volunteers. This enabled me to travel overland to remote and interesting parts of the country.

I also became fascinated by Sudan's recent history, especially the Mahdiya years that preceded the Anglo-Egyptian Sudan – actually more Anglo than Egyptian. In 1973 a young Sudanese army officer, Ismat Hasan Zulfo, published a much praised book on the battle of Omdurman. Zulfo had gone through all the available material in English and Arabic, and had interviewed a handful of survivors in their nineties. His book was long (six hundred pages) and detailed. I translated the book and visited the battlefield north of Omdurman with him. I also read widely in English and Arabic on the background.

Living in Omdurman, I was conscious of the Mahdiya in a very personal way. My house backed on to the house of Sadiq al-Mahdi, the political heir of the Mahdist tradition. The landlord of the British Council premises in Omdurman was Abd al-Salam al-Khalifa Abdullahi, the posthumous son of the man whom Kitchener's army had humiliated in 1898. I was very much aware of the Mahdist interpretation of the history of the previous century.

Outside my British Council duties I read, studied and scribbled.

The Hicks Pasha Expedition

In the 1970s during the winter months, the Anglican church in Khartoum used to arrange a monthly lecture. I gave three – in January 1975, January 1976 and January 1977. All were on the military history of the Mahdiya years. The first was on the Battle of Omdurman, the second on Gordon and the Siege of Khartoum. The third was about the Hicks Pasha Expedition, the least known of the three military engagements. In December 1976 I had walked over the site of the final massacre in Kordofan, and, scrabbling in the ground, had exposed bones and buttons belonging to the Egyptian soldiers. I had polished one button, and actually wore it as I gave the lecture.

All three talks were reproduced in *Three Sudanese Battles*, published by the Institute of African and Asian Studies in the University of Khartoum in 1977 – though it actually did not appear until 1979. This article appeared in *The Army Quarterly* in October 1978.)

The month of December 1883 was a month of panic among the foreign community in Khartoum. In the early 1880s Khartoum was the capital of the Sudanese dependencies of the Khedive, the ruler of Egypt. Sudan had been an Egyptian colony since the 1820s. The rule had been established to exploit the alleged mineral wealth – especially gold – of the country. In fact it supplied slaves and soldiers for the Khedive's army. Khartoum on the Nile and el Obeid in Kordofan became important commercial centres dealing with slaves, ivory, gum and ostrich feathers. Egyptian rule was based on a series of garrison towns and military outposts, penetrating the rural areas only to extract taxes. Certain aspects of industrial Europe were introduced to the Sudan for the first time, such as steamers, postal services, the telegraph, railways, hospitals and schools. The foreign community was a mixed bunch. There was a wealthy class of Egyptian merchants and officials including Copts who were clerks, traders and accountants. The Europeans included Greeks, Austrians, Italians and some British subjects, including Maltese and the odd Indian. There were also Jews, Syrians, Algerians and Ethiopians.

For the previous two years a religiously motivated anti-foreign movement, led by the Mahdi, had been spreading like wildfire in the west of the Sudan. Successive military expeditions had been despatched only to meet disaster. The second city of the country, el Obeid in Kordofan, had fallen, and in the course of 1883 a large military expedition was prepared and equipped. The foreign community had pinned their hopes of relief from this threat on the latest expedition led by General William Hicks, an Englishman, and containing about 7,000 soldiers. On 13 November a rumour reached Khartoum that

Hicks was 'supposed to have beaten the Mahdi in seven battles and to be at el Obeid.' Eleven days later came news that the total force had been annihilated. The Mahdi was reported to have 300,000 fighters with rifles and artillery. As *The Times* correspondent in Khartoum wrote desperately, 'We have only 2,000 soldiers, no retreat, and the town and the country to the Red Sea [is] red hot for the rebels.'

The news precipitated a flight from the capital. The French Consul, M Marquet, packed his valuables, which included mirrors, cut glass, silver, champagne, hock, green peas, asparagus, strawberries and pineapple, and left the city. Other foreigners rushed down to Berber before the river route was cut off, and then east to Suakin on the Red Sea – the usual route to and from Khartoum in those days.

The news caused consternation in Cairo, the capital of the Khedive's dominions, and dismay in London. The British had recently occupied Egypt, and a series of advisers were in indirect control of the machinery of government. The news of the disaster in London and Cairo led to the sending to Khartoum of General Gordon with objectives that were ill defined, indeed irreconcilable. He arrived in February 1884. The events of the siege and fall of Khartoum are well known. The memory of the death of Gordon was an important driving force in the reconquest of the Sudan, 1896-98, and in the British dominated colonial rule that was to shape so many things that became familiar to British visitors to the Sudan in the first generation of Sudanese independence.

In the next few pages I wish to consider what went wrong with the expedition that was totally annihilated at Shaykan in Kordofan on 5 November 1883, and which led to such momentous consequences.

Outside the towns of the Sudan Egyptian imperial authority was weak. The government was associated with the harsh recruitment of young men for military service, with arbitrary, capricious and excessive levying of taxes, with interference in trade – and especially the slave trade. Tribal authority prevailed. Islamic piety was intense and owed little to Egyptian influence. In Northern Kordofan the Kababish tribe patrolled the trade routes to Egypt and maintained a distant alliance with the government. To the south the various Baqqara cattle-rearing tribes had little to gain from having anything to do with the government. The Baqqara were to provide the Mahdi with his strongest support in the early years. In the south of Kordofan the Nuba Mountains stood out, harbouring thirty or so tribes who had avoided Islamisation and

Arabisation. These mountains provided the raw materials for the slave trade. They also provided a refuge for those fleeing from taxation and justice. In central Kordofan, around el Obeid and Bara, were many tribes including immigrants from the west and the north.

Limited government control, the ennoblement of the idea of the warrior and the glorification of fighting, led to frequent conflict between tribes, between families and between individuals. Government authority in the 1860s and 1870s, however, was improved by the development of the telegraph and the consequent speedier despatch of soldiers to trouble spots. But for the people of Kordofan, the tribesmen, the warriors, the slavers and the holy men, extra reminders of Egyptian rule were irksome. The province was ripe for revolt. Support for a charismatic and theocratic challenger to Egyptian rule was natural.

The challenge to Egyptian rule was centred on a Dongolawi religious teacher called Muhammad Ahmad, who declared himself the *Mahdi al-Muntazar*, the Expected Rightly-Guided One, at Aba Island on the White Nile, two hundred miles south of Khartoum, in June 1881. His Call attracted attention from the White Nile tribes. The Mahdi was invited to come to Khartoum to account for himself. He declined. In August a small military force was sent to face him. The Mahdists ambushed and destroyed the force. The following morning, the Mahdi with a few hundred followers crossed the White Nile to the west and migrated to Qadir in the southern Nuba Mountains, about ninety miles north of the garrison town of Fashoda. The migration took place during the rainy season and started in the fasting month of Ramadan, times of maximum inconvenience to a government that might try to mobilise troops quickly. When a larger government force came to Aba Island they found the place deserted.

In December 1881 the Governor of Fashoda, acting without instructions from Khartoum, sent an army of 1,500 men towards Qadir. On the way they were ambushed and almost all were killed.

Another government army was caught in a state of unreadiness near Qadir the following June, and the Mahdi with 8,000 men won an overwhelming victory. This was the government's third reverse and the Mahdi's most spectacular gain so far. Word spread and support from Kordofan and Darfur flocked to him.

For some years the Mahdi had been building up support in Kordofan. Before his Call he had paid two visits to el Obeid. Support came from holy men, from dissident tribesmen and from merchants out of favour with the government. All were able to mobilise large numbers of men. The Mahdi, in his first year after his Call, had written to these people appointing *amir*s, canvassing support and urging them to come to him and pay allegiance. During 1882, the Mahdi's supporters reduced and obliterated all the isolated garrisons in Kordofan.

The towns of Bara and el Obeid now stood out as desirable prizes. Inside el Obeid a merchant at loggerheads with the Governor invited the Mahdi, then at Qadir, to come to the city. As the Mahdi approached, many inhabitants left to join him. In July and August the Mahdi made his way to el Obeid on foot, as a gesture of humility. He settled at Kaba on 1 September.

On the following Friday the Mahdists attempted to storm the town. The Mahdi put his faith in swords and sticks, but the firepower of the town's defenders was able to show its superiority. There was, even so, fierce fighting for many hours. The Mahdi and his forces were beaten off and the government forces, in the words of an eye-witness, 'swept the nomad Arabs away like sweeping hay'. The Mahdists lost about 10,000 soldiers. This was a serious setback for the Mahdi.

Aware how vulnerable he was after this unsuccessful Friday assault, the Mahdi sent for the captured firearms kept at Qadir. He arranged for Hamdan Abu Anja, a veteran of many wars, to lead an armed battalion. This was called the *jihādiya*, and the soldiers in it were largely ex-slaves and Southern Sudanese. They underwent training and, in years to come, were to receive regular pay. The Mahdi's army was based on numerous units of different sizes called *raya*s (standards). The leader of a standard was either a tribal leader, or a prominent merchant, or a man with some following. Al-Manna Isma'il, for example, a holy man, was able in a few months to raise a following of 10,000. The merchants of el Obeid used to have private armies of hundreds of men. The fighters formed themselves into rows on the pattern of rows of worshippers, and followed their commander as the worshippers followed their imam. The divine nature of the Mahdi's Call made fighting a religious duty, thereby calling on self-discipline, loyalty and devotion to the cause.

After the Friday battle the Mahdists tightened their siege round el Obeid, and also Bara. This depressed the defenders in both towns, for hope of relief was cut off. All access to el Obeid was severed and food became short. People died of hunger, malnutrition and dysentery. In early January Bara surrendered. The garrison and its commander, al-Nur Angara, were recruited into the

Mahdist army. They came south to el Obeid and called on the besieged to surrender. On 17 January 1883 el Obeid fell to the Mahdists.

The Governor General in Khartoum, Abd al-Qadir Pasha Hilmi, was blamed for the fall of el Obeid, and was recalled to Cairo. Abd al-Qadir in fact had been a vigorous commander and had done much to restore the government's authority. He constructed defences in Khartoum and had recruited many more soldiers. He advised the abandonment of the west of the country and the strengthening of defences along the White Nile. In place of Abd al-Qadir, three men, all new to central Sudan, were sent. Ala al-Din Pasha Siddiq was appointed civil Governor General. The former military functions were assumed by Sulaiman Pasha Niyazi. Both these men were Circassians, and Ala al-Din had seen service in Eastern Sudan. The post of Chief of Staff went to an Englishman, William Hicks, known as Hicks Pasha.

It is useful at this stage to consider the British involvement in the Sudan in 1883. In 1882 a British military expedition had occupied Egypt, defeating the Egyptian army under Urabi Pasha. The pretext was to restore the authority of the Khedive. The Egyptian army was disbanded and British advisers came to sort out the muddle and debts incurred by the Egyptian government. The structure of Egyptian administration was maintained. The British government argued that they were responsible only for Egypt. Nevertheless they took a lively interest in the fate of Hicks, and indeed Hicks's channel of communication with his employers, the Egyptian government, was through Sir Edward Malet, the British Consul General in Cairo. Malet tried to convince the Egyptian Prime Minister, Sharif Pasha, that 'Her Majesty's Government are in no way responsible for the operations in the Soudan which have been undertaken under the authority of His Highness's Government, or for the appointment or actions of General Hicks.' The Egyptian government, irked by military occupation and foreign interference, was anxious to stress its independence and tended to take a 'forward' line. It was sceptical of the British government's disinterest, and anticipated financial support. Gladstone's government, however, had come to power after deploring the imperialist adventures of its predecessor. It was embarrassed by its own foreign adventure in Egypt, which added to its domestic troubles. Moreover, another of Gladstone's political principles was retrenchment of the economy. When Malet sent reports on the Sudan and Hicks's shortage of financial support, the relevant documents were passed round the Cabinet. The Chancellor of the

Exchequer commented, 'I don't like the look of these papers.'

Colonel William Hicks had spent thirty years in the Indian army. In 1883 he was fifty-three years old, and had seen service in a number of Indian campaigns, including the Mutiny, and the Napier Expedition in Abyssinia in 1867-68. He became a Lieutenant Colonel in 1875 and retired from the service in 1880 with the honorary rank of Colonel, for pension purposes. Hicks was made a *fariq*, roughly Lieutenant General, in the Egyptian army and sent to the Sudan in February 1883 accompanied by an army and a number of European and Egyptian officers. He arrived in Khartoum in early March, and in the following months was busy patrolling the White Nile.

During the next four months Hicks remained based in Khartoum, training his men, appealing for more men, more money, more munitions, more provisions. The Mahdi was consolidating his position in Kordofan, and Hicks was under pressure from the Cairo government to undertake an expedition to the west. He was daunted by the task. 'The force we have is not sufficient to undertake the Kordofan campaign,' he wrote. 'Every ounce of food must be taken from here. We march through a hostile country, inhabited by powerful tribes. The lines of communication must be kept open, and depots must be formed which must be sufficiently garrisoned. Each convoy will require escort. Our available strength will be under 6,000; of these many will be likely to be sick after the fever season.'

Hicks felt that his authority was limited. Sulaiman Pasha Niyazi was expected to refer to him on military matters. Hicks complained through Malet to the Egyptian government, and, under the threat of resignation, got his way: Sulaiman Pasha was transferred to the Eastern Sudan. Hicks now, whatever his misgivings about the Kordofan expedition, was robbed of his excuse to resign. He prepared for the march into Kordofan, and moved his army up to Duwaym, 130 miles south of Khartoum, ready to head west.

Hicks was in charge of about 8,000 men. 7,000 regular soldiers were divided into four battalions. These soldiers were mainly Egyptian, though there were a number of 'blacks' – Southerners and Nubans. The Egyptians were largely the remnants of Urabi's army who had fought against the British the previous year. Nearly 2,000 of them had been rejected earlier for military service 'because of slight physical defects'. They had received basic training in Khartoum, but morale was low. Supplies had been late in arriving, and there had already been threats of mutiny. The senior officers were Egyptian and European.

Six European officers accompanied the expedition. Hicks's Chief of Staff was Colonel Arthur Farquhar, formerly of the Coldstream Guards. He is described as 'bold and dashing'. However, he was somewhat inflexible, relying on a compass and charging through thick forest, rather than on common sense and riding round it. A German Baron, Major Gotz von Seckendorff, had accompanied Hicks in the Abyssinian campaign. He was fat and quick-tempered. The intelligence officer was Major Edward Evans, the only British officer who knew Arabic. He had been in business in the Red Sea and had been in the Sudan before. He used to translate Hicks's addresses to the soldiers. An Austrian, Captain Herlth, was a cavalry man. He kept a diary during the expedition. This has been lost, but was seen by a European prisoner of the Mahdi, Father Joseph Ohrwalder, who produced what he could remember of it in his book, *Ten Years' Captivity in the Mahdi's Camp*.

Among the European civilians who accompanied the expedition were two newspapermen. The Irishman Edmund O'Donovan of the *Daily News* had travelled extensively. He was once arrested in Constantinople for insulting the Sultan and arrived in the Sudan wearing Turkish dress. Frank Vizetelly of the *Illustrated London News* had walked from Suakin to Khartoum and was planning to walk south through Africa before he got diverted to the Hicks Pasha Expedition.

The expedition was accompanied by 2,000 civilians and camp followers. Some had official positions, like Georges Bey as he is known – the Greek Gheorgis Dimitrious Douloughli – who was Chief Physician and Surgeon General to the forces in the Sudan. Others were brought in to help in setting up an administration in el Obeid after victory. These included Busati Bey Madani, who had been Inspector of Finances for the Sudan, Mahmud Ahmadani, a former Egyptian Governor of Khartoum, and Hamad al-Tilib, Chief of the Appeal Court in Khartoum. One other civilian who came with the expedition was Abd al-Rahman Ban Naga. His father was an el Obeid merchant who had thrown in his lot with the Mahdi. He 'had been made to accompany the expedition to use his good offices with his father and thereby to facilitate the task of the expedition.'

The soldiers were armed with Remington rifles and there were four long Krupp guns, six five-barrel Nordenfeldt machine guns and ten short-range cannons. All food and much water were carried. Food included sacks of biscuits, barley and rice. Water was in iron tanks. This was to supplement water found on the route, for, as one of the officers said, there were '20,000 water drinkers'. Apart from the humans, there were about 14,000 beasts. The expedition started with 5,500 camels, but there was a high mortality rate with them. Of 5,000 horses that set out, most died by a week before the final battle. The 3,000 mules and 1,000 donkeys were tougher, however.

The expedition gathered at Duwaym in September 1883. It was accompanied by the new Governor General of the Sudan, Ala al-Din Pasha Siddiq. At once disagreement broke out between him and Hicks over the route to el Obeid. Hicks argued that they should go due west to Bara and then south to el Obeid. The Kababish of northern Kordofan were more sympathetic to the Egyptian government. Ala al-Din argued they should head south west from Duwaim to the valley, Khor Abu Habl, and follow that towards el Obeid, passing settlements where there was ample water. The availability of water would be offset by the potential hostility of the tribes. Moreover the southern route was longer. Ala al-Din's authority prevailed.

The expedition left Duwaym on 27 September. Hicks wanted to leave a hundred or so men at each place they spent a night. These would guarantee a line of retreat and supply. Again the Governor General overruled him, arguing that the 'force at our disposal is not large enough to allow of its being divided.' Hicks conceded: 'I should in garrisoning these posts be only weakening my fighting force without gaining any advantage.'

At el Obeid the Mahdi operated an effective intelligence system. He had the sympathy of most people on Hicks's route. After Hicks left Duwaym the Mahdi sent Muhammad Uthman Abu Qirja, Abd al-Halim Musa'id and Umar Ilyas with 3,000 men to dog the expedition. They were not to engage in fighting, but to skirmish and harry the force. Hicks and his men found the villages they passed through were deserted, the camps where they slept were occupied after they left and the wells they came upon were either dry or filled with earth.

External pressures compounded internal tensions. The day after leaving Duwaym, Hicks, irritated by some administrative blunder, threatened to quit. He was in frequent disagreement with the senior Egyptian officer, Husayn Pasha. On 8 October he was squabbling with Colonel Farquhar over the issue of orders. From 10 October, stragglers were picked off. The force was obliged to stick close together and no soldier was allowed to leave the camp unarmed. The beasts were unable to roam and find grass. Camels had to eat whatever they could find within the squares. Their saddles were cushioned by straw pallets. In their hunger the camels ate the straw. The wooden saddles then chafed the skin and caused painful wounds. On 15 October more than one hundred camels died from thirst, the result, according to Hicks, of incompetence in arrangements for water distribution.

Morale, already low, was made lower by a nagging thirst which was aggravated by excessive eating of peanuts. At Rahad the force rested for five or six days near the large tract of water that still exists. Not far away the Mahdists camped, but they disappeared when Hicks moved on. Fires sprang up everywhere. The expedition was aware that the enemy's numbers were increasing daily. On 30 October they left Rahad. The following day on a five-mile march they were continually sniped at. After two days they reached Alluba.

The drama of these final days in October 1883 took place in a triangle whose base is the line between Alluba and Birka, both about thirty-five miles south of el Obeid. Birka – the word means pool – is a large lake around which are a number of settlements. The lake could satisfy the needs of an army. The apex of the triangle is el Obeid. The lower part, now sliced by the railway, was a thick bush forest of *kitir* trees. Ten miles north of Alluba on the way to el Obeid lies the forest of Shaykan, the word being an Arabic dialect plural of *shawka*, a thorn. The *kitir* bush grows thorns up to three inches long and very tough. About twelve miles north of Alluba is another lake, which, unlike Birka, is seasonal. This is Fula al-Masarin, meaning the pool of the entrails, from a battle that took place before, 'when the entrails of the slain were picked out by vultures.'

On Thursday, 1 November and Friday, 2 November Hicks remained at Alluba. His own scouts, in whom he had diminishing confidence, brought to him several hundred copies of a proclamation of the Mahdi in which he was urged to put his trust in Allah, the Prophet Muhammad and the Mahdi rather than in cannons and firepower. As many of these proclamations as possible were burnt. Hicks planned to move west to the abundant water at Birka.

His movements were reported regularly to the Mahdi. On 1 November the Mahdi left el Obeid and moved south with an estimated 50,000 men, and spent the night at Firtingal, half way between el Obeid and Birka. He was aware of Hicks's plans and sent his right hand man, the Khalifa Abdullahi, with Mahmud Abd al-Qadir on to Birka. On 2 November, while the Mahdi was still at Firtingal, Mahdist forces under the Khalifa Abdullahi occupied the lake at Birka. Later the same day this information was relayed to Hicks fifteen miles away.

The following morning – Saturday the third – Hicks left Alluba at dawn, heading north towards Fula al-Masarin. After ten miles they constructed a strong zariba (stockade) and camped. A number of the Mahdi's men were at Ji'aybat. When they heard that Hicks was moving north, they marched east through the forest until they 'came on the enemy's camp fires winking ... through the trees.' They camped close by. The Mahdi, meanwhile, left Firtingal and went on to Birka. Some of his men were not as confident as their commanding position would justify. One man, Hajj Ibrahim, said to the Mahdi:

'They are making for el Obeid to seize our women. Ought we not to go there beforehand?'

The Mahdi answered with riddles. He spat on his hand.

'What is that?'

'Spittle', said Hajj Ibrahim.

The Mahdi threw it on to the ground, where it soon evaporated.

'We are the ground and the Turks' – by which he meant Hicks's army – 'are the spittle. If a bird flies where does it land?'

'On the ground,' answered Hajj Ibrahim.

'The Turks are the bird and we are the ground. So rest assured. Believe in the power of Allah, not of the Turks. Monday will be the day of reckoning. If any one of you on that day is late, because he has to repair his sandal, then he will not see them alive.'

The following day, Sunday, 4 November 1883, Hicks's army left the zariba in a tight square although they were all aware that they were surrounded. Hamdan Abu Anja, with the firing force, the *jihādiya*, moved into the space they had left, blocking retreat. They attacked the rear. The first battalion in front wheeled round and attempted to drive the Mahdists back. But their square was broken. Many camels carrying water fell outside the square. So hot was the fire that they could not be recovered. Guns too were lost for the same reason. Hicks ordered the band to play. (It is possible they played the Khedivial anthem that had been composed by Verdi.) But camels, mules and men were dropping constantly, and the feeble attempt to raise morale was abandoned. According to Captain Herlth's diary, 'We are all cramped up together, so the bullets cannot fail to strike.' Among those killed in this action was the Greek doctor, Georges Bey.

The Mahdi called off the assault. Morale in the Egyptian army was at its lowest. Some of the merchants conspired to mutiny. Already a few days earlier,

Abd al-Rahman Ban Naga had been caught writing 'a letter to his father, whom he knew to be with the rebels, asking his advice as to whether he should desert.' The merchants, led by Qinawi Bey, whom the Governor General proposed to appoint Governor of Bahr al-Ghazal, planned to seize arms and break out of the square. This mutiny was thwarted by Busati Bey Madani. Hicks called a meeting of the officers and asked for constructive suggestions. Nobody answered. Hicks decided to trust in God.

At 10 am the following morning, Monday, 5 November, Hicks and his army left their campsite in three squares, forming an equilateral triangle, each square three hundred yards from the next. In the middle of each square was the baggage and ammunition. Hicks and his staff were in front, followed by what was left of the artillery and four cannons. Then there was the first square, and after that the two others. Horsemen made a show of guarding the rear and flanks.

At al-Fula, a mile away, the Mahdi called his senior commanders, the *amir*s. He led the army in prayer and ordered Abu Qirja and Abd al-Halim Musa'id to attack the rear. Abd al-Rahman al-Nujumi, supported by the Khalifa Abdullahi and his brother, Ya'qub, and the Khalifa Ali wad Hilu, were to attack the van.

In the general assault the fighting was fierce. Hicks's army, surrounded as they were, shot wildly, killing some of their own men, but the Mahdists lost several hundred men. Hicks cut his way through to the left, and the Governor General, Ala al-Din, was killed trying to reach him. The overwhelming superiority in numbers and morale of the Mahdists left the issue in no doubt. The whole of Hicks's army, with the exception of two junior officers and about three hundred men, were killed – perhaps 7,000 all told. Years later, one survivor recalled how he managed to flee with others to the south. He was pursued, but 'they were too busy collecting loot to bother about us.' A number of days were spent looting the dead soldiers. Weapons, ammunition and supplies were taken and divided, one fifth to the Mahdi and the rest for the Mahdist state treasury.

Hicks Pasha has been immune from criticism. He died a soldier's death and has been seen as a poor man's General Gordon – a martyr to other people's political errors. However, this narrative has shown that Hicks had considerable defects as a general. He showed little leadership and was unable to impose his will unquestioningly upon the other officers. He got involved in unseemly squabbles with his Chief of Staff and the senior Egyptian officer. On the eve of battle, bankrupt in ideas himself, he appealed for suggestions from his staff. It is difficult to imagine Gordon or Kitchener, the Mahdi or the Khalifa Abdullahi showing such lack of authority. In some ways this was hardly surprising. In the Indian army, Hicks never rose higher than Lieutenant Colonel. He was promoted rapidly as an aging man. His last battle experience was as brigade major in Abyssinia sixteen years earlier. Indeed, his characteristics were those of a junior officer – anxiety to cooperate with colleagues and fussiness over administrative detail. These traits are commendable in a junior officer, but less appropriate in a general.

By contrast, the Mahdi showed considerable talent as a military leader. He exploited every natural advantage of the environment. He was able to delegate. He showed great restraint in waiting for the Expedition to get so far before delivering the coup de grace – although in this he was probably mindful of the Friday disaster at el Obeid a year before. Above all he showed qualities of leadership, never doubting his destiny, keeping morale high.

The nature of the campaign was singular. A leading Sudanese historian, Professor Mekki Shibeika, has written that, a few days after leading Duwaym, the expedition was 'virtually in a state of moving siege'. This vivid image helps us see how the Mahdi's tactics employed at el Obeid were applied to the Hicks Pasha Expedition.

The consequences of the battle of Shaykan were far reaching. The Mahdi was on the crest of a wave. He at once cast his eyes towards Khartoum and wrote to the inhabitants of the capital calling for their allegiance. He acquired an international reputation and was to receive delegations from the Hijaz, from India and from Morocco.

For the Khartoum government it was a further disaster. At once all garrisons south of Khartoum, with the exception of Sinnar, were withdrawn. Government authority collapsed in the west and the south. The sequence of events that led to General Gordon coming to Khartoum was set in train. The memory of the disaster of Hicks and the death of Gordon was to influence the reconquest fifteen years later in 1898, after more than a decade of Sudanese independence.

In 1899 Kordofan was restored to Egyptian – or rather Anglo-Egyptian – authority. In spite of the disintegration of the Mahdist state in Kordofan in 1898-99, for several years the new Condominium government was sensitive about their security in the west. In the winter of 1905-06, the Governor

General, Sir Reginald Wingate, visited the Shaykan battlefield. After his visit he wrote: 'I have no hesitation in hazarding the opinion that, had the efforts to relieve el Obeid been conducted by a far more numerous and efficient force, the result would have been the same.' Two years later, Wingate expressed his anxiety in a private letter: 'I shall always feel rather nervous about our situation in Kordofan: indeed, if a similar rising to that which took place in 1883 occurred any time before the Railway is completed … it would probably be impossible to relieve our isolated garrisons with any reasonable chance of success.'

The railway to el Obeid was completed in 1911. The line was extended to Darfur in the 1950s. It divides Birka from the battlefield. There is a railway station called Shaykan. The site of the battle has monuments to both sides. Where the main fighting took place, light digging on the ground in the 1970s uncovered fragments of bones, buttons, pieces of equipment and parts of armaments. They served as grim reminders of the awful tragedy that took place there in November 1883.

The Battle of Omdurman

This was the first of three talks I gave in Khartoum. The audience included members of the British Army Training Team and Sudanese army officers, as well as staff of the University of Khartoum and members of the British expatriate community. There were two distinguished Sudanese in the audience, and they were given places of honour at the front. One was Abd al-Salam, son of the Khalifa Abdullahi, a central character of the drama of the battle. The other was Hasan al-Turabi, distinguished Islamic scholar and leader for the last forty years of the Islamists in the country. I spoke from a lectern. I was anxious to avoid offence with the cross on the front of the lectern, and draped over it maps of the battlefield. But it was a night with a high wind, and as I spoke the wind ripped the maps away. I was most concerned about seeming to thrust the cross in the faces of these distinguished Muslim gentlemen. But I need not have worried. They were totally understanding and keen to allay my own distress.

In addition to the battlefield north of Omdurman, I had in 1974 been to Umm Dibaykarat, south west of Kosti, where the Khalifa Abdullahi had finally met his end. The Landrover I was in came upon three huts in the middle of nowhere. From one of them emerged a tall, elderly gentleman in glasses who addressed me in English. He was Muhammad, another son of the Khalifa. He had been prominent in one of the first organised revolts against the Anglo-Egyptian Condominium in 1924 and exiled to Egypt. He had come to spend his final years by the tomb of his father. He occupied one of the huts, his wife another and servants the third. We walked together over to some graves. One was of his father, the Khalifa Abdullahi, another of the Khalifa Ali wad Hilu. The graves were surrounded by a thorn fence, and under a tree nearby was a young woman chained to the tree. The Khalifa's son told me she was crazed, and her family had brought her there, hoping for blessings from the proximity of the Khalifa's remains. The Khalifa's son provided her with food and drink.

With a few stylistic amendments this appeared in *Three Sudanese Battles*, published by the Institute of African and Asian Studies in the University of Khartoum in 1977. It was also published in *The Army Quarterly* in July 1977.

The battle of Omdurman, which took place in about five hours on the morning of Friday, 2 September 1898, was an episode in the history of Afro-European relations. It was an incident in the general advance of European control of the African interior in the years between 1880 and 1914. The battle was fought by a joint Anglo-Egyptian force, of which all the senior officers were British, against the supporters of the ruler of the Sudan, the Khalifa Abdullahi.

The story of the battle and the two-year campaign preceding it was told by several journalists who were with the Anglo-Egyptian forces, including G W Steevens and Winston Churchill. Churchill's account, *The River War*, was published in two volumes in 1899, and was, deservedly, a best seller. An abridged one-volume edition was published in 1930 and the book has been reprinted regularly ever since. Later accounts of the battle have relied heavily on the work of these two writers, supplemented by the official reports published by the Director of Intelligence of the Anglo-Egyptian force, Sir Reginald Wingate. The story of the battle has been retold frequently including in two books published in 1973, *Omdurman* by Philip Ziegler, and *Dervish* by Philip Warner. Substantially, the story they tell is that first told by Churchill, Wingate and company.

In 1973 a young Sudanese army officer, Ismat Hasan Zulfo, published a long account of the battle with the title *Karari*, as the battle is known in the Sudan. He discussed the political, military and social background of the battle and explained the Khalifa's tactics sympathetically, though not uncritically. Between 1973 and 1975 I translated the book into English. In the course of this task I had frequent and lengthy discussions with the author and visited the battlefield with him. This paper relies much on Zulfo's work.

Why was there a battle on the plains of Karari, four miles north of Omdurman, in 1898?

From 1821 the Sudan was controlled by an Egyptian regime. In the early 1880s there was increasing resistance which found a leader in a holy man from Dongola called Muhammad Ahmad, who proclaimed himself the Mahdi, the Rightly Guided One. At his base at Aba Island, two hundred miles south of Khartoum on the White Nile, he defeated a small government army that was sent to crush him. After his success, he withdrew to Kordofan, gained enormous popular support and secured more victories over government forces, though armed only with swords and spears, and in early 1883, after a siege, he captured el Obeid, the most important city in the west of the Sudan. The Egyptian government became alarmed and sent out an expeditionary force from Cairo to crush him. The force was led by a British officer from the Indian army, Hicks Pasha. Hicks had innumerable problems before he set out from Khartoum for Kordofan. But the Mahdi's forces tracked him, harried him and dragged him further and further west. Finally his army was massacred at Shaykan, some twenty-five miles south of el Obeid.

Meanwhile, Egypt had fallen under effective British control and the situation in the Sudan became something of a British responsibility. General Charles George Gordon was sent out to evacuate Egyptian forces remaining in the country. He arrived at Khartoum in the spring of 1884. The Mahdi besieged the city and in January 1885 Khartoum fell and Gordon was killed.

With the fall of Khartoum, the Mahdi's control extended over most of the Sudan. A theocratic state was established with its capital at Omdurman, hitherto a fishing village and the site of the Mahdi's camp. The regime became known as the Mahdiya. The Mahdi himself died in June 1885, still in his forties, and the control of the state was assumed by his successor, a Baqqara of the Ta'aisha tribe of Southern Darfur called Abdullahi. He was known as the Khalifa, the Successor.

Although Gordon had been sent out by the British government, there was no direct British control or interest in the Sudan. A British Gordon Relief Expedition had been sent to rescue him but arrived two days after the fall of the city. They withdrew, and Egyptian control in the Sudan was limited to Wadi Halfa in the north and Suakin in the east. The Egyptian army had been humiliated by the rout of Hicks Pasha and was reorganised by British officers headed by a Sirdar or Commander in Chief. The new Egyptian army thwarted a Mahdist invasion of Egypt led by Abd al-Rahman wad al-Nujumi in 1887, and held the frontier against irregular raids.

In the Sudan the Khalifa strengthened his rule. He brought in as his closest advisors members of his family and tribe and other western Sudanese. The Mahdi's family and the riverain tribes felt somewhat out of the picture and attempted to take over. The coup failed and the rule of the westerners was reinforced. During these years there was much suffering in the Sudan: a run of bad harvests led to famine. The Khalifa was involved in bloody, albeit successful, wars in Ethiopia, and in civil insurrection in Darfur. However, after about 1892 the situation seemed temporarily to improve and there was a degree of prosperity and security.

In Cairo three British officials were closely watching the situation. As the new Consul General, Evelyn Baring, later Earl of Cromer, was effective ruler of Egypt. He was cool, intelligent and methodical, and ran the country through a series of British advisors attached to Egyptian government departments. He looked forward to a renewal of Egyptian (and thereby British) control of the Sudan, but not yet. Balancing Egypt's budgets was a higher priority. In 1894 Kitchener was appointed Sirdar of the Egyptian army. Kitchener was then forty-four, an Arabist, ambitious and highly strung. He had been attached to the Gordon Relief Expedition in 1885 and looked forward eagerly to avenging, as he saw it, the murder of General Gordon, who had been, like Kitchener, a Royal Engineer. His Director of Intelligence was another Arabist, Colonel F R (Reginald) Wingate. Wingate interviewed Sudanese traders in Egypt and built up a vast detailed picture of the Sudan and especially events in Omdurman. He organised a propaganda campaign against the Khalifa and bombarded the

War Office in London with his reports. Wingate had published a great book, *Mahdiism and the Egyptian Sudan* in 1891, to rouse British public opinion. In the following years he translated, edited, perhaps even ghosted two accounts by Europeans who had been imprisoned in Omdurman. One was by a Catholic priest, Father Ohrwalder. The other was *Fire and Sword in the Sudan* by the Austrian adventurer, Rudolf Slatin, who had been alternately prisoner and confidant of the Khalifa.

Kitchener and Wingate sought to persuade Cromer and through him the British government to launch a campaign against the Khalifa. In the spring of 1896 things suddenly worked their way. In Eritrea, an Italian army was defeated by an Ethiopian army at Adowa. The Italians wanted a British demonstration to distract the Khalifa's attention and to shore up European morale. The British government approved a limited expedition to recapture Dongola.

By August 1896, after an easy campaign, Dongola was occupied by a combined Anglo-Egyptian force. Their position was consolidated. Small expeditions were made as far as Merowe. Kitchener hoped that the Dongola expeditions were the prelude to bigger things, visited London, and secured approval for a further advance. A railway was constructed, against all professional and military advice, from Wadi Halfa through the desert to Abu Hamad. As the railway advanced, Abu Hamad was seized by a force coming from Merowe, and then a group of irregulars went further south and seized Berber. Berber had been the centre of an important Mahdist garrison, and occupied a strategic point at the junction of the Nile and the route to the Red Sea. Kitchener took the risk of holding on to Berber even though his supply line was far from secure. Gunboats were brought up to Berber, and by Christmas 1897 a fort was being built at the junction of the river Atbara and the river Nile.

The Khalifa in Omdurman was being kept informed of the apparently inexorable advance. After the fall of Dongola he sent for his cousin, Mahmud wad Ahmad, who was at the time crushing a revolt in the west. The Khalifa and Mahmud were very much aware of the route that had been taken by the Gordon Relief Expedition in 1885, from Dongola to Debba and Korti and then across the Bayuda desert to Metemma opposite Shendi. Metemma was clearly a most important strategic spot on the junction of the desert route and the Nile route to Khartoum. The people of Metemma, largely of the Ja'li tribe, were asked to evacuate the town to make way for Mahmud's army. The Ja'li leader, Abdullah

Sa'd, refused. Mahmud and his army went north in the spring of 1897 and wiped them out, thereby alienating the Ja'li tribe who occupied the villages between Khartoum and Berber, providing many of the merchants who plied between Sudan and Egypt. Not surprisingly many Ja'li threw their lot in with the invaders.

In February 1898 Mahmud went further north. He was joined by Osman Digna, Mahdist amir of East Sudan, who was a veteran of many irregular campaigns against British and Egyptian troops based in Suakin. Mahmud aimed to take Berber. He bypassed Fort Atbara but as he crossed the river, a force left the Fort and moved one day's journey up the river. Mahmud settled himself in a huge zariba – a camp surrounded by thorn bushes. The distance from his zariba to Berber over the desert was too great for a one-day march. He had to deal with the force sent out, or withdraw. After a fortnight's wait, on Good Friday 1898, Kitchener moved on to Mahmud's zariba. Mahmud's army of 15,000 was defeated. Osman Digna slipped away with his men to eastern Sudan. Mahmud was taken prisoner to Berber, and there displayed in chains.

Kitchener with his army and his gunboats waited for three months in Atbara. A second British brigade joined them. The delay was for the Nile to rise. A high Nile would facilitate the passage of the gunboats through the cataract at Sabaluka gorge, thirty miles north of Omdurman.

At Sabaluka the Khalifa had had constructed a series of forts at the northern entrance to the gorge. The Khalifa's intelligence chief, Abd al-Baqi Abd al-Wakil, was based here, and his men kept Omdurman fully informed of the nature, movements and positions of the invading force. Occasionally they skirmished, but generally the Anglo-Egyptian force had the disconcerting experience of seeing Mahdist forces in the distance watching them and vanishing. As Kitchener moved south on the west bank, the Khalifa ordered the abandonment of the Sabaluka forts. This seems to be one of the first major miscalculations made by the Khalifa. He feared that his own supply line would be overstretched, and dreaded another disaster to his forces, preferring to have one big decisive battle outside Omdurman. But with the abandonment of Sabaluka the way was cleared for the gunboats to advance right up to Omdurman.

At the end of August the Anglo-Egyptian force advanced in full battle order. The night of 31 August was spent at Sururab. The following morning after torrential rain they marched over the hills of Karari to al-Ijaija and set up a large zariba.

On 1 September 1898 too, a large force of irregulars, largely Ja'li and Shaiqi tribesmen but officered by British and Egyptians, moved up the east bank to present-day North Khartoum. With the assistance of gunboats, the Khalifa's defensive positions were stormed and sites were secured for the invaders' artillery and particularly their Howitzers. Lyddite shells were despatched over the river and smashed the roof of the Mahdi's tomb, spiritual centre of Omdurman.

While Kitchener was taking these initiatives, the Khalifa had been mobilising all his available forces. On the morning of Thursday, 1 September a great army moved out from the west of the city and settled west of Surkab hill.

Then for fourteen hours two armies confronted each other.

The dynamic for the Mahdist state had been religious, a reformed Islam, though based on traditional values. Islam has never been pacifist. The early spread of Islam was based on military conquest and the warrior is ennobled with the prospect of bliss for himself and his kin if he falls as a martyr in a holy war against infidels.

In the Sudan in an apparently informal social life, religion calls on powers of discipline and organisation. When we see Sudanese Muslims praying, men form themselves spontaneously into neat rows behind a leader in prayer, the imam. It is a most moving experience to attend a Muslim festival. A space with hundreds of men milling around will, within one or two minutes, become a series of rows. The actions of praying – kneeling, bowing, standing – are performed in as regular and disciplined a way as well-drilled soldiers on a parade ground. Such groups of worshippers behind the imam formed the basic fighting unit in the Mahdi's forces. Such organisation and discipline had borne fruit in the early military successes of the Mahdiya. Like groups of worshippers the number of these basic groups could vary enormously in size.

The early campaigns of the Mahdiya, especially the campaign against Hicks Pasha, were basically guerrilla campaigns. As Hicks pushed into the west, horsemen harassed his army day and night. Wells on their path were filled up. Local guides misled them and they became thoroughly disheartened. When they were dazed with thirst and frustration, the Mahdi's forces besieged them in a wood and wiped them out. The siege of Khartoum was a similar waiting game with the Mahdi waiting for his enemy to become weak and demoralised and only when a Relief Expedition was approaching did he finally pounce. The campaigns of Osman Digna in the Red Sea area were marked by ambushes. The Mahdist armies had a successful tradition of irregular warfare. Only when their armies confronted another well-disciplined force, as at Toski in 1889 and Atbara in April 1898, were they worsted.

By September 1898 what were the Khalifa's fighting forces? In one sense all men were warriors supposedly ready to fight when called upon. In fact the Khalifa did have a full-time army. The main garrison was based at al-Kara, on the Omdurman side of the present While Nile bridge. The garrison was in two parts. The Mulazimin, a word meaning companion, or, today, lieutenant, had originally been the Khalifa's private guard. In 1898 they were commanded by the Khalifa's son, Osman Shaikh al-Din, a wayward youth of about twenty-four. The mulazimin were well-armed usually with Remington rifles that had been looted from Hicks's army or from Khartoum, or from Ethiopia. The rest of the regular fighting forces were under the command of Ibrahim al-Khalil, a cousin of the Khalifa and brother of Mahmud wad Ahmad. Ibrahim was a bit of a martinet, keen on endless drilling and on bad terms with Shaikh al-Din. These soldiers were trained, paid and fed by the Mahdist state.

The Khalifa's reserves were usually divided into large forces called *raya*s or standards. The Black Standard was the largest and was commanded by Ya'qub, the Khalifa's brother, a scholarly man, utterly loyal to the Khalifa, a good organiser of the army and administration – in short, the Khalifa's prime minister. The men in the Black Standard were largely from the west of the Sudan, and were divided into smaller units based on tribe or subtribe. These smaller units were led – as in prayers – by either (in descending order of size and priority) an *amīr*, a *ra's miya* (centurion) or a *muqaddam* (captain). There were two other standards during the Mahdiya. The Red Standard had been made up of Dongolawis and was commanded by the Khalifa Muhammad Sharif, a younger relation of the Mahdi, but after the revolt of the riverain tribes this standard was suppressed, to be revived shortly before the battle of Omdurman. The third standard was the Green Standard, led by the Khalifa Ali wad Hilu, who came from the White Nile area near present day Kosti. He had been a holy man and was one of the first supporters of the Mahdi. The standards were usually not armed, and were seen as the forces that got to grips with the enemy with sword and spear.

The Khalifa and his brother Ya'qub were at the head of an elaborate chain of command that covered the state's needs. Many of the lower officials, clerks and particularly technicians, were taken over from the Egyptian regime, the

Turkiya. There was a well-constructed bureaucracy, a treasury, a postal service, factories for soap, a printing press, an ammunition factory and a mint.

It is difficult to determine with precision the size of the Khalifa's army at the battle of Omdurman. Those who saw the army on 1 September 1898 reckoned the force to be about 30,000. But after the battle the official figure issued by Kitchener and Wingate had swollen to 52,000. Most historians since then have accepted this figure. Wingate based his figures on evidence found among Ya'qub's papers. But these papers were not up to date, and consisted of a roll call of the Omdurman garrison dating back to before the campaign in the north.

The Mulazimin were reckoned by Wingate to be 14,000 strong. This was accepted by Churchill and others, although Broadwood, who fought against them, reckoned their number only 10,000.

The Kara garrison that fought under Ibrahim al-Khalil and Osman Azraq is generally estimated at from 10-15,000.

The Green Standard was presented by Wingate as 5,000 strong, though other sources, including eye witnesses, put it at less than 3,000.

The Black Standard's size has, following Wingate, traditionally been put at 14,000, but the commander of the British division, General Gatacre, gave the figure of 12,000, a figure also supported by other eye witnesses.

The Red Standard was about a hundred strong and took virtually no part in the fighting. The other small unit, Osman Digna's men, is estimated variously at between seven hundred and over 3,000.

If we add the 2,000 men with the Khalifa's headquarters we are left with estimates of the whole army varying between 37,000 and 54,000. There is insufficient evidence for us to state categorically the size of the Khalifa's army. However, one can assert that the hitherto accepted figure of 52,000 is open to question, and there is plenty of evidence to suggest a smaller figure. In spite of the universal conscription imposed by the Khalifa in Omdurman, we must note the many factors that hindered his mobilisation. The experience of Mahmud's army had demoralised many who sought retirement rather than an apparently futile struggle against overwhelming odds. The ravages of previous wars – in the north, in Ethiopia and in the west – had limited the capacity of the Khalifa to bring out numbers that might have been available ten years earlier. Nor must we forget that the demoralisation at the series of reverses in the north had sapped the enthusiasm and the loyalty of not a few who deserted to the enemy.

The Khalifa's army was armed with Remingtons, Martini Henrys and elephant guns. The Remington rifles were breech-loaded and dated from earlier campaigns. They had been poorly maintained and were antiquated when compared with what the Anglo-Egyptian force had. The 1880s and 1890s in Europe saw a great development in weaponry. Accuracy and speed had improved as well as range of fire and capacity for destruction. Ammunition was manufactured in the Khalifa's state – at four different factories – but this was not of the same quality as that taken over from the previous regime. Ya'qub forbad the continued use of the old ammunition and Shaikh al-Din hoarded it for the use of his mulazimin. The Mahdists saw rifles as an inadequate substitute for hand-to-hand fighting. Fire power was seen not as a means of destruction but rather as cover for an assaulting force that was armed with swords and spears.

The Khalifa's army consisted of about thirty-five pieces – Gatlings, Nordenfeldts, mitrailleuse and mountain guns. With the exception of two mountain guns, all were left in Omdurman during the battle, in the forts facing the gunboats or in the armoury. It was felt that artillery should be used for piercing fortified places and not for killing people.

Such was the strength of the Khalifa's force on 1 September 1898.

The Anglo-Egyptian force is better known and can be quickly dealt with. At the battle there were 20,000 men divided into six brigades and two cavalry regiments, a camel corps and six artillery batteries. In the zariba, going in a clockwise direction, there was the 2nd British brigade under Lyttelton, then Wauchope's 1st brigade, Maxwell's brigade consisting of one Egyptian and three Sudanese battalions, Macdonald's brigade with three Sudanese battalions and one Egyptian infantry battalion, then Lewis's brigade with four Egyptian battalions. At the back was Collinson's all-Egyptian brigade looking after field hospitals, baggage and ammunition. On the river were six patrolling gunboats. The artillery both on the gunboats and round the zariba consisted of the latest models – Maxims and five inch Howitzers. The infantry was armed with up to date Lee Metford rifles.

The scene of the fighting was bounded by the river in the east, the desert in the west, the city in the south and the hills of Karari in the north. The battlefield was dominated by Jabal Surkab, called by British writers Surgham, a hill about one hundred metres above the plain with a ridge extending eastwards to the Nile. The plain sloped gently to the river, with a large number of khors, seasonal watercourses, that were at the time of the battle still damp and muddy.

Kitchener realised that he had a great advantage if there were to be a daytime engagement. His modern weapons with their accuracy and long range would be able to deal easily with an army advancing over the clear open country in front of his zariba. On the other hand man to man combat would offset these advantages. When the Khalifa stopped to the west of Surkab and smoke was seen rising as the Mahdist forces prepared food and brewed tea, Kitchener feared that a night offensive was probable. This was indeed the Khalifa's intention at the time, and a council held in the early afternoon by the Khalifa and his closest advisors confirmed this.

Kitchener's intelligence, however, managed to secure a couple of individuals who went over to the Khalifa's camp and spread the word that Kitchener was going to attack at night. Night fell with each side expecting and fearing an assault from the other. Kitchener's army had some searchlights which scoured the plain, another infernal weapon that bewildered the Khalifa.

Late that night the Khalifa held another council. Doubts were expressed about a night offensive, and argument was polarised between the Khalifa's cousin, Ibrahim al-Khalil, and his son, Shaikh al-Din. Ibrahim al-Khalil had spied out the land and felt there was a good chance of a successful storming of the zariba with his well-trained soldiers. Ibrahim was supported by Osman Azraq and Osman Digna. Shaikh al-Din opposed this. A quarrel flared up between them. Shaikh al-Din felt that the Black Standard, full of irregular and ill-trained soldiers from the west of the Sudan, could not be controlled. He had his comparatively well-armed force and wanted a day assault so he could direct his fire over the plain. 'Let us not', he said, 'be like mice or foxes slinking into their holes by day and peeping out at night.'

The Khalifa backed his son and the night offensive was abandoned. In making this decision, the Khalifa lost the battle. In his thirteen years as ruler, he had never been a commander in the field and had lost any sense of the advances in modern weapons and tactics. His last field experience had been with the slow firing rifles and cumbersome cannons of Hicks, nearly all of which had a limited range of fire. He had never been able to assess the effect of Maxim guns. He had seen no shrapnel with its splinters that would shower down on soldiers. He did not know case shot with its capacity for destruction at short range. Finally, he was not to know that a direct assault in broad daylight without strong cover was suicidal after the introduction of the Lee Metford rifle with its capacity to produce a vast amount of concentrated fire.

In arguing to make use of his mulazimin fire in daylight, Shaikh al-Din was playing into Kitchener's hands, with the irony that Kitchener preferred a daytime fight for the same reasons.

After the council, the Khalifa developed a plan for a daytime assault. It was to be in two stages. The enemy should be persuaded to come out of the zariba and away from their fortified position. This would be done by a direct assault by the professional soldiers of Osman Azraq and Ibrahim al-Khalil. Then the Black Standard would rush on the Anglo-Egyptian army and – it was hoped – cut them to pieces, sheltered by the fire from Shaikh al-Din's mulazimin.

But things were to work out otherwise.

Now this is where the story really begins. Before dawn Kitchener sent his cavalry out to look for the enemy. At 5.55 am they reported that the Khalifa's army was advancing, and withdrew into the zariba. Ibrahim al-Khalil brought troops over the ridge, and for nearly two miles charged over the open ground at the zariba. At the same time Osman Azraq, with about 6,000 men, went north of Surkab and charged at the centre of the zariba. At 6.45 am the 32nd Field battery opened fire and a few minutes later the Anglo-Egyptian infantry opened fire with long range volleys. An awful massacre followed. One unit of Osman Azraq's force managed to find cover among the winding depressions and bring down a few of the soldiers in the zariba. The field battery was brought to concentrate on them and they were wiped out. This first assault was a complete failure. The attack was over by 8.20 am.

While this was going on, Shaikh al-Din's mulazimin had advanced to the Karari hills and there was a clash with the Anglo-Egyptian cavalry commanded by Broadwood. Kitchener ordered Broadwood to return to the zariba. Broadwood sent the camels back. They stumbled over the rocky ground and were almost overtaken, but for the timely arrival of a patrolling gunboat that destroyed the attackers. Broadwood defied Kitchener and retreated to the north, drawing with him Shaikh al-Din and the mulazimin. Thus the Khalifa's most effective fighting force became literally *hors de combat*.

At 8.30 am there was a lull. One third of the Khalifa's army had hurled itself against the new artillery. One third had withdrawn from the battlefield in useless pursuit of Broadwood's cavalry. One third remained intact quietly behind Surkab. It is not clear how far Kitchener at this time was aware of the situation. The plain was strewn with slain men, wounded men, and others struggling and heading for Omdurman. Kitchener now wanted to get to

Omdurman before these soldiers, and accordingly sent out the 21st Lancers to clear the plain. But the Lancers were to fall into a trap.

Khor Abu Sunt is a deep khor running from just south of Surkab to the Nile. Osman Digna with his Hadendowa spearmen occupied this khor. Reinforcements were joining him from west of Surkab. Osman Digna prepared the trap. The Lancers, a proud cavalry regiment seeking glory, trotted out of the zariba. Osman Digna placed a few hundred of his men on the north of the khor. The Lancers saw this row of men, and the commander, Colonel Martin, thought it would be easy enough to scatter them with a textbook charge. They lined up, a drum roll signalled and the Lancers' charge began.

But as they approached the khor the situation changed dramatically. They suddenly realised that the enemy was not just a line of men, but there was also a throng of several hundred fighting men within the body of the khor. It was too late to check the horses in their charge. The Lancers forced their way through the khor but not without a grapple between equally matched combatants. There was no opportunity to demonstrate superior firepower. It was sword against sword and man against man. The troops on the furthest right confronted the mass of reinforcements at the thickest point and suffered heavy casualties. Another troop led by journalist-soldier, the twenty-three-year-old Lieutenant Winston Churchill, charged and broke through the less dense ranks of the Hadendowa. But one troop on the far left rushed ahead and broke through with ease. The survivors reached the far side. They were harried, but succeeded in shaking off their enemy and after a short gallop got some hundreds of yards out of reach.

This clash caused more casualties to the Anglo-Egyptian army than any other part of the battle. Twenty-one out of the twenty-seven British killed lost their lives in this engagement. However, the Lancers' charge captured the imagination and was seen as a great feat of arms instead of the fatuous blunder it actually was.

Around 9 am Kitchener sent the brigades out of the zariba. They spread out and faced south. The far right was occupied by Macdonald and his Sudanese battalions. Macdonald was a Scot, a Highlander who had risen through the ranks and was an exacting trainer of Egyptian and Sudanese soldiers. As the army advanced, Macdonald stretched further to the west. At about 9.30 he spotted the Black Standard behind Surkab facing him. The Black Standard was waiting for fire cover from Shaikh al-Din and the mulazimin. But the latter were several miles to the north fruitlessly pursuing Broadwood. The idea had been for the firepower to cover an assault. Ya'qub had kept his standard concealed and it remained quiet. Maxwell's brigade also spotted the Black Standard after storming Surkab. Kitchener quickly swung the brigades round. Maxwell and Lewis prepared to fire on the flank of the Black Standard. Wauchope's British brigade was sent to fill up the gap between Macdonald and Lewis.

Ya'qub waited impatiently for Shaikh al-Din. At last, at 9.50 am, after any advantage of surprise caused by the Black Standard's concealment had been thrown away, the Black Standard launched its offensive at Macdonald's battalion. It was fired on by the brigade ahead of it and from the hill on its right. It had no firepower of its own and was not covered at all. Inevitably it was a desperate and suicidal assault.

At 10.15, as the Black standard assault was dying away, the mulazimin reappeared and, with the Green Standard, a second assault was launched on Macdonald's brigade. Macdonald with great skill managed to order his battalions to turn around ninety degrees to face this new threat. Months of drill were vindicated and the new assault was parried with the assistance of extra fire from a battalion of Wauchope's brigade.

At 11.30 Kitchener ordered a cease-fire. Successive waves of courageous but ineffectual offensives had all been smashed. The brigades resumed their march towards Omdurman. They rested by Khor Shambat for an hour or so, and entered the city facing minimal resistance. By nightfall Kitchener and his staff were camping in the open ground of the Khalifa's Mosque. The battle was over.

There were 11,000 of the Khalifa's army killed on the battlefield, 16,000 wounded. Among the dead were Ya'qub, Ibrahim al-Khalil and Osman Azraq. The Anglo-Egyptian forces suffered fifty-six dead and 434 wounded.

The Khalifa himself managed to get away from the battlefield. He entered the city and then vanished to the south and then to the west. For over a year he evaded capture and wandered around Kordofan, joined by the Khalifa Ali wad Hilu, his son Shaikh al-Din and by Osman Digna. At one point he had an army of 6,000. Eventually, in November 1899, he was cornered by an expedition led by Wingate. He put up a token resistance and was killed at Umm Dibaykarat, about thirty miles west of Aba Island. The Khalifa Ali wad Hilu was killed at his side. Shaikh al-Din was wounded and taken prisoner to die in captivity. Osman Digna slipped away once again but was captured in 1900 in the Red Sea Hills. He lived in captivity to a great age and died at Wadi Halfa in 1926.

Did the Khalifa have a chance?

The reasons for the Khalifa's defeat have become clear in the course of this account. Kitchener's army was better drilled, better organised, better trained, better armed than the Khalifa's. Yet the advantages Kitchener had were all the greater thanks to a catalogue of miscalculations on the part of the Khalifa. The withdrawal from Sabaluka, the choice of the open plain of Karari as a battlefield, the decision to fight by day, the failure to impose a sense of responsibility on Shaikh al-Din – all assisted Kitchener. When the two sides engaged as they might have done in a night attack, as they did in Khor Abu Sunt, as they could have done in house to house fighting in Omdurman: then Kitchener's advantages were reduced and the proportion of casualties were more equal.

The Khalifa had a rational plan of fighting the battle. It can be argued that his organisation was not resilient enough to sustain such a plan. Shaikh al-Din allowed himself to be dragged away from the battlefield. There was no means of communication between the units more effective than a string of gallopers. Thus the Black Standard's assault was an isolated venture, and hence easily dealt with.

The Khalifa's failure can be seen in a broader strategic context. He seems to have been paralysed by Kitchener's relentless advance with all the terrible tricks of nineteenth century technology – railways, gunboats, searchlights, new weaponry. Yet Kitchener took some great risks that made him vulnerable. His supply line for food, ammunition and reinforcements was one single-track railway line. Why was this not blown up? Why was the invading army not harried more with the assassination of isolated sentries? A kind of psychological warfare was practised in the evacuation of places just before the invaders arrived – at Dongola, Berber and Sabaluka. But the final stand was made at a site favourable to the enemy. Guerilla warfare, intelligently conducted, can exhaust and occupy the attention of a large army. But Mahmud's massacre of Ja'liyin at Metemma alienated potential guerrilla fighters.

The Khalifa lost another opportunity when he declined to withdraw from Omdurman altogether to the west. The Khalifa would have been in the area of his greatest support. If Kitchener had been dragged out to Kordofan the cost in money and men would have been frightful. His mobility would have been limited and his gunboats useless. But the Khalifa, it seems, had elected to be a secular leader with a capital around the Mahdi's tomb. The strength of the early Mahdiya had been in its mobility. Loyalty was to an idea or a tribal leader, not to a place. The Khalifa had, as it were, inherited the machinery of the old Egyptian regime without any compensating gain.

Kitchener's political bases were not secure. The campaign was being run on a shoestring, and Kitchener was keen to get returns for every penny spent. If the Khalifa had been able to spin out the campaign then he would have eroded Kitchener's political bases both in Cairo and in London. The support that the Khalifa, after his defeat and humiliation on the plains of Karari, received from Kordofan for more than a year is an indication of the potential resources the Khalifa failed to exploit.

But such speculation is idle. In history it is hard enough to find out what happened without wondering what might have happened. There seemed an inevitability in the Anglo-Egyptian victory. British interest in Egypt pressed for control of all the Nile waters. The British were not prepared to leave a potential enemy, a possible ally of the French, astride the Nile.

The control of the Nile settled the political map of Africa for two generations until, in 1956, Sudan became the first of African nations to become free of European imperialism. The effects of Kitchener's victory over the Khalifa were undone, but the memories lingered on.

'Dervish Wars'

In book reviews I have always tried to be kind. I am aware of the efforts put into the composition of tens of thousands of words. However, I made an exception with this book. I felt irritated at the author's ethnocentricity, his carelessness and the fact that the Sudanese were being patronised or marginalised. The book reviewed was *Dervish Wars: Gordon and Kitchener in the Sudan 1880-1898* by Robin Neillands, published by John Murray, London, 1996. The review appeared in *Asian Affairs* in February 1997.

Robin Neillands has a deserved reputation as a historian of the British army. In *Dervish Wars* he has concentrated on the wars in Egypt and the Sudan, and mostly in the Sudan, from Wolseley's victory at Tell el-Kebir to Kitchener's trouncing of the Khalifa Abdullahi at Omdurman in 1898. He tells a good story and has a feel for the issues of the British Victorian army – controversies over reform, the Queen's direct albeit sentimental interest, the major significance of Wolseley. He is also excellent on the personality and leadership qualities of Kitchener, and fascinating on talented though unfortunate mavericks like Valentine Baker and Hector Macdonald. But this is a book that, in spirit, could have been written eighty years ago. He acknowledges – as did Winston Churchill in *The River War* published in 1899, and A B Theobald who was writing fifty years later – positive aspects of Mahdism, but his treatment of the Sudan and the Sudanese ignores a good deal of recent scholarship that has explored the dynamics of the Mahdist state, most notably the work of P M Holt and Ismat Hasan Zulfo, which have appeared in English. There has also been much work published in Arabic that offers a different approach.

This ethnocentricity makes him careless about many matters of detail in Egypt and the Sudan. Granted that there can be variations in the transliteration of Arab names, but there are limits. He confuses Caucasians and Circassians. The Egyptian annexation of the Sudan was in 1821 not 1831. The Governors General of the Sudan before Gordon were Isma'il Ayub and Ra'uf Pasha, not Ismail Ayat and Rais Pasha. He confuses Nuba with the Nuba Mountains. Neither had anything to do with the Armenian Egyptian Prime Minister Nubar Pasha whom Neillands calls Nuba Pasha. The Mahdi was not a 'desert dwelling Arab' but a riverain craftsman. His successor was the Khalifa Abdullahi not the Kalifa Abdalla Abd Allah and his 'palace' was not 'by the river'. The Khalifa's son was Osman Shaikh al-Din not Osman-al-Din.

This carelessness is not confined to matters Egyptian and Sudanese. Edward

Cardwell was Secretary for War, not Secretary of State for War. Hicks Pasha was not a 'British General'. He was a Lieutenant Colonel in the Indian Army from which he retired with the honorary rank of Colonel for pension purposes. Soldiers who were recruited to the Egyptian army after the British occupation were raised in rank and Hicks was made *fariq*, roughly Lieutenant General. The journalist in Khartoum during the siege was Frank Power not Powers and Kitchener's brigadier at Omdurman was Lyttelton not Lyttleton. And some of the most checkable points of British history are treated with misleading negligence. It must be hard to get more mistakes into nineteen words on page 173: 'Gladstone had returned to office in 1886 and finally retired in 1895. Lord Salisbury and the Conservatives took office. . .'

We expect better from John Murray. And we are still left with an old-fashioned approach to a tale that is certainly worth retelling but only in the light of late twentieth century research and insights.

The Scars Of Culture

This is a review of the book, *Shulūkh* by Yusuf Fadl Hasan, published by the University of Khartoum Press, 1976. It appeared in the *Times Literary Supplement* on 13 January 1978. I was told it was the first review in that journal of a book written in Arabic.

Most Northern Sudanese of the Nile valley of a certain age have scar-markings on their cheeks. These marks are an intimate, unwritten part of the traditional culture. Foreigners are often inhibited from prying into something that seems very personal but they may notice that it is as rare in the North for a young Sudanese of twenty to have these cuts as it is for a Sudanese of fifty to be without them. In one generation the custom seems to be dying out.

It was in danger of disappearing without a trace until Yusuf Fadl Hasan decided to bring together notes and observations he had made on the phenomenon. Professor Hasan is the Director of the Institute of African and Asian Studies at the University of Khartoum. The Institute has been collecting oral and linguistic material, and coordinating various studies – history, anthropology, archaeology, language studies, folklore and ethnography. As a result new light is being thrown on hitherto dark corners such as African migration, the Islamisation of the Sudan and the fading away of Christian Nubia.

In *Shulūkh* Professor Hasan has recorded the available evidence on the facial markings from poetry, written sources in Arabic and other languages and his own personal observation. The cuts (*shulūkh*) in Sudan of the Nile valley are seen on Meroitic statues and would appear to have been a Nubian characteristic. According to Professor Hasan, the custom was transmitted by Nubian mothers to the offspring of Nubian-Arab marriages and became a mark of Arabism. Those unmarked were regarded with disapproval as slaves or gypsies.

There is more evidence for the practice of cuts in the last two centuries. Professor Hasan argues that different tribes had distinguishing marks, borrowed often from camel brandings. The decline and dissolution of the Funj Sultanate of Sinnar in the eighteenth and early nineteenth centuries led to a regrouping of allegiances. New loyalties were to religious brotherhoods (*tarīqa*s) rather than to tribes. Collective identification was demonstrated by differing *shulūkh*. An H-like cut was called 'Shaikh al-Tayyib's ladder' and was generally, but not exclusively, the mark of the Sammani tariqa. A T cut was called 'Wad Hasuna's stick'. Sometimes the T was made to look like a cross and could be an unconscious survival from Christian Nubia.

Marks for identification were mainly for men. Women would seldom leave the tribal or brotherhood homeland and there would thus be less need for identification. Nevertheless *shulūkh* on women's faces were widespread and were used to enhance the beauty of the face. Long, broad and deep cuts on a fleshy cheek were greatly prized. The practice of *shallākha*, face cutting, became a profession like that of the circumciser or midwife – a skilful art associated with the intimacies and rites of passage of domestic life.

Professor Hasan's book is brief and enlightening. A series of line drawings (with rather unhelpful captions) illustrate the text. Professor Hasan is a historian and has aimed to classify his evidence and to detect a pattern of continuity. He refrains from asking more searching questions. Why was it necessary to have visible means of identification? How far is the custom analogous to female circumcision? The *shulūkh* are on the way out: was the custom maintained under British rule as an assertion of Sudanism? Female circumcision persisted as a similar assertion. Since independence such assertions are perhaps less necessary. Professor Hasan steers clear of these questions but he has most competently preserved in beautiful Arabic a fragment of African social history. *Shulūkh* arouse much curiosity outside the Sudan and a translation (with better captions) would be useful.

Greenlaw's Suakin

This is a review of *The Coral Buildings of Suakin* by Jean Pierre Greenlaw, published by Oriel Press, London, in 1976. The review appeared in *Sudanow*, a monthly English language magazine published by the Sudanese Ministry of Information, in November 1976.

In Khartoum the retreat of the British during colonial times was an extraordinarily exclusive club, called outrageously the Sudan Club – membership was open only to British passport holders. Peter Shinnie told me that Jean Pierre Greenlaw was the first member to turn up at the bar of the Sudan Club wearing his shirt outside, and not tucked into his trousers.

Jean Pierre Greenlaw first came to the Sudan in the 1930s to build up the Art Department at Bakht er Ruda Institute of Education. He was the first head of what is now the School of Fine and Applied Arts in the Khartoum Polytechnic. From the 1940s he frequently visited Suakin where he recorded in his sketchpad the buildings and their interiors.

The Coral Buildings of Suakin, published by Oriel Press, is the result of more than thirty years work. Its publication has been aided by a grant from the Sudanese National Council for Research. The book is short but is lavishly illustrated by Greenlaw's drawings. There are no photographs. The drawings illustrate the detail of the woodwork, the screens, the method of construction, the decoration in stone and the tools used, in a way denied to the camera.

Greenlaw has seen Suakin in the last thirty years of its dilapidation. His pen has succeeded in producing an imaginative reconstruction of the interiors from fragments of woodwork and decoration. The drawings have a commentary in which he describes the town, outlines its history and defines the characteristics of the Suakin style, which reached its peak in the 1880s. The houses, he says, 'made full use of the local material resources without waste or destruction to the environment, were economical to build and maintain and there was nothing to go wrong, no plumbing or wiring. The fabric was an excellent insulator from extremes of temperature and would last indefinitely if properly maintained and the outer skin of plaster kept intact.'

The Islamic city and port of Suakin was contained on an almost circular island. Social habits determined many of its architectural features such as the separate women's quarters and the finely designed areas for entertainment. As a port Suakin reflected distant parts of the world. Its most characteristic feature, the wooden screened window, the *roshan*, is known in other parts of the Arab world as the *mashrabiya*. Roshan is a Persian word and the original designers of the Suakin roshans were craftsmen from Bokhara. The heavy wood used is called *jawi* and used to be brought from Java. Suakin culture was unique but eclectic, taking what was fittest from all parts of the world.

During the late nineteenth century Egyptian styles, sometimes remotely derived from Europe, were introduced. These were often unsuited to the area, and buildings of the Egyptian style have deteriorated more rapidly than those in the older style. Technologically inappropriate innovations upset the Suakin harmony and unity, a unity that, in Greenlaw's view, 'betokens deep social agreement and a corporate belief which accompanies the all-pervading metaphysical system and religion of Islam.'

The decline of Suakin became rapid and inevitable after the foundation in 1906 of Port Sudan. Suakin is forty miles away: too far for it to be a suburb of the new city, too near for it to be an alternative port. Port Sudan became the railhead, and Suakin's vast, elaborate *wakāla* or caravanserai, constructed as recently as 1881 for camel caravans, became obsolete. Port Sudan became the local administrative headquarters, drawing off the decision makers, the merchant houses and the forward looking from Suakin. Port Sudan's deeper docks were suitable for international liners, displacing Suakin's port and jetties constructed for Indian Ocean dhows. The slow, relentless disintegration of Suakin invokes ecstasies of melancholia, like Palmyra in Syria. It touches a universal chord reminding us of the transitory nature of civilisation, recalling Macaulay's imaginary New Zealander who in a future century sketches the ruins of St Paul's Cathedral.

Did it have to be like this? Is there any point in restoring Suakin unless the town has a vital function? Some buildings – like the *muhāfaza*, the old provincial headquarters – have been preserved. Most of the others have tumbled into ruin. There is little justification for the expenditure of vast sums to restore or maintain them. The tragedy of Suakin is the loss of the interiors. They are unique. They could have been preserved on a large scale without undue cost or organisation. It is to be hoped that a Suakin salvage operation can concentrate on what is left of the roshans, the grilles, the woodwork, the doors, the doorways and the furniture.

Jean-Pierre Greenlaw's book is a superb record of what has been lost and of what might yet be saved in part.

Mohamed Omer Beshir

Mohamed Omer Beshir (MOB) was a great friend in the Sudan. I wrote his obituary for *The Guardian* but this was a more personal piece written for *Emirates News*. It appeared on 7 March 1992. I was living and working in Abu Dhabi at the time.

Forty days ago today Mohamed Omer Beshir died in Khartoum. Mohamed was a scholar, a Sudanese patriot, a writer, a historian, an educationalist, a graduate of the University College of Khartoum, of Queen's College Belfast and of Linacre College in the University of Oxford. He was a former Academic Secretary and Principal of the University of Khartoum, a Senior Fellow of the Institute of African and Asian Studies, an Ambassador. He was an honorary doctor of the University of Hull and founder and Chancellor of the Ahlia University of Omdurman.

A dozen books in English and scores of articles and lectures explained to the world aspects of Sudan's past and present. MOB, as he was widely known, wrote first on education in the Sudan. Spreading opportunities for education was a central theme throughout his life.

In 1964 MOB had an administrative post in the University of Khartoum. In the autumn of that year a popular rising dominated by university staff, students and graduates led to the downfall of the military regime of General Abboud which had intensified the civil war between Northern and Southern Sudan. The new civilian Prime Minister was Sirr al-Khatim al-Khalifa whose earlier career had been as an educationalist in Southern Sudan. Sirr al-Khatim inaugurated a Round Table Conference to discuss the conflict. MOB was the Secretary General. His book, *The Southern Sudan, Background to Conflict*, was the first of several to explain the complexities of the issue.

I first got to know MOB in 1971 when I started a six-year spell in the Sudan. Unlike so many of his generation he never took a permanent job outside the country, in spite of governments that he scorned. He had his books. He had his projects. He had his friends. He inspired two generations of Sudanese with an enthusiasm for the recording of Sudan's past. There was nothing elitist about historical research. He was closely concerned with collecting oral evidence of people's involvement in the events of the past. This included the memories of the grandparents of his students, which could be recorded, documented and stored.

111

In explaining his own country to the world, MOB was more than an academic. His house in Manshia was an open house for scholars and visitors to Khartoum. Thousands went there for breakfast or dinner, prepared by his patient and placid wife, Sikkina. MOB as a host was unforgettable and his parties were joyous occasions. Shrieks of high-pitched laughter would come from him as he talked volubly in Arabic and English about some fantasy or some absurdity. He could listen to and talk to anybody, old or young, educated or illiterate, and make each person feel important. He always had time for my infant son, Paul, telling him Sudanese riddles.

I have one abiding memory. An old Australian called Fred March was living in quiet retirement in a suburb of Khartoum. Old Fred was in his nineties and had been the official driver of Sir Lee Stack, Governor General of the Sudan, when he was assassinated in Cairo in 1924. Now here was an interesting piece of living history. I went with MOB to call on Old Fred who was living with his Eritrean wife, twenty years his junior and with whom he spoke in Italian. We went into the shaded internal veranda of his house and sat and were offered tea. Old Fred was deaf, but polite and friendly. We edged the conversation to the past and to the event of which he had been a major witness.

Old Fred's friendliness vanished and he gruffly made it quite clear that he was not going to talk about that at all. Embarrassed silence. We felt we were impertinent intruders and sipped our tea. MOB saw on the wall the picture of a young man on a motorbike taken in about 1910. MOB broke the silence by asking about it. Old Fred's friendliness returned. 'That's me on my Norton. I was the first man to ride a motorbike at more than 100 miles an hour,' he said proudly. MOB had no interest in such matters but quizzed him on his motorcycling career. Trophies were brought out, and it seemed that Fred's motorcycling achievements were the only things in the world that interested MOB. We left as friends but never learned any more about the assassination of Sir Lee Stack.

In the last year of his life, MOB became very ill from cancer. His last project was a MOB Memorial Library to which he wanted his friends to contribute. Over the New Year, a month before he died, he went to Oxford – a city he loved passionately – hoping for a cure. It was not possible and he returned to Sudan to die.

A friend, learning that MOB was at death's door and knew it, phoned him a few days before the end, full of grief. But MOB was cheerful, giggling weakly. His last words to the old friend were, 'We'll all meet up in the Horse and Jockey'

– recalling a pub in North Oxford. What a way to die! We all feel the loss but can rejoice in memories of a wonderful man.

Arabia

I caught up with my University of Keele contemporary, Ahmad al-Duaij, in 1971 on a visit to Kuwait, my first to Arabia. Kuwait was much more interesting than I had expected.

I spent four years in Yemen from 1980 to 1984. It was a difficult country to get to know. There was a lack of cultural ambiguity that marked the countries of the Eastern Mediterranean, where an outsider could find a role. In Yemen, an outsider was defined as a foreigner, an alien and an infidel. This was especially the case in the capital, Sana'a. But the history, architecture and landscape were all absorbing.

I was in Tunisia for four years after Yemen. I was then posted to Abu Dhabi, the capital of the United Arab Emirates. I did not want to go there. I wanted to work in a country that has a history, and shuddered at working in a materialistic oil-rich state. I was quite wrong in my reluctance to go. The Emirates are certainly new, but in Abu Dhabi and Dubai, there was an international community, with very interesting people from all Arab countries. And there was a gentleness and modesty about the nationals whom I knew. From there I travelled to the other Gulf countries for work or pleasure.

Since I left the British Council I have made frequent visits to Saudi Arabia and the United Arab Emirates as a cultural consultant.

Tim Mackintosh-Smith

Tim Mackintosh-Smith first came to the Yemen in 1982. He was at the University of Oxford, reading Arabic, but chose to spend a year in Sana'a. The British Council had just started an English language teaching centre and Tim had already obtained the minimum qualification to teach English, and we were delighted to employ him. He went back to complete his degree at Oxford where his tutors were puzzled by his fluent Yemeni Arabic. He returned to Sana'a and has, as far as I can gather, been based there ever since. In the late 1990s he wrote a brilliant book on the country: *Yemen: Travels in Dictionary Land*, published by John Murray, London, in 1997.

I reviewed it together with a book by Kevin Rushby, another former teacher of English at the British Council in Sana'a, who was there after my time. His book: *Eating the Flowers of Paradise: A Journey through the Drug Fields of Ethiopia and Yemen*, was published by Constable, London, in 1998. The review appeared in *Asian Affairs* in 1999.

In the 1980s the British Council's new English Language Teaching Centre in Sana'a was fortunate in attracting several remarkable teachers, among them the authors of these two books, both making their debuts as travel writers. Tim Mackintosh-Smith first went to Yemen in 1982 and has been in Sana'a more or less ever since. Kevin Rushby has lived and taught in Sudan and Malaysia as well as Yemen. Both overlapped and were friends. Each appears, not too obtrusively, in the other's book. Tim accompanies Kevin on some wanderings in the mountains above Hodeida. Kevin was with Tim on a fabulous trip to Socotra. Neither covers exactly the same ground.

Yemen: Travels in Dictionary Land is a whimsical yet scholarly collection of accounts of journeys Mackintosh-Smith has made over the years. A graduate of Arabic, he has steeped himself in the chronicles and literature of medieval and early modern Yemen. He admits that he 'treads a thin line between seriousness and frivolity'. Sometimes the reader is unsure which century we are in. But Mackintosh-Smith's observations of the people of Yemen include an imaginative appreciation of the value systems, cultural reference points and perspective of his hosts. He is frequently uproariously funny. Some of his adventures are a mixture of deep human interest, suspense and farce. By far his most enthralling chapter is about the trip to the island of Socotra, perhaps the least known inhabited corner of the Arab world. He sails there on a *sambūk* that is more seaworthy than it appears and wanders over the island, discoursing on the people, the flora, its history and the way of life of today's Socotrans. His book is a compulsive and excellent read, given greatly added value by etchings drawn by Martin Yeoman, who is equally deft with personalities, scenes or buildings. My only regret is that he has not drawn a portrait of the author.

The title of Kevin Rushby's book refers defiantly to the plant *qāt*, chewed as a stimulant in Yemen, Somalia and Ethiopia. He is a defender of the habit and writes with the aesthetic of a wine buff about its varieties. The chewing of *qāt*, at segregated parties, has been the principal social activity of Yemenis for several centuries. As Kevin Rushby says: 'At a conservative estimate, it accounts for one third of the gross national product, politicians take decisions on it, businessmen strike deals over it, even Texan oil men will force themselves to accept bouquets of it, "exchanging green gold for black gold"; from the centre of the capital to the outermost desert reaches tribesmen will accept judgments made by men with *qāt* in their cheeks. It has consumed my money, decided my friends, chosen my house, taught me some Arabic, and given me a love for the country more powerful than my own.' One could add that a substantial minority of Yemenis deplore the habit, seeing it as a drain on resources and productivity, a factor in malnutrition in children and a major cause of injuries and deaths in road accidents caused by drivers under the influence of *qāt*.

The purchase or consumption of *qāt* is in the background of most of the encounters Rushby records in his journey from Addis Ababa to Sana'a Each incident is superbly recorded. Captivated by the detail of each incident on the way, we lose interest in the destination of the journey.

Both writers are not afraid to reveal attitudes that are politically incorrect. Mackintosh-Smith states the case for the exclusion of women. Kevin Rushby makes excuses for slavery. Both extol *qāt*.

Yemen: Travels in Dictionary Land is likely to be a classic of Yemen travels. Mackintosh-Smith is the Hugh Scott of the 1990s. Both Scott and Mackintosh-Smith are easily distracted to consider the symbolic, the meaningful and the grotesque. Kevin Rushby could write about any place with distinction, wit and humanity. Both books are essential reading for anyone who plans to visit or to understand contemporary Yemen.

Tim spent the next few years devoting himself to the work and travels of Ibn Battutah. In 2001 he produced the first volume of a trilogy, *Travels with a Tangerine: A Journey in the Footnotes of Ibn Battutah*, published by John Murray in 2001. The review I wrote appeared in *Asian Affairs* in 2001.

Tim Mackintosh-Smith's first book, *Yemen: Travels in Dictionary Land*, was awarded the 1998 Thomas Cook/*Daily Telegraph* Travel Book Award. That was a very personal book, with an account that revolved around the author's long residence in and love for the Yemen. With this book, Mackintosh-Smith joins the select band of outstanding British writers – Kinglake, Robert Curzon, Doughty, Freya Stark, Thesiger, Colin Thubron and William Dalrymple – who have described their encounters with the Arab world and western Asia.

The formula of this second book *Travels with a Tangerine* is simple: its execution outstanding. Readers of his earlier book *Travels in Dictionary Land* will recall how Mackintosh-Smith saw Yemen through the eyes of medieval Arab writers. In this book he concentrates on the travels of Ibn Battutah, the fourteenth century traveller born in Tangier – hence Tangerine. He has made himself thoroughly familiar with Ibn Battutah's work and starts his quest in his predecessor's birthplace. He traces the great man's travels to Egypt, Syria, Oman, Anatolia, the Crimea and Istanbul/Constantinople. He has also read up the Arab and European travel writings of Ibn Battutah's contemporaries, and we are drawn into the mental and cultural framework of the fourteenth century. Reminders of the modern and contemporary world (that is, any time after 1350 AD) become tiresomely irrelevant.

Ibn Battutah was a great visitor to the tombs and shrines of Islamic saints. The author locates these tombs, some almost lost without trace. Others can just about be identified and some, such as the tomb of al-Shadhili, are to this day objects of pilgrimage in a way that Ibn Battutah would have recognised. Indeed our contemporary traveller's determined search for al-Shadhili's tomb in Upper Egypt is a brilliant piece of reportage. He notes the quiet piety of today's pilgrims, the blend of menace and good humour in the behaviour of the Egyptian police, the significant and the inconsequential and the continuity of faith and practice. It is a world rarely observed by Europeans and non-Muslims.

Mackintosh-Smith describes his pursuit of Ibn Battutah's travels in little known corners of Asia, such as the Kuria Muria islands off Oman and the cities of the Crimea. He wears both his Christian identity and his scholarship lightly, but when he meets a fellow Battutah enthusiast or a descendant of one of Ibn Battutah's acquaintances we can share the delight at the encounter.

The narrator has developed a language that is distinctly his own. He has a fondness for esoteric words – obeah, gloop, gurning and Thesmophoriazousae, for example – that, like Doughty's language, help the reader enter an unfamiliar world. He also has a skill in wordplay: a brass band inflicts grievous bodily harmony; someone with Turkish blood has a touch of the tarbush. But there are deeper reflections on the nature of time and travel and the human condition. His empathies are universal. We learn a lot about the author himself, but he is not an intrusive narrator. We see the contemporary world through his historically-sensitive eyes. He notes the somewhat comic enforcement of Qaboosian political correctness in the remoter parts of Oman. He discusses the theory of the mid-fourteenth century Black Death reaching Europe from a Crimean port, just a few years after Ibn Battutah's visit there. He notes the return of the Tatars to Crimea after their forced migration by Stalin, a return that is leading to a revival of Islam and a restoration of the mosques.

There is a hint of a further volume of travels in Ibn Battutah's wake further East. This reviewer is already impatient.

The United Arab Emirates

Although Abu Dhabi and Dubai are extraordinarily modern cities, there are deep roots, and things are not what they seem. The Gulf is an outlet of the Indian Ocean. The country, like the other Gulf states, is based on innovation, and is a pan-Arab place in a remarkable way. People from all Arab countries are working there. I left in 1992 but have made numerous visits there since, and feel very much at home. The book reviewed is *The United Arab Emirates: A Study in Survival* by Christopher M Davidson, published by Rienner, Boulder, Co and London, 2005. This review appeared in *Asian Affairs* in 2007.

The United Arab Emirates (UAE) has been one of the most remarkable polities of the twentieth century. At its birth in 1971 few would have predicted its fortunes. Not all of the seven emirates seemed to be committed to the confederation, and indeed one of the emirates, Ras al-Khaimah, delayed joining up for a few months. Monarchy was unfashionable and the survival of Nasserism posed an ideological threat to the distributive capitalism that characterised the UAE.

Dr Davidson of the University of Durham has spent time in the Emirates, teaching at the English medium Zayed University. Many of his sources, referring to public opinion and social prejudices, are laconically described as based on 'personal interviews'. The book is a political scientist's analysis of the achievements and challenges of the country. He traces some of the features of the contemporary UAE political culture to the years before oil wealth. The paramount dominance of the ruling families was derived from legitimacy conferred by the 'truce' treaties with the British, going back to the early nineteenth century. These treaties 'effectively froze a snapshot of local power struggles and established formerly elastic territorial boundaries'. The Gulf was part of a wider Indian Ocean world and the presence of large numbers of non-nationals from south Asia is nothing new. Nor is the nature of the 'rentier state' whereby the government has an income not dependent on taxing its citizens. The families had long obtained rent from guano-collecting expeditions, fishing licences, and airport landing rights from Imperial Airways.

Since independence the ruling families have concentrated on consolidating their power and wealth, but, at the same time, have legitimised that authority by providing a sophisticated welfare state and handouts to nationals. The country relies on professional services from northern Arabs, South Asians and Europeans and on Asian immigrant labour. Colossal disparities of wealth and the denial of basic human rights to immigrant workers are accepted because the vast majority of non-nationals in the UAE are better off than they would be in their own countries. Even taxi drivers from the North West Frontier and Bangladeshi labourers are able to send remittances to their families back home. There is no shortage of people wanting to work in the UAE.

The book assesses the effectiveness of the federation. Local loyalties are strong, and people who live in the northern Emirates and work in the capital, Abu Dhabi, will prefer to return home every weekend. Each state clings on to its legal and economic identity. Buses take passengers from Abu Dhabi to Dubai but are not permitted to return with passengers from Dubai to Abu Dhabi. Dubai has been allowed to go over the top with its flamboyant and hedonistic consumerism and Sharjah has been able to see itself as the cultural and educational centre. The charisma of the late Shaikh Zayed, backed by untold wealth, has allowed Abu Dhabi to secure the adherence of the smaller emirates. Dissidents, if they are non-nationals, are speedily and ruthlessly deported; if they are nationals, they are ignored or co-opted into the system. Most people are happy making money or enjoying themselves.

Davidson brings out the astuteness, vision and dynamism of some of the members of the ruling families. Tactical concessions have been made, opportunities seized. Shaikh Muhammad bin Rashid Al Maktum and Shaikh Abdullah bin Zayed Al Nahyan (or Nuhayyan, as Davidson transliterates the name) have both called for a greater openness in the press, and have embraced the information revolution. But the pace of change has led to cultural dislocation. An Arab-Islamic identity is asserted though it has only been in the last half century that there has been any significant cultural orientation towards Cairo or Damascus, instead of Iran or India. The Arabic language is seen as under threat. In 1999 a survey indicated that forty-seven per cent of the students preferred English as their exclusive medium of instruction, more than twice the number of those who preferred Arabic. English is the language of the private sector, of hotels and the expanding tourist industry.

This volume is an admirable survey of the lights and shades of the Emirates. A tendency to use some of the jargon of the social sciences may puzzle the general reader who would otherwise understand much about an Arab country where the development over the last generation has been exciting, and where things, against all the odds, work well and where the future continues to look promising.

The Peace Maker

During my time as Director of the British Council in the United Arab Emirates I organised an exhibition of photographs of the Emirates taken by Wilfred Thesiger in the 1940s. I invited Thesiger, then – in February 1990 – just short of eighty, to come for the opening. He had visited the Emirates in 1977 and hated the modernity, describing Abu Dhabi as an 'Arabian nightmare'. But the 1990 visit was the first of several he made in his old age. I wrote an account of the 1990 visit in *Thesiger's Return*, published by Motivate Publishing in 1992. This essay was about one of his old friends from the Rashid tribe, and appeared in *Meetings with Remarkable Muslims*, edited by Barnaby Rogerson and Rose Baring, published by Eland Publishing, London, in 2005.

In 1990, Wilfred Thesiger returned to Abu Dhabi to attend the opening of an exhibition of his photographs, arranged by the British Council. He had known the town and the region over forty years earlier during his great journeys across the Empty Quarter of south east Arabia. Thesiger had known and loved pre-oil Arabia and its people.

We had brought over from Oman two of Thesiger's companions during his historic explorations, Bin Kabina and Bin Ghubaisha. Thesiger dedicated *Arabian Sands*, describing those years, to them. They had then been teenagers. Now they were bearded patriarchs in their sixties. One morning Thesiger said, 'The man I'd really like to see is Musallim bin al-Kamam. I haven't seen him for over forty years. His picture is on the spine of the dust-jacket of the first edition of *Arabian Sands*.'

In *Arabian Sands* Musallim is described – in the late 1940s – as being middle aged, but he must only have seemed so, for he was then in his late twenties, ten years younger than Thesiger. He was born into the Rashid tribe of Dhofar, the son of a minor sheikh. He and his father acquired reputations as peacemakers among tribes. His father had given assistance to Bertram Thomas in his desert travels in the 1920s. A generation later Musallim provided similar services for Thesiger. He knew all about the tribes and their conflicts, was resourceful and wise and very well known. A story tells how in Inner Oman in 1947 Thesiger was pointed out as a Christian, and an old man said, 'Is he the Christian who travelled last year with bin al-Kamam and the Rashidi to the Hadhramaut?'

Musallim helped Thesiger with contacts but never travelled across the Empty Quarter with him. However his quiet authority and dignity left an enduring impact on Thesiger and all who met him and spoke with him. He was a good listener, patient and curious, and could make friends with anyone.

As such he had all the qualities of a negotiator and in the following decades he negotiated treaties with tribes all over southern Arabia, and travelled from Yemen to Baghdad.

An hour after Thesiger expressed the wish to see Musallim, I was in my office when the phone rang. The caller was from the British Embassy. 'We have a Musallim bin al-Kamam here who wishes to see Umbarak bin London.' (This was the name by which Thesiger was known in those parts.) I immediately went to the Embassy, and met a man clutching a camel stick. He was perhaps seventy, neatly built, lithe of body and bright of eye. He had heard about the exhibition, travelled over from Oman, and wanted to see Wilfred. For the next week Musallim was with Wilfred every day.

His Arabic was difficult to follow. My Arabic – he said – was like that of a Syrian school teacher. I do not know if he went to school but I remember him writing his name for me, slowly and with effort: Musallim's skills were in speaking, listening and acting on evidence thus acquired. Reading and writing were inessential to his way of life. He had not lost an iota of his integrity in adapting to the transformations of the late twentieth century, looking at them with detached curiosity and acceptance: it was all part of the unfathomable purpose of God. After Thesiger left, Musallim often dropped into our house, bringing some dates from Dhofar, meeting my family, including my widowed mother-in-law, whom, he told me, he would like to marry. This offer was made without irony. For him, the world was full of extraordinary things and becoming my step-father-in-law was no stranger than, for example, the modern island city of Abu Dhabi, which he had known when it had only one tree and no building taller than the residence of the then Ruler.

On one occasion, I accompanied him to call on Edward Henderson at that residence, in the early 1990s the Centre for Documentation. Musallim had known Edward Henderson in Dubai in the 1940s. The guards at the gate challenged Musallim as we went past, but not me. I was in a western suit. He was in Bedu clothes, neat and clean, but clearly not a recognisable part of bourgeois *modern* Abu Dhabi. I felt furious. This man had been a legend in southern Arabia over forty years earlier. Even the President of the United Arab Emirates, Shaikh Zayed, would have treated him with respect. But Musallim was not angry. He smiled tolerantly at what I thought was ignorant and insulting behaviour.

Musallim never gave notice of any visit. On the outskirts of Abu Dhabi there was a community of Rashid tribesmen. I would always, after a visit, take him where he wanted to go, and we generally ended up there. He would sit in the passenger seat of the car, clutching his camel stick and squatting with his feet up, as if he was sitting on the ground.

He invited me to Dhofar and I did see him and his family at Thumrait, fifty miles from Salala. They lived in a breeze block government house, with a couple of camels in the enclosure. His son was working with an oil company and was later to study at Loughborough University of Technology. Musallim and his son suggested we take a few days off and travel with the camels into the Empty Quarter. A fascinating idea, but, for my pattern of life, quite impossible. But it was proposed as if it was the simplest idea in the world. It seemed to make Thesiger's pioneering explorations somehow an extended picnic.

I saw Musallim for the last time at Muscat airport. He was not well and was going to India for treatment at Omani government expense. He died soon afterwards. But on that last sad encounter there was a smile, a cheerful and curious acceptance of the manifold wonders of the world. Flying across the Indian Ocean. Peace-making among warring tribes. Camel riding in the Empty Quarter. Calling on strange Ingiliz friends in Abu Dhabi. A son studying modern management at a place called Loughborough. Musallim's tranquil and tolerant friendliness made him one of the most remarkable people I have met. Life has been the richer for having known him.

Muslims In Britain

In the late 1970s I read some of the novels of Marmaduke Pickthall. Reading his work and examining his life led to my writing a book, *Marmaduke Pickthall British Muslim*, published by Quartet Books, London, in 1986. Pickthall became a Muslim during the First World War and I researched the British Muslim community of which he immediately became a leading member. I retained an interest in the links between British Muslims and the wider Muslim world. My last task with the British Council was to organise a conference on the mutual relationship between Britain and Islam.

The Background of British Muslims

This is a review of an excellent and comprehensive study of Muslims in Britain. The book is *The 'Infidel Within': Muslims in Britain since 1800* by Humayun Ansari, published by C Hurst and Company, London, 2004. The review appeared in *Asian Affairs* in 2005.

This is a most authoritative guide to Muslims in Britain. The book falls into two parts. The first covers the history of Muslims in Britain before 1945. The second is a survey of issues dealing with the large-scale immigration of Muslims, largely from South Asia, from the 1950s to the 1990s. The author examines all aspects of issues confronting Muslims. Very little is omitted.

It is possible to trace a Muslim presence in Britain back to Tudor times – individuals from Morocco or Turkey. The recent work of Nabil Matar has recorded the close relations with the Muslim world in the sixteenth and seventeenth centuries – raids by Barbary pirates on the southern coasts of England and Ireland, kidnappings, enslavements and ransoming of captives as well as more peaceful diplomatic and commercial relations with the Ottoman Empire. But isolated individuals became a trickle in the eighteenth century. There were groups – rather than communities – of Muslims in the nineteenth: Moroccan and Syrian merchants in Manchester, and Somali and Yemeni lascars that settled in the ports. Early immigrants assimilated well. Ansari is excellent in bringing out fascinating individuals such as Sake Dean Mohaamed [*sic*], an Indian who settled in Brighton, eloped with an Irish girl and established a successful shampooing and herbal vapour baths business. He is buried in St Nicholas's churchyard and his family was so assimilated that his grandson, the Rev James Kerriman Mohamed, became vicar of Hove. Other colourful early Muslims who settled included Duse Muhammad Ali, probably Ethiopian, though Ansari claims he was Egyptian. Duse was a professional actor and became a champion of Egyptian nationalism in Cromer's time. He later became involved in pan-Africanism. Ansari also writes on Munshi Abdul Karim, who became a trusted servant of the elderly Queen Victoria and gave her lessons in Hindustani. Like John Brown twenty years earlier, his closeness to the Queen caused resentment in the rest of the household as well as political suspicions that he was spying on behalf of Afghanistan. We shall never know the full story for, after his death, the courtiers made a bonfire of his personal papers.

British Muslims, until the large-scale post-war immigration, were often quite prosperous. The community included wealthy transient South Asians (such as Muhammad Ali Jinnah) and a number of converts, often middle class folk, who had worked or travelled in Muslim countries. But Ansari draws attention to less successful Muslims. Mayhew's *London Labour and London Poor* catalogues Muslims who had fallen on hard times.

The second larger part of the book is thematic rather than chronological. Ansari analyses the different communities and their varying ways of adaptation to their host country. The first generation that came from South Asia in the 1950s and 1960s were far readier to assimilate. There is a bizarre reflection of the British in India in the early nineteenth century. Once wives were brought out from the homeland, adaptable individuals became a detached more inward looking community, or a series of communities. Ansari emphasizes the range of opinion and strategies among Muslims in Britain. In spite of individuals who claim to speak for British Muslims, Islam is one of competing markers of identity – competing with class, location, family and above all ethnic origin. Most Muslims (who registered and went to the polls) have until now voted Labour. (In the United States, Arabs have tended to vote Republican.) After the Iraq war this may change, but the Islamic Party has made minimal impact in constituencies where there are large numbers of Muslim voters. The Muslim Council of Britain has tried to act as an umbrella organisation but many Muslims wish to be seen as British people who just happen to be Muslim. One Muslim – Abd'Elkader Farrah – has been principal designer with the Royal Shakespeare Company, another – Nasser Hussain – has captained the English cricket team. Local government and (increasingly) the media are full of people with Muslim names.

Muslims who have migrated to Britain vary in their links with home. Arabs have in general seen themselves as in transit, being seasonal or transient migrants. Twenty years ago commentators identified 'the myth of return': Muslims from South Asia saw themselves as temporary migrants who would go back and could not quite accept that they had become part of Britain. Links are still retained with homelands. The home country is a pool for finding marriage partners. Some do return. Property prices in Sylhet in Bangladesh, I have learned, have rocketed, thanks to Bangladeshis returning, having made their pile in Britain. Ansari writes with authority about all the issues of today's young Muslims – education, the *hijab*, arranged marriages, the generation gap, employment, the use of the internet, the political extremists. He writes with sympathy, without pushing any line, and it is hard to see how such a work could be bettered.

130

Islamic Influence on Architecture in Britain 1800-2000

This was a lecture I gave at the Felix Meritis Foundation in Amsterdam in January 2000.

For over two centuries architects in Britain has found inspiration from the classical world of Islam. Until the end of the nineteenth century this influence was mediated by non-Muslims. Britain, like the rest of Europe, was eclectic and catholic in finding inspiration from outside Europe: ancient Egypt, China, India, the Middle East. More recently the influences have been moulded by Muslims themselves. There is nothing alien or new about Islamic influences in Britain. Close connections between the Islamic world and Britain go back for over four centuries through trade, diplomacy, travel, art and scholarship. In the early seventeenth century there is a record of a community of Muslims in London – though there is no record of a mosque.

The eighteenth century was a great age for building. Styles often reflected a philosophical curiosity about the rest of the world. Three features from the Islamic world were developed in this century. One has been totally indigenised, the second has persisted and the third disappeared as fantasy and has reappeared in the last hundred years as the major symbol of the faith of a community.

The first is the kiosk. The word and the concept are derived from Turkey where it was a small garden house, structurally independent of any other building. The kiosk provided a comfort and an intimacy often missing from a larger building. Over the years the kiosk has become an urban one-purpose, free-standing construction – a newsagent's stall or a telephone booth. Few are aware of its origins from the Islamic world.

The second is the *hammam*, the Turkish baths. In the Islamic world the baths were linked with the obligation of cleansing and purification. But they transferred to Europe without the religious associations. Only in the nineteenth century was there any attempt to build baths with an Islamic style of architecture.

The baths followed other domestic social innovations derived from the Islamic east, such as the coffeehouse. Coffee came to Britain in the early seventeenth century. The first coffeehouse opened in 1650. They then spread like internet cafes in the 1990s. By 1700 there were reckoned to be 3,000 in London alone. Less publicly visible, but similarly popular from the eighteenth century were the sofa, the ottoman and the divan – all concepts imported from Turkey.

The third borrowing was the mosque itself. In 1767 the architectural pattern book of William Wright, *Grotesque Architecture or Rural Amusement*, proposed different models of mosque for 'garden embellishments'. 'Mosques' were built in the gardens of country estates such as at Kew, to the west of London. They were not built as places of Muslim assembly.

Although there are records and architects' drawings of such mosques, I do not think any have survived. Such buildings are the physical equivalent of the oriental tale, comparable with the extraordinary impact of *The Arabian Nights*, of which there were eighty separate editions in the eighteenth century. Characters such as Sindbad the Sailor and Aladdin became part of British culture. The first pantomime of Aladdin was presented in London in 1813.

Britain's closest contacts with the Islamic world during the eighteenth and nineteenth centuries were with India. Popular interest in things Indian was aroused by the trial of a former Governor General of India, Warren Hastings, between 1788 and 1795. Individual merchants were captivated by the Islamic architecture of India. Many who made huge fortunes reproduced their fantasies in their homelands.

The vogue for the 'Indian style' at the beginning of the nineteenth century relied on artists' drawings that were produced in expensive limited folio editions. One pioneer was William Hodges who produced *Select Views in India* between 1785 and 1788. He was impressed by what he called 'Moorish grandeur' and argued – as had the architect of St Paul's Cathedral, Sir Christopher Wren – a historic connection between Islamic architecture and the Gothic arch. More influential were Thomas Daniell and his nephew, William, who produced a collection of sketches, *Oriental Scenery*, between 1797 and 1808, based on their travels in South Asia.

One of the earliest outstanding outcomes of Indian Islamic architecture was the country house built for Sir Charles Cockerell at Sezincote in Gloucestershire. It has onion domes, corner pavilions and minaret-like towers. The architect, Humphrey Repton, never went to India but did consult Thomas Daniell.

The supreme example of Indian Islamic architecture is the Royal Pavilion at Brighton. Palatial stables had been constructed for the Prince Regent, later

King George IV, by William Porden. In 1797 he had presented at the Royal Academy: 'a Design for a Place of Amusement in the style of the Mahometan Architecture of Hindustan'. (This overlap of amusement and Islamic architecture will recur.) But the architect for the Pavilion was John Nash. Nash used the Daniells's *Oriental Scenery*, but his patron, the Prince Regent, had ideas of his own. The result is an amazing mixture of styles – Indian Islamic, Hindu and Chinese. The eclectic influence of the Pavilion spread throughout the country and the century. The poet, Thomas Moore, mocked these fantasies:

> The same long masquerade of rooms,
> Tricked in such different, quaint costumes,
> . . .
> You'd swear Egyptians, Moors and Turks
> Bearing good taste some deadly malice,
> Had clubbed to raise a pic-nic palace.

Touches of 'oriental' influences, derived from Islamic originals – horseshoe arches and arabesque decoration – were employed in all manner of public buildings from water towers to lighthouses.

The other great influence from the Islamic world came from the far west, from Andalusia. William Chambers built a palace at Kew called Alhambra in the 1750s (now lost), but it was only after the Napoleonic wars that people in Britain became enthused by Islamic Spain, partly by the writings of Washington Irving. Then, in 1815, James Cavanagh wrote *The Arabian Antiquities of Spain*. David Roberts, best known for his pictures of the Near East, also produced architectural sketches of Alhambra. Indeed the direct and indirect influences from the Islamic world on public space in Britain in the nineteenth century were enormous. Owen Jones popularised Andalusian models. He was principal designer for the Great Exhibition and his *Grammar of Ornament* is still in print.

Thanks to the development of steam-driven ships, travel to the Middle East became easier from the 1830s. Egypt was on the route to India and became part of a European-dominated global economy. The well-known oriental paintings of the period were one aspect of a cultural discovery of the Arab Islamic world. The 1840s saw the publication of a number of popular works of travel, such as *Eothen* by A W Kinglake. The novelist and Post Office official, Anthony Trollope, who travelled to Cairo on post office business, wrote in *Doctor Thorne*, published in 1852, how Frank Gresham did the usual things after university, 'going up the Nile, crossing over to Mount Sinai, thence over the long desert to Jerusalem, and home by Damascus, Beyrout and Constantinople, bringing back a long beard, a red cap, and a chibouk'. In addition to red caps and chibouks, travellers also brought back ideas of design and notions of space and leisure.

There are two outstanding, self-conscious, surviving attempts at producing Arab architecture in the nineteenth century. Leighton House, in West Kensington, London, was built in 1865 for the artist Lord Leighton. Leighton had travelled in the Near East and spent time studying Damascus houses. He imported tiles from Damascus for his London home, installed fountains and decorated his rooms with quotations from the Holy Koran. The second example is the Arab Room at Cardiff Castle, South Wales, designed by William Burges, for the fabulously rich Marquess of Bute. Bute had travelled to the Near East and wanted a fantasy building. Burges had also travelled to Turkey where he examined and studied the mosques. At Cardiff he demonstrated virtuosity with domed ceilings, stained glass, coloured tile work and spectacular Moorish arches.

By the middle of the nineteenth century fantasy was yielding place to faith. The first religious buildings to owe inspiration to Islamic models were actually synagogues. Newly prosperous Jewish communities rejected the idea of Gothic with negative medieval Christian associations and opted for a Moorish revival style, recalling a happier Jewish time in Andalusia. There are good examples in Liverpool and in Bradford where the synagogue, now in the heart of the Muslim area, has a horseshoe arched doorway and horizontal banding of alternate colours of stone.

Some architects who travelled in the Near East imported ideas also into churches. The architect of Christ Church Streatham in south London – built in 1842 – had studied the Islamic buildings of Egypt and consciously modelled the west doorway on a Mamluk iwan that opens on to the courtyard of the Sultan Hasan Mosque in Cairo. That architect, J W Wild, also designed St Mark's Church in Alexandria.

Muslims in the nineteenth century used to hold communal prayers either in private homes, in rented halls or in public places like Hyde Park Corner or Leicester Square. The first purpose-built mosque in Britain was at Woking, south of London. It was built in 1889 with funds left by the Ruler of Bhopal using designs by a non-Muslim British architect, W I Chambers.

By 1900 Britain was becoming a centre for the further education of wealthy Indians. The British ruling classes in India had cordial relations with Indian rulers, mostly Muslims, ruling over fragments of the old Mughal Empire. Some of the Indian upper classes came to Britain for residence and pleasure as well as for education. Other Muslims, who migrated to Britain during the nineteenth and early twentieth centuries, were sailors from Bengal, Yemen and Somalia, and merchants from Morocco and Syria. Before 1914 there were established Muslim communities in London and Liverpool. The Jubilees of 1887 and 1897 brought hundreds of Indian Muslim soldiers to Britain, and in the First World War Britain saw thousands of Indian soldiers en route to theatres of war in Europe and throughout the Empire. The Royal Pavilion in Brighton became a hospital for wounded Indian troops. Did the Indo-Islamic fantasy architecture make them feel more at home?

The major migrations took place in the second half of the twentieth century, mostly from South Asia. Most British Muslims today are British by birth. Muslim populations are largely urban. West London has become a place where Arab Muslims come for holidays or to invest in banks, business or property. Iraqi refugees tend to be in outer west London, Turks and Kurds in Hackney. Older communities of Yemenis settled in Cardiff, Tyneside, Birmingham and Sheffield. All have left their mark on public space in Britain today. But although faith was determining buildings, a fantastic element with its overtones of pleasure has persisted. Cinemas took over theatres with names like Alhambra and Grenada, and even Mecca. In the 1950s, with the rise of television, these palaces of popular pleasure were converted to ballrooms or bingo halls.

Today there are about 1,200 mosques and praying areas in Britain. About one hundred have been purpose built. The others have been conversions of houses, warehouses and cinemas. Richly carpeted rooms where shoes are shed, calligraphic texts and the addition of some decoration have helped to islamise the building. In the 1960s the architect, Gulzar Haider, arrived in Britain from Pakistan and attended prayers at a Wimbledon house. 'There was no *mihrab* niche, just a depression in a side wall, a cold fireplace with a checkerboard border of green and brown ceramic tiles.' Twenty-five years later he returned to the house-mosque which was now 'wrapped with a glazed finish; arched windows sat squeezed into what seemed like an endless line of sharp crescents; and there were a number of token domes, whose profile came less from any architectural tradition than from illustrations of the "Arabian Nights"'.

The Brighton area has Muslims from many backgrounds, speaking thirty-nine languages. Of the three Brighton mosques one is a former private house that has been a Jewish school, another is a converted shop, the third a floor above shops. At nearby Hastings the mosque is a converted church. Inland

Crawley has a purpose-built mosque. This pattern is representative of all Britain. Those areas with large concentrations of Muslims – London, Birmingham, Bradford, Edinburgh – have purpose-built mosques, showpiece buildings, sometimes constructed with funding from the Arab world. The Islamic Cultural Centre and Regent's Park Mosque is the best known in Britain. It was pioneered in the 1930s by London-based Ambassadors from the Islamic world and some British politicians, who often had an imperial background. Crown Estates land was granted to the Muslim community, a grant that reciprocated the award by the Egyptian government of a site in Cairo for an Anglican cathedral.

Proposals for the building of a mosque, however, encountered problems and delays. Permission to build was granted in the 1970s and a competition to tender was won by the British (non-Muslim) architect, Sir Frederick Gibberd. Its design is derived from a number of Islamic sources. The low drum-like dome could be Iranian, the minaret Middle Eastern. The prayer hall is limited in space with room for 965 worshippers but the entrance hall, courtyard and marquees can accommodate 4,500.

The Regent's Park Mosque is well-known, even fashionable. Three miles to the east is the London Borough of Tower Hamlets. This has for centuries been a working-class area and first home of new immigrants to Britain. Huguenot silk-weavers in the seventeenth and eighteenth centuries, Irish Catholics in the eighteenth and nineteenth, Russian and Polish Jews – and also Chinese – one hundred years ago, and now Bangladeshis. There are two major mosques. One was purpose built in the late 1960s. The second, in Brick Lane, was built in 1742 for Huguenot worship. It later became a Methodist chapel and after 1895 an ultra-orthodox synagogue. In the 1970s it was bought by Bangladesh businessmen for conversion as a mosque.

The Manningham area of Bradford is almost totally Muslim. Of over thirty mosques in the city of Bradford, four have been purpose-built, two are former cinemas, three are former churches and nine are converted industrial premises. The Darfield Street mosque is still under construction and is likely to be the largest. The architect, Neil Waghorne, has a clear vision of how the mosque will develop. He has studied Turkish architecture and has been inspired by the Süleymaniye mosque in Istanbul. A doorway has stalactite (*muqarnas*) decoration, carved from Yorkshire stone by a local stonemason. The whole building is a fascinating combination of Islamic inspiration and local non-Muslim craftsmanship.

Let us conclude. Muslim influences on British architecture have been persistent, pervasive if indirect for several centuries. There has been no aversion to borrowing or adapting Islamic cultural phenomena. Secondly, the connection between Britain and Islamic architecture has been one of partnership. Non-Muslim British architects have built prestigious British mosques. These architects are in a long tradition of observing and replicating original Islamic buildings. The 'orientalist' architecture is re-worked in the interests of today's British Muslim community.

Finally, are Islamic architectural forms adapting to a British environment? Could it be that a typical British mosque displays the enterprising re-working of an existing structure – house, church, factory or cinema? Or is it an imaginative use of local talent and local materials?

138

People

It was my ambition when I was at school to write obituaries for *The Times*. In the 1970s I wrote eight obituaries for *The Times* of prominent Sudanese. In the 1990s I switched to *The Guardian*. The following are mostly reprinted from that paper, but they include one or two other assessments of people whom I have admired or known.

Edward Gibbon

I first read *Decline and Fall of the Roman Empire* in Ankara in 1962, and was enthralled by the prose. It was also interesting to read it in Turkey, for Gibbon had a fascination with the Eastern Mediterranean world. I was invited to contribute to *Encyclopedia of Islamic Religion and Civilisation*, edited by Ian Richard Netton, and wrote three biographical essays – on Gibbon, on Abdullah Yusuf Ali and Marmaduke Pickthall. The encyclopaedia was published in 2008.

Edward Gibbon is one of the world's greatest historians. A product of the European Enlightenment, his comprehensive presentation of twelve centuries of post-classical history has formed the minds of west Europeans for over two hundred years. Although he never visited the lands of Islam he had a lifelong fascination for the Arab world, from the days of his childhood reading of *The Arabian Nights*.

Gibbon was born in Putney in western London in 1737 to a comfortable middle-class family. He was sickly as a child, but read voraciously in history and literature. He went to Westminster School and on to Magdalen College, Oxford with, as he said in his *Memoirs*, 'a stock of erudition that might have puzzled a Doctor, and a degree of ignorance of which a schoolboy would have been ashamed'. At Oxford he had an unfulfilled wish to study Arabic. Wide reading led him to question his family Protestant beliefs and, at the age of seventeen, he became a Roman Catholic. His horrified father sent him to Switzerland to study under a Calvinistic pastor. This worked and Gibbon returned to the Protestant fold. But he stayed on in Switzerland for five years and became soaked in European classical scholarship. His reading bore fruit in his first book, written in French, an essay on the study of literature, published in 1761.

By now he was back in England, wintering in London and spending the summer on active service with the Hampshire grenadiers. In 1763 he set off for a year's European travel. In Rome, 'musing amid the ruins of the Capitol', he conceived the idea of writing his *Decline and Fall of the Roman Empire*. This was to occupy most of his energies for the next twenty years. Most, but not all. He became a Member of Parliament in 1774 and took office in the government of Lord North, as Commissioner of Trade and Plantations.

The first volume was published in 1776, the year of the US Declaration of Independence and of Adam Smith's *Wealth of Nations*. Volumes II and III were published in 1781; the last three volumes in 1788. The work was an instant success and Gibbon enjoyed fame for the rest of his life. He died in London in 1794. His *Memoirs* were published posthumously two years later.

His great history contains a million and a half words. The first four volumes trace Roman history in detail from the late second to the early seventh century. The last two volumes gallop through the next eight centuries to the conquest of Constantinople/Istanbul by the Ottoman Turks in 1453.

Gibbon was a methodical scholar. He relied on printed sources and fitted into a tradition of 'philosophical history'. The antiquary delved among primary sources; the philosopher reviewed their works to present his gentlemanly conclusions to his public. Gibbon was totally familiar with available sources in English, French and Latin – history, literature and published documents. He was less assured in other languages – German, Italian and Greek.

His work is mostly a narrative, chronological history, though he breaks off to follow through themes that cross centuries: Roman law, the rise of Sassanid Persia or the rise of Christianity. His two chapters on the rise of the Church angered the established clergy. Gibbon's youthful religious upheavals left him with a deep scepticism about supernatural claims. He applauded the tolerant polytheism of the Roman Empire, where religion was 'considered by people as equally true, by the philosopher as equally false, and by the magistrate, as equally useful'. Church historians before Gibbon saw the rise of the Christian church as the fulfilment of God's purpose. Gibbon argued that may be so, but he also attributed secondary causes for the success of the church and examined the social and political context of that success. But he never lost an opportunity to be sarcastic about Christian claims and the frailties of popes and churchmen. His jibes were often in witty and scurrilous footnotes: a literary habit developed by Richard Burton a century later in his translation of *A Thousand and One Nights*.

His warm account of the rise of Islam, 'one of the most memorable revolutions which have impressed a new and lasting character on the nations of the globe', may be seen as part of his habit of belittling Christianity. For his account, he relies on translations, usually into French, of Arabic sources, on George Sale's translation of the Koran, on English scholars such as Ockley, Prideaux and Pococke, and on the writings of travellers to Islamic lands. The latter, 'in the present decay of religious fervour', were 'edified by the profound humility and attention of the Turks and Persians'. Gibbon was eloquent on the merits of the Prophet Muhammad:

His memory was capacious and retentive, his wit easy and social, his imagination sublime, his judgment clear, rapid and decisive. He possessed the courage both of thought and action, and, although his designs might gradually expand with success, the first idea which he entertained of his divine mission bears the stamp of an original and superior genius.

As with his account of the rise of Christianity, he does not acknowledge divine favour for Islam's success. He places the Prophet's mission in a social and historical context. But he is cordial towards the tenets of Islamic faith: 'A philosophic theist might subscribe to the popular creed of the Mohammedans: a creed too sublime perhaps for our present faculties'. He is generally fair on the philosophic bases of Islam: 'The God of nature has written his existence on all his works, and his law in the heart of man.'

Gibbon's sympathetic treatment of Islam came at an important historic moment. Britain was, in his generation, undertaking political responsibilities for millions of Muslims in India. Writings on Islam in Britain henceforth became, in general, less polemical. Gibbon's rationalism, genial curiosity and majestic prose have had an impact on most historians, many writers and thousands of readers over the last two centuries.

Violet Marie Gordon MBE

The life of Violet Gordon is a complete contrast to that of Edward Gibbon. She was a teacher in Turkey for twenty-nine years, and wielded a great influence on my development. After she died, I wrote this appreciation for *New Horizons*, the magazine for former employees of the British Council. It appeared in 2005.

Vi Gordon who died on 5 November 2005 in her mid nineties was one of the most remarkable people I have known. She was with the British Council for twenty-nine years, from 1942 to 1971, all the time in one posting: Lecturer, Ankara. I met her in 1963, during my first job, teaching Mathematics at Ankara College. She was a wonderful raconteur and I became enchanted by her conversation, her life and her career.

Vi was a Scot, a Catholic and a Conservative. Physically slight but mentally animated, she was the soul of kindness. She originally came from Huntly between Inverness and Aberdeen. During the 1930s, Vi was teaching English in the west of England. She was always an enterprising young lady and taught herself to fly a plane. When war broke out she volunteered to serve as a pilot in the Royal Air Force. Her patriotic request was turned down because, as a teacher, she was in a reserved occupation. Then, in early 1942, the RAF started to employ pilots from the United States.

'I was absolutely livid', she told me, still angry twenty years later, her hands quivering with rage as she lit a fresh cigarette with the stub of the one she had just finished. '*I decided there and then never to work in Britain again.* Och, it was not easy to find a job abroad in 1942 but I answered an advertisement in a newspaper for the post of Lecturer in English at the University of Ankara, to be recruited by the British Council. I got the job and have been here ever since. Mind you, it was none too easy to reach Turkey in the middle of the war. I had to go on a liner to West Africa. We were torpedoed on the way. But we were rescued and got to Lagos. Then across the middle of Africa to southern Sudan, all the way down the Nile to Alexandria and then over to Turkey.'

She had travelled all over the Middle East, and especially in eastern Turkey. She was an authority on Armenian and Seljuk architecture, the geology and the flora and fauna of the country, and the literature of nineteenth century travellers to Anatolia. She was an accomplished photographer, and some of her pictures were used in books by Lord Kinross and David Talbot Rice. She had also travelled in the Arab countries to the south. She went to Jordan in the early 1950s and was able to hire an aeroplane in Amman and flew herself to Petra. She showed me photos she took of the castle of Kerak. It was clear that she had flown round and round, at a fairly low altitude, snapping away. The hire of the plane had almost exhausted her funds and she had to return to Ankara by train, travelling fourth class.

Vi Gordon was at home abroad. At home she was at sea. Most summers she would drive back to an ancient mother in the north of Scotland. She had no problem getting as far as England but she had difficulties reaching Scotland from England. 'I cross over to Dover,' she told me, 'and always stay with my sister in Faversham. That bit's easy enough. Then the next morning I set off. I don't like driving through London. The roads are always changing and I can never understand the maps. What I do is find a lorry that has painted on it the name of a town which I know to be north of London – Oldham or Leeds or Northampton – and follow it. I stick to it like a limpet, hoping it's going to the place painted on it, until we are well past Greater London. I am then able to get my bearings and find my way to the A1 and so on up to Huntly.'

I was not a good teacher and I had problems controlling a class of fourteen year olds. I told Vi about this. She told me that she too had had problems with discipline when she started. 'I was teaching a class at the University and there was this big lout of a man at the back who was, with malice aforethought, deliberately undermining my lecture. I got fed up with this and went up to him. He was much bigger than me but I slapped him across the face like that' – her hand sliced through the air and I almost had to duck myself – 'and then the other way. And again and again. I went back to the front of the class. There was total silence. They could not cope with the situation. I was tiny. He was huge. Honour prevented him from exerting his superior strength against me in front of the other students. I got away with it and have never had any trouble since.' It was not a solution I felt I could apply to my dilemma.

Vi enriched my time in Turkey and stimulated interest in all things Middle Eastern. Towards the end of my year in Ankara I fell ill and she insisted that I move to her flat. I had the pleasure of her conversation and the run of her library every day for a fortnight as I convalesced.

She retired in 1971 to her house in the middle of the Aberdeenshire countryside. She always had a freezer full of food because former Turkish students would often drop in with their families, 'and if they have come so far you canna just point them in the direction of a restaurant.'

145

Farid Hanania

I only knew Farid Hanania from conversations with his son, the novelist, Tony Hanania. This obituary appeared in *The Guardian* on 24 August 2007.

In the summer of 1932, a young anglophile Palestinian came to England with the aim of studying law. The bursar of Queens' College, Cambridge, told him to get two references. His parents had known the former High Commissioner of the Mandate of Palestine, Sir Herbert Samuel, who replied immediately. Then the Palestinian recalled that a writer who had come to Jerusalem and met his family had written a book called *The New Jerusalem*. Inquiries at a bookshop identified the writer as G K Chesterton. The newcomer invited himself to tea with Mr and Mrs Chesterton at Beaconsfield, Buckinghamshire, and was thus able to produce the second letter of recommendation.

The would-be student, Farid Hanania, who has died at the age of ninety-eight, went on to a distinguished academic career as Professor of International Law at the American University of Beirut (AUB). A man of great charm, he did much to advance AUB's reputation for academic independence. Through his hospitality, he helped to improve relations between Arabs and foreigners during a period that many look back on as Beirut's golden age. His life story reflects the tragedies that have afflicted the Christian communities of Palestine since the fall of the Ottoman Empire.

Farid was the son of an Orthodox priest of Jerusalem, from one of its oldest Christian families. As a boy, he saw Allenby enter the city in 1917, and went to St George's School, attached to Jerusalem's Anglican cathedral. He was captain of soccer and cricket, and went on to AUB to do a degree in Business Administration. But he yearned for a British qualification, and after Cambridge became – he believed – the first Arab to be called to the English bar.

During the Second World War he broadcast for the BBC Arabic service, offsetting the influence of the strident pro-Axis broadcasts from the Italian radio station at Bari. Farid returned to Jerusalem after the war, only to escape death narrowly when the King David Hotel was blown up by pro-Zionist militants in 1946. He moved to Beirut and was Professor of International Law from 1946 to 1977, during which time he served as Faculty Dean for twelve years. As Dean, he effectively raised money from the Rockefeller and Ford

Foundations, securing AUB's reputation as the leading university at the time in the Middle East. At the same time he resisted US attempts to have university staff dismissed for alleged anti-American activities. His house on the campus became a meeting place for Arab nationalists, Beirut socialites and foreign diplomats, journalists and visitors. Guests included the explorer, St John Philby, and his spy son, Kim, Arnold Toynbee, John Julius Norwich and Jawaharlal Nehru. Among his student contacts were Walid Jumblat and George Habash.

After retirement, Farid lived in Winchester and then in south-west France where he worked on his memoirs. He was twice married, both times to British teachers working in Beirut. He is survived by his second wife, Prue, his daughter, Caroline, a film production designer, and Tony, a novelist.

Ulfat Idilbi

I translated two of Ulfat Idilbi's novels while I was working in Damascus between 1992 and 1997. I got to know her during visits to her flat on the slopes of Mount Qasyun with fantastic views over the city of Damascus. Her house was full of mirrors and chairs that evoked an Ottoman past. She retained her beauty and elegance into her old age. I also called on her in Paris. This obituary appeared in *The Guardian* on 19 April 2007.

Ulfat Idilbi, who has died in Paris at the age of ninety-four, was one of Syria's best loved writers of fiction, and a feminist for half a century. Although she came from a privileged family, her sympathies were far from being elitist, and her strongly articulated messages were in harmony with the Arab nationalist secular regime that has governed Syria for the last forty years.

Idilbi was born in Ottoman Damascus, in 1912, the daughter of Najiba and Abu'l-Khair Umar Pasha. She was profoundly affected as a teenager by the Syrian revolt against the French Mandate rule in the 1920s, which led to France's bombing of Damascus. She became a nationalist and educated herself by reading widely the books in the library of her author uncle, Kazem Daghestani.

At the age of seventeen, she married a German-trained physiologist, Dr Hamdi al-Idilbi. Normally, married women retained their family names, but Ulfat rejected what she saw as a patriarchal custom and insisted on being known as Mrs Idilbi. She started writing and publishing stories in magazines in her teens. In 1948, she won a prize for a short story, awarded by the BBC Arabic Service, and the first of several volumes of her stories was published in 1954, introduced by the master of the modern Arab short story, the Egyptian Mahmud Taymur.

She is best known for her novel, *Dimashq ya Basmat al-Huzn*, published in 1980 when Ulfat was approaching seventy. It was translated into English as *Sabriya: Damascus Bitter-Sweet*, and published in 1995. This tells the story of a young girl who grows up in the 1920s and develops national and female consciousness. The former is suppressed by the French, the latter by her family. The girl hangs herself in the beautiful courtyard of the family house, leaving a diary that forms the bulk of the novel. 'My countrymen demand freedom,' Sabriya, the central character says, 'but cannot even give it to one another. Half the nation remains bound by chains imposed by you men.' The story has been serialised on Syrian television.

A second novel that has been translated as *Grandfather's Tale* (1998) recreates the world of nineteenth century Damascus. Many of her short stories deal with women who suffer, operate and survive by manipulating within a limited private world.

Idilbi was also a lecturer and essayist, on social, educational and literary issues. She was physically minute tiny, and a chain smoker – another gesture of emancipation.

Her old age was saddened by the death in 1995 of her son, the banker Ziad Idilbi, and she divided her later years between Damascus and Paris, where she lived with her daughter. She is survived by that daughter and by a son.

Peter Shinnie

Peter Shinnie was a personal friend for over thirty years. He was a most remarkable man as I hope the obituary that was published on 30 October 2007 in *The Guardian* indicates.

Professor Peter Shinnie, who has died aged ninety-two, was one of the founders of African archaeology. His professional career spanned seventy years, during which time he was an RAF pilot and intelligence officer, a member of the Communist and Scottish National Parties, an administrator, an inspiring – if demanding – teacher, a pioneering researcher and a gifted writer.

Born in London, the son of an Aberdonian doctor, he went to Westminster School and on to Christ Church, Oxford, to read Egyptology. His first exposure to archaeology was at Maiden Castle, Dorset, with Mortimer Wheeler, as one of a number of gifted apprentice archaeologists – others included Stuart Piggott, J Desmond Clark, Beatrice de Cardi and Rachel Maxwell-Hyslop.

At Oxford, he learned to fly with the university air squadron and was active in the university Communist club, whose members then included Denis Healey and Iris Murdoch. His intense undergraduate life – he also learnt modern Greek – resulted in a third-class degree, but he stayed on at Oxford as a £3 a week Communist Party organiser, and a temporary assistant at the Ashmolean Museum. He joined the RAF when war broke out, flying bombers, then serving in intelligence on air photography interpretation and finally in the battle for Athens, where he was tempted to stay on after the war.

With peace, he returned to the Ashmolean and spent a season working with Leonard Woolley on the Bronze Age site at Tell el Atshana in Turkey, near the Syrian border. This gave him his first exposure to Arabic and helped him secure his first permanent job as Assistant Commissioner for Archaeology in the Anglo-Egyptian Sudan. His boss was A J Arkell, an authority on prehistoric Sudan. Over the next ten years Shinnie explored Nubian studies and started his work on Meroe, the literate civilisation that scattered the Nile valley with pyramids and other impressive masonry. He succeeded Arkell as Commissioner, set up the antiquities museum in Khartoum, founded the journal *Kush*, and was punctilious in writing up surveys and digs.

With the Sudanisation of senior posts, Shinnie had to move on. He was the archaeologist on the Oxford Exploration Society's 1955 survey of Socotra, off the Horn of Africa, and served as Director of Antiquities in Uganda for two years. In 1958 he was appointed Professor of Archaeology at the university in newly independent Ghana, succeeding A W Lawrence, T E's brother. For almost half a century, Ghana remained a major focus of Shinnie's interests. His second wife, Ama, was an Asante from Kumasi and the Shinnies spent part of most years there for the rest of his life. He surveyed capitals of the medieval states of West Africa and researched the languages and cultures of northern Ghana.

His interests in the Nile Valley were sustained. From 1965 he spent the first of eleven seasons at Meroe and returned, more permanently, to be Professor of Archaeology at the University of Khartoum in 1966. His best known work, *Meroe*, in the Ancient Peoples and Places series, was published in 1967, but the next decade allowed Shinnie to place Meroe into the broader context of ancient Africa. In both Ghana and Sudan, Shinnie trained a generation of African archaeologists and contributed to a continental approach to Africa's history and archaeology. His intellectual energies were prodigious and he was interested, not just in the buildings and the artefacts of an elite, but in the whole civilisation. Plunged into a senior post in the Sudan he acquired skills as an inspiring and imaginative manager. For Africans his work placed the blip of European colonialism into a wider context.

Shinnie left Sudan in 1970 and moved to Canada, being appointed to a chair at the University of Calgary. The Canada Council was generous in supporting his work, and during the next twenty to thirty years he took teams of Canadians and Americans to Ghana and Sudan. His last major field project was to combine archaeology with the study of oral traditions and build up a picture of the early Asante state, from the ninth century AD onwards.

Peter was always delightful company, mentally curious and alert to the end, enjoying conversation, gossip, literature and wine. His early leftwing passions mellowed to a broad liberal humanism. He married twice. Margaret was a fellow archaeologist and collaborated with him in the Sudan. She was the mother of his three children, one of whom, Nick, died in 2004. The marriage ended in divorce. His second wife, Ama, survives him.

By chance I was in Calgary in September 2007 and was invited to contribute to the commemoration at the University of Calgary of Peter's life and work. I had been with Peter in Calgary three years earlier. One evening at dinner at the house of Robin Thelwall and Rebecca Bradley we all tried to get Peter to talk about his relationship with Iris Murdoch before the Second

151

World War. We were too polite to ask him directly if he had been one of her lovers. He knew what we were getting at and was too much of the British gentleman to talk openly about such things. But his eyes twinkled. He went so far as to say, 'Well I was three years older than Iris and had a position in the Communist Party of authority over her.' We got no further in our prurient curiosity. But the following is the text of my tribute to Peter Shinnie at the commemoration.

When I first went to the Sudan in 1971 my PhD supervisor, Jack Simmons, told me to look out for Peter Shinnie. Jack and Peter had been contemporaries at both school and Christ Church, Oxford. So for me Peter was a kind of academic uncle. I got to know him and Ama well during the six years I was in the Sudan in the 1970s and made several visits to his dig at Kabbushiya. There was another remarkable link in that Margaret and Peter's children all lived within a mile or so of my then UK base on the Essex Suffolk border.

Peter was always fascinating to talk to. He enjoyed wine, conversation and gossip that was rarely ill-natured. There was an acute eye for social nuances and an informed curiosity about Africa and the Mediterranean worlds. He combined wisdom with a mischievous sense of humour. I continued to see him from time to time during the 1980s and 1990s. In 1984 he stayed with us in Yemen and we met up on our occasional visits to Calgary.

I would like to recall and share two or three particular memories.

In 1976 an older Sudan archaeologist, Sir Laurence Kirwan, Director of the Royal Geographical Society, visited the Sudan and it fell to me to take him to the site of Musawwarat and on to Peter's dig at Kabbushiya, staying overnight. Kirwan was very much an establishment figure. Peter was the ex-Communist. I had had lunch earlier in London with Larry Kirwan who had been very critical of Peter – politically unreliable and professionally unsound. Peter had also confided to me an unfavourable view of Larry – presumptuous, a man of poor judgment.

I was consequently full of impish curiosity and some anxiety as to how these two great men, both in their sixties, would get on together. Would sparks fly? Would there be embarrassing pauses in the conversation? I need not have worried. Both men got on famously, chatting away and savagely rubbishing the work and reputation of an even older Sudan archaeologist, A J Arkell.

Peter had been the archaeologist on the celebrated British universities' expedition to the Island of Socotra off Yemen in the 1950s. A few years ago – when Peter was in his late eighties – there was another expedition to Socotra and I remember having dinner with Peter who was very distressed, indeed indignant, that he had not been invited to take part in that expedition.

One of my last memories was when my wife, Theresa, and I were here in Calgary three years ago, staying with Rebecca Bradley and Robin Thelwall.

Ama and Peter came to dinner and Peter was in sparkling form as we quizzed him about Iris Murdoch and the Oxford Communist Party in the late 1930s. As he got up from the table Peter pretended to be a feeble and old man. It was a hilarious performance. There was something Falstaffian about him, in the way he mocked fate, and dealt with the world, frailty and illness, and ultimately death, on his own terms.

He enriched the lives of us all.

Lord Henniker

Sir John Henniker was Director General of the British Council from 1968 to 1971. In 1971 I was a junior official of the British Council in Jordan when Henniker made a pastoral visit. Ten years earlier he had been the British Ambassador in Amman and had counselled Hussein against marrying Toni Gardiner. The marriage went ahead and she became the mother of Jordan's current king, Abdullah II. King Hussein bore no grudge and, on Sir John's arrival in Amman, made a palace available to him. I was in charge of my Director General's transport arrangements during the visit, and all my careful plans were thrown into confusion by the king's generous gesture.

Thirty years later we were living near the Hennikers' Suffolk home and I met up with him again. He was still an impressive personality, but sadly aged. Walking around his estate I reflected on that advice Henniker had given to the king. Toni Gardiner, like Henniker, came from Suffolk. Her father was a Colonel who came from Ipswich. In his memoirs, Henniker said that the advice to King Hussein was taken on his own initiative. Did Henniker have a Suffolk grandee's disapproval of a misalliance in the marriage?

This obituary appeared in *The Guardian* on 4 May 2004.

Everything that the 8th Baron Henniker, who has died aged eighty-eight, did, as soldier, public servant and diplomat, was done with panache and to applause, until he became Director General of the British Council in his fifties. The panache went on to the end; but the last decades of his life did not seem to live up to the promise of earlier years.

John Henniker-Major was born to a family that, in the eighteenth century, achieved prosperity, a barony and a Suffolk estate. In the nineteenth and twentieth centuries, Hennikers served their country in politics and the armed forces. Agricultural depressions and taxation saw a decline in their fortunes by the First World War. John was sent to Stowe school and went on to Trinity College, Cambridge, where he studied modern languages.

In 1938 he joined the Foreign Office, which with reluctance released him to join the army in 1941. He served in North Africa, was wounded in Libya and hospitalised in Cairo. From there, he was recruited by Brigadier Fitzroy Maclean to join his mission to occupied Yugoslavia, and, for two years, worked with a distinguished group of officers that included Bill Deakin, Randolph Churchill and – improbably – Evelyn Waugh. Their task, to make contact with the charismatic, communist guerrilla leader Tito, has been told in Maclean's *Eastern Approaches* and Deakin's *Embattled Mountain*.

At the end of the war, Henniker-Major, now a major with a military cross, reopened the British Embassy in Belgrade before spending two years as

Assistant Private Secretary to the Foreign Secretary Ernest Bevin, a man whom he loved.

A posting in Buenos Aires was followed by the sensitive task – at the age of thirty-seven – of heading the Foreign Office's Personnel Department. Henniker-Major held this post for seven years, steadying a profession that was still reeling from the defections of Guy Burgess and Donald Maclean, and was soon to reel again from the Suez crisis of 1956. More positively, he completed the integration of different structures – consular, commercial consular, Levant, China, Siam and Japan consular – into one unified diplomatic service. In achieving this, his affability and interest in people were great assets.

During the 1960s, he became, successively, ambassador to Jordan and Denmark. In Jordan, a delicate task was trying to dissuade King Hussein from marrying the daughter of a Suffolk colonel; Henniker-Major failed, but so did the marriage (though the fruit of the marriage is now King Abdullah II).

After Copenhagen, he trod water as an Under-Secretary in London, and then, in 1968, as Sir John Henniker – the Major being dropped – he was appointed Director General of the British Council by an informal mechanism overseen by the Chairman, the discreet Lord Bridges. By the time Henniker took over, however, Bridges had been replaced by the less tactful Lord Fulton.

From the beginning, Henniker encountered coolness on the part of senior staff, which, over the months, turned to sullenness, even non-cooperation. The objection had nothing to do with his performance; it was to the way he was appointed. He was an outsider and perceived as a Foreign Office imposition.

Junior staff, by contrast, saw the new DG as a breath of fresh air. If he had a query, he would bypass senior management. A junior colleague would be amazed, answering the phone, to hear the words, 'Henniker here', followed by a direct question. Physically a large man, he made everyone feel important, and was a great success on overseas tours. But as months turned into years, the senior staff found an ally in Lord Fulton, who, in 1972, invited Henniker to resign on the pretext of his first wife's failing health. Henniker felt his career was in tatters; indeed, he never took a major public post again. He was for six years a director of the Wates Foundation, and threw himself into issues of humanitarian relief, especially activities that improved the lives of vulnerable people.

On his father's death in 1980, he became Lord Henniker and, in the late 1980s, was briefly a Liberal Democrat spokesman in the House of Lords. He also inherited the 2,000-acre estate of Thornham Magna, in north Suffolk. The totally impractical, 95-roomed hall had burned down in 1953, and Henniker moved into a smaller house, formerly occupied by the land agent.

Over the next two decades, Henniker and his second wife, Julia, transformed the estate into an asset for the community. The woods and parklands were opened up to the public, and obsolete outhouses were turned into workspaces and employment opportunities for small businesses. A field study centre was opened in 1985, and local schoolchildren were able to learn about the ecology of the estate. Today, a restored walled garden, with eighteenth-century greenhouses, provides horticultural courses, and a venue for concerts and lectures.

After a back operation in 1998, Henniker was reluctantly persuaded to talk about his life and dictate his memoirs. The result was a breezy and modest autobiography, *Painful Extractions*, published in 2002.

Henniker was twice happily married. His first marriage, in 1946, to a Canadian, Margaret Osla Benning, ended with her death in 1974. He is survived by Julia, whom he married in 1976, and by the two sons and one daughter of his first marriage.

Abd al-Salam al-Ujaili

Abd al-Salam al-Ujaili was a Syrian writer, better known in France than in Britain. This obituary appeared in *The Guardian* on 20 April 2006.

Abd al-Salam al-Ujaili, who has died in his late eighties, was one of the Arab world's most accomplished short-story writers. Collections of his translated work have been published in France and Spain, though only a few stories have appeared in English.

Ujaili was born in the city of al-Raqqa, in northern Syria, to a family that was still semi-nomadic. His education in Aleppo was interrupted by illness and he spent four years at home, becoming a voracious reader of Arabic literature, history and religion. When he resumed his schooling, he amazed everyone by his ability to recite poetry from memory.

He started writing in his early teens – poetry and a play (though he had never been to the theatre) – and his first publication was a story which he sent off to the Egyptian magazine, *al-Risala*, in 1936. During the Second World War, he studied medicine at Damascus University, while writing anonymously for Syrian and Arab literary magazines. His identity was only disclosed when one publication won a prize.

After qualifying, he based his life in al-Raqqa. He was elected to the Syrian National Assembly in 1948 and volunteered to fight for the defence of Palestine. Though he did not care for political or military life, he was, for six months in 1962, concurrently Minister of Culture, Information and Foreign Affairs.

He preferred to spend time practicing medicine in the Euphrates valley of eastern Syria, often refusing to charge poorer patients, occasionally visiting Aleppo or Damascus to give lectures. His first volume of short stories was published in 1948; a poetry collection followed in 1951. In the next forty years, he published twenty volumes of short stories, ten of essays and travel writing, and two novels.

Ujaili's tales illustrate the dilemmas of modern life. He drew on his experiences as a doctor for his plots, and many are located in the Euphrates valley. Earlier stories read as if they should be spoken aloud; later stories touch on how bureaucracy and the police state affect ordinary people. They all have a profound humanity and are written in simple, but forceful Arabic.

He married in 1958 and had four children. The death of his eldest son in a road accident was followed by divorce.

Nazik al-Mala'ika

I knew Nazik al-Mala'ika only by reputation. *The Guardian* asked me to write her obituary. This appeared on 6 August 2007.

Nazik al-Mala'ika who has died aged eighty-three was one of the most influential Arab poets of the twentieth century. Her life and work reflected the history of her native Iraq – idealism, hope, disappointment, exile, depression. Like others of her generation she was influenced by English poetry and pioneered the breakaway from the formalistic classical modes of poetry that had prevailed in Arabic poetry for more than a thousand years.

She was born into a liberal Baghdad family: her father was a teacher of grammar and her mother an early Arab feminist poet. At the age of ten, Nazik showed a poem to her father. He tossed it aside. There was an error and he told her she had to master the grammar of the language first. This she did, and went to the Baghdad Teachers' Training College to do a degree in Arabic, simultaneously studying English at the British Council. She developed an interest in drama and contemporary Arab music.

Her first poetry collection was *The Lovers of the Night*, (1947). She expressed an idealism that was tinged with pessimism and fear of disillusion. Nature and 'the night' became a pervasive theme. Her second collection, *Sparks and Ashes* (1949), was more revolutionary. In her introduction she argued that traditional Arab forms of verse inhibited Arabic poetry from attaining the heights of other world literatures. In her poems she dealt with the themes that moved her contemporaries – nationalism, social and feminist issues, honour killings and alienation.

In the following years she pursued her education in the United States. A career of teaching in Iraq was sandwiched between one year studying literary criticism at Princeton and two years, from 1954 to 1956, studying for an MA in comparative literature at the University of Wisconsin at Madison. Her third collection of poetry, *Depth of the Wave* (1957), mixed both traditional forms and the newer free verse.

Her pessimism was suspended by the revolution in July 1958, when the Hashemite kingdom was replaced by a republic. But disillusion with the succeeding brutal regime soon set in, and Nazik moved to Beirut in 1959. She returned to Iraq in 1964 with her husband, Dr Abd al-Hadi Mahbuba. He headed the new University of Basra, where she was appointed Professor of Arabic. But in 1970 she went again into exile and moved to the University of Kuwait, which was to be her base for nearly twenty years. She published her last three collections in the 1970s. Her later verse continued to experiment. Her romanticism – much affected by the work of Keats – was replaced by a gloomy concern with nationalism and religion.

In 1990 she retired to Cairo and lived a reclusive life, clouded by illness. Her husband died in 2005. She is survived by one son.

Fatma Moussa Mahmoud

I only met Professor Moussa Mahmoud twice, but admired her from afar. She was one of those people who bestride two cultures, adding something of value to both. One of the reasons I write obituaries is to celebrate people such as Professor Moussa Mahmoud. Her life and work should be known to a wider circle than academics and people with an interest in the Egyptian cultural scene. This obituary was published in *The Guardian* on 21 December 2007.

Fatma Moussa Mahmoud, who has died aged eighty, was a pioneering academic who explored and strengthened connections between the literary cultures of Egypt and Britain. The head of English departments at universities in Egypt and in Saudi Arabia, her scholarly output was prodigious.

Apart from themes of English literature, she wrote about the contemporary Arab literary scene and was an early translator of the Nobel prize-winning author Naguib Mahfouz. Her translation of his *Miramar* (1978) has been reissued repeatedly, and her translation of *King Lear* into Arabic (1985) was performed at the Egyptian National Theatre in 2004 to tremendous acclaim. For Moussa, it was her proudest moment.

Moussa Mahmoud was born in Cairo, the eldest child of a merchant from Upper Egypt and his wife, who came from Alexandria. From her early childhood she was a voracious reader. Although there was no English in her home, she mastered the language at the Princess Fawzia secondary school, which had a 6,000-volume library in Arabic and English. Determined to study the arts at university and to be a writer, she was told that it was a career for men, not women. 'Are you going to be an effendi, Fatma?'

Cairo University, then the King Fouad I University, had some British staff teaching English, but anti-British feeling in the postwar years led to riots and a subsequent drop in their numbers. When the British left the Faculty in 1952, Moussa Mahmoud and Magdi Wahba, both first class honours graduates, were appointed to the staff.

By now Moussa Mahmoud was married to Mustafa Soueif, an academic and clinical psychologist, and combined the roles of academic, wife and, in the course of time, mother of three children. The family came to London during the 1950s and Moussa Mahmoud completed a PhD at Westfield College in 1957 on the oriental tale in English fiction.

She returned to Cairo University as lecturer and then Professor and head of the English department. She was now publishing articles and books on aspects of English literature that related to Egypt and to Arab-related themes – on the eighteenth century orientalist Sir William Jones, on the influence of *The Arabian Nights*, and on William Beckford's *Vathek*.

An inspirational and demanding teacher, her passion was communicating Arab literature to the Anglo-Saxon foreigner and vice versa as could be seen in the titles of two of her books. In the early 1970s she published *The Modern Egyptian Novel* and also a collection of her Arabic essays, *Bain Adabain* (Between Two Literatures).

In 1972 she was briefly seconded to Saudi Arabia and was involved in the establishment of higher education for women, returning as Professor of English and Director of the Research Centre at the King Saud University Women's College (1981-92). Meanwhile her scholarly output was both vast and varied.

As Professor Emeritus at the University of Cairo after 1992, she edited an encyclopaedia on the theatre, chaired the Committee for English Translation at the Higher Council for Culture and was the leading light of PEN, the international association of writers, in Egypt. Her novelist daughter, Ahdaf Soueif, was by then living in London.

In her seventies, Moussa Mahmoud undertook the translation into Arabic of *The Map of Love*, Soueif's novel that was shortlisted for the 1999 Booker Prize. The Arabic version appeared in 2001.

In her younger days, Fatma Moussa Mahmoud, while supporting imprisoned relatives, did not take part in demonstrations that toppled the monarchy. But she became increasingly politicised after the first Gulf War, joining her daughter on the march in London against the invasion of Iraq in February 2003.

She is survived by her husband and three children.

Nizar Kabbani

I never met Nizar Kabbani but knew members of his family. He cast a poetic shadow over the whole Arab world during his lifetime. This obituary appeared in *The Guardian* on 1 May 1998.

With the death of Nizar Kabbani at the age of seventy-five, the Arab world has lost one of its most popular poets, one who expressed in simple but searing language the aspirations, frustrations, anger and visions of millions of Arabs. In particular, Kabbani's work explored the themes of love and freedom, especially as experienced by women.

Kabbani was born in Damascus to a gifted and comfortable, but not wealthy family. A great uncle, Abu Khalil Qabbani, was a pioneer of the theatre in late nineteenth century Damascus. His niece is the London-based writer, Rana Kabbani. He was deeply affected as a teenager by the death of his sister, Wisal, who committed suicide because she was unable to marry the man she loved.

Kabbani wrote poetry from an early age. While still a very young man, he published his first volume of love poetry at his own expense, or rather at the expense of his illiterate mother, who, recognising her son's talent, sold some of her jewellery to provide the cash. The publication caused a minor scandal among the conservative bourgeoisie of Damascus.

After studying law at the Syrian University, he joined the diplomatic service of the newly independent Syrian state, and served in embassies in Cairo, London, Beijing and Madrid. During this professional period he produced a volume of poetry almost every year. He was skilful both in a classical form as well as in modernist free verse. But he also developed a style of his own. He extended poetic language to include the language of everyday speech, and his words had a direct appeal to literate and unlettered alike.

Most of his poetic themes were about love, and embodied an assault on social and sexual taboos. His view was that social and national liberation was meaningless without sexual liberation. He wrote usually in the first person, often using the voices of women, exploring the themes of betrayed love, frustrated love, even lesbian love. His message was that women should be free to live, work and love as they choose. A Kabbani poem might be like a squib, a firecracker of feeling:

You ask me the date of my birth
Write this down.
And now you know: my birthday
Occurred when you began to love me.

One of his most celebrated poems of social protest was 'Bread, Hashish and a Moon', written in 1954. In this he described the conditions of poverty of the Arab masses. The publication of the poem led to a debate in the Syrian parliament with some members wanting to put Kabbani on trial, and others wanting him to be expelled from government service.

Of his overseas postings, it was his longest, in Madrid, that had most impact on his poetry. The Umayyads had ruled an Islamic empire from Damascus in the first centuries of Islam and it was an Umayyad who had fled to Andalusia to rule in Cordoba. Kabbani was passionately mindful of the link:

Walking through Cordoba's narrow alleys
I kept searching in my pockets, hoping to find
The key to our house in Damascus.

Kabbani left the diplomatic service in 1966 and set up his own publishing house in Beirut, working also as editor and journalist. His poems by now were popular throughout the Arab world and had been set to music and sung by all the leading singers of the time. His readings both on radio and television reached millions. A public reading in the Sudan had an audience of 10,000. But from 1967, with the Arab defeat at the hands of Israel, there was a new tone in his poetry, which, from being revolutionary in social and literary terms, became more political and very angry.

My grieved country, in a flash
You changed me from a poet who wrote love poems
To a poet who writes with a knife.

Another celebrated poem, 'Marginalia to the Book of the Setback', was an attack on the empty rhetoric of the Arab governments in the months leading up to the June 1967 war:

Our shouting is louder than our actions,
Our swords are taller than us,
This is our tragedy.

Kabbani stayed in Beirut well into the civil war. His first marriage to a Syrian had ended in divorce. His second wife, Bilqis, an Iraqi teacher, was killed in a car bomb in 1981, a death which – like that of his mother – inspired poetry that expressed a mature appreciation of women as individuals rather than as symbols for social emancipation. His autobiography, *My Story with Poetry*, was published in 1972.

After his wife's death, he moved to Switzerland, then France before settling in London. He received many literary awards and reckoned that over ten million volumes of his verse had been sold. Much of his later poetry savaged the tyranny, corruption and abuse of power of Arab governments, and in most Arab countries his poetry has, at one time, been banned.

Yet those governments, nervously aware of his mass appeal, courted him. He attended poetry festivals in Baghdad under the patronage of Saddam Hussain. In the early 1990s, he visited Damascus and, in spite of his apparent criticism of the regime, a public lecture and reading he gave was attended by a son of the President.

Two volumes of translations of his poetry into English have been published.

Such has been the allure of Arabic words that Kabbani's poetry will long outlast the men of power against whom he railed:

If an audience could be arranged
And also my safe return
This is what I'd tell the Sultan
If I were given safety
From the Sultan's armed guards
I would say, O Sultan,
The reason you've lost wars twice
Is because you've been walled in from
Mankind's cause and voice.

Nizar Kabbani is survived by two daughters and a son.

Paul Bergne

I studied Arabic with Paul Bergne at the Middle East Centre for Arab Studies in the village of Shemlan Lebanon from September 1970 to July 1971. I was in the same class as Paul and was in awe of his brilliant capacity to absorb effortlessly the complexities of Arabic. He was also an amusing, delightful and modest companion. This obituary appeared in *The Guardian* on 17 April 2007.

Paul Bergne, who has died aged seventy from cancer, was the British diplomatic and intelligence services' most talented linguist of his generation. A former ambassador to Uzbekistan and Tajikistan, in 2001 he was brought out of retirement by Prime Minister Tony Blair to be special envoy to Afghanistan where he used his linguistic and diplomatic skills with the Northern Alliance, the grouping which opposed the Taliban.

Paul was the son of Bill Bergne and Diana Holman Hunt, a granddaughter of the painter. He was educated at Winchester College and read Archaeology at Trinity College, Cambridge. After graduation he travelled in Iran as a film cameraman. He joined MI6 at the age of twenty-two, and his skills as a linguist – acquired in boyhood – soon became apparent. His first posting in Vienna, where he met his Silesian wife Suzanne, was followed by a year off to study Russian and Persian. A posting in Iran gave him the opportunity to perfect his Persian, but he also took the chance to learn some Azeri, the language of Azerbaijan, which gave him the key to other Turkic languages. In 1970 he studied Arabic for 18 months at the Middle East Centre for Arab Studies in Lebanon. He wrote Arabic in the flowing ornate Farsi script he had learned in Tehran and would also score an extraordinary one hundred per cent in tests and examinations.

In the 1970s he was posted to Abu Dhabi and Cairo, and in 1980 served in the embassy in Athens – Greek was one of his European languages. In 1984 Ken Whitty of the British Council was killed in Athens by terrorists and it was said that Paul had been the intended target. Paul was quickly transferred to an entirely different region – to Hong Kong, where he picked up Chinese.

Between 1988 and 1992 he was in the Cabinet Office in London and was able to provide expert advice on central Asia during the break-up of the Soviet Union. He first retired in 1992 but was recalled the following year to be Britain's first ambassador to Uzbekistan, covering, from 1994, Tajikistan as well. Paul knew all the relevant languages, though modestly claimed he was not terribly fluent in Uzbeki. He opened the embassy in a Tashkent hotel room and had a former Soviet biological weapons expert as his cook.

After a second retirement, he was taken on by the research department in the Foreign and Commonwealth Office, and also developed a career as a scholar and broadcaster. He became a Senior Research Fellow of St Antony's College, Oxford, from 1997, and was the founding director of the Oxford Centre for the Caspian and Central Asia. He wrote numerous articles on the region but his only book, *The Birth of Tajikistan – National Identity and the Origins of the Republic*, is being published posthumously. This tells the story of the Soviet takeover of the region, how Tajikistan was first an autonomous region before acquiring the status of a full Soviet republic in 1929.

Paul was a man of wide interests. He retained a professional interest in archaeology, and was a great coin collector, and was an authority on the coins of the eastern Mediterranean and central Asia. Few were able, as he was, to decipher all the scripts.

In the autumn of 2001, after the launch of the multilateral invasion to topple the Taliban regime following 9/11, Paul was asked by Tony Blair to go at short notice to northern Afghanistan and make contact with members of the invaders' local partners, the Northern Alliance, and persuade them to act on behalf of the people of Afghanistan as a whole, rather than simply in their own (Uzbeki) ethnic interest. Working with the UN representative, he endeavoured to allay suspicions the Northern Alliance had of Afghanistan's majority Pashtun speakers, whom they saw as tainted with the Taliban message. The Alliance had possession of the area by the Bagram air base, near Kabul, and were furious that UK troops were landing without having secured their consent. According to Paul, they were within an ace of firing on their British allies. He managed to defuse the situation.

Acting as the Prime Minister's special envoy did not inhibit Paul from being a signatory to the letter sent by retired ambassadors in April 2004 to Tony Blair expressing deepening concern about British foreign policy over the Arab-Israeli dispute and the intervention in Iraq. One of his last publications was a review in *Asian Affairs* (March 2007) of the memoir of a successor as ambassador to Uzbekistan, Craig Murray. He was sympathetic with Murray's reactions: 'Acquaintance with the excesses of the Uzbek government is enough to make any decent person's blood boil.' He was less sympathetic with Murray's personal behaviour. Paul preferred to be equally outspoken about human rights, but within the framework of the privileged position of diplomat and ambassador.

He is survived by his wife, a son and a daughter.

Faris Glubb

Faris Glubb was a personal friend for over thirty years. He was living in Amman Jordan when I was working there between 1968 and 1970, and in Beirut Lebanon when I was studying Arabic in Lebanon. We must have seen each other at least once a week. I learnt a great deal about the Arab world from him.

In 1973 he took me to have lunch with his father, Glubb Pasha, at Mayfield in Sussex. I had for the previous five years known Faris as Faris, but his father addressed him as Godfrey. Now here was a problem of social etiquette. Would I be implicitly correcting his father by insisting on calling Faris Faris? Or would I be challenging Faris's sense of identity by calling him Godfrey? As usual I fudged the dilemma.

This appeared in *The Guardian* on 17 May 2004.

Faris Glubb, who has died as a result of a road accident in Kuwait at the age of sixty-four, was a journalist, poet, political activist, Muslim and translator. The only blood-child of Sir John Bagot Glubb (Glubb Pasha) and Lady Glubb, he was born in Jerusalem. His father was commander of the Arab Legion, the army recruited from the bedouin in the service of the Amir of Transjordan, Abdullah, later King Abdullah I of Jordan.

His parents were evangelical Christians and he was christened Godfrey after the first sovereign of the 1099 crusader state. Faris, however, did not adopt his parents' faith. He spent his childhood with the bedouin soldiers in Amman, absorbing both Arabic and the Islamic faith. He said he never felt he was anything other than a Muslim and declared his faith as soon as he was, in accordance with Islamic precept, mature enough to do so. Thereafter, outside the family, the name Faris replaced Godfrey.

Sent to England to be educated at Wellington, he was deeply unhappy. He ran away, not to any British relations, but to the office of the Military Attaché at the Jordanian Embassy in London. He went on to the School of Oriental and African Studies to read Arabic and became involved in political activism in the 1960s with the Bertrand Russell Foundation and the Popular Front for the Liberation of Oman and the Arabian Gulf, working with the Omani opposition at the United Nations in New York.

After teaching and broadcasting in Tunisia, he moved, with his wife, Sharon, and young son, Mubarak, in 1967 to Amman, just eleven years after his father had been dismissed by King Hussein. He taught at a school for Palestinian refugees and then worked with the Hashemite Broadcasting Service and became a stringer for CBS News.

As a young Muslim friend of revolutionaries, he was a contrast to his father, the conservative Christian apologist for the British Empire. But there was much in common between father and son. Each lived a life that was faith-driven. Both had humility and an intense sense of justice, especially for Palestinians. Both had a message that had to be communicated to others, the Pasha through his many books and Faris through his journalism.

Faris moved to Beirut and during the 1970s covered the Lebanese civil war, first for CBS, then, as 'Michael O'Sullivan' for the *Daily Mail* and also for Arab news agencies. His Islamic faith, his Arabic and instinctive rapport with Arab politics, his close relations with the Popular Front for the Liberation of Palestine and its representative in Beirut, the writer Ghasan Kanafani, as well as a total fearlessness gave him access and insight denied to most other western journalists. In addition to journalism, he also developed an alternative career as translator of Palestinian stories and poetry. He also wrote his own poetry, both in Arabic and in English.

With the Israeli expulsion of the Palestinian leadership from Lebanon in 1982, Faris also left, moving with his second wife, Salwa, a Palestinian, to Cyprus, from where he covered the Middle East. In 1994 he moved to Kuwait and worked as translator, then senior editor, for Kuna, the Kuwait News Agency.

At the time of his death he had almost completed a PhD at SOAS on relations between Saladin and King Richard the Lionheart, based on documents at the Vatican. He was active in Islamic human rights organisations and was in demand as an eloquent commentator on Islam and the Arab world. He had a firm faith and his earnestness was tempered with an anarchic sense of humour.

He is survived by his mother, his son Mubarak, otherwise Mark, from his first marriage, and by his daughters Sarah and Darina from his second marriage.

Sa'dallah Wannus

Sa'dallah Wannus was another Syrian writer who became a friend. I knew him only in his last years, when he was slowly and distressingly dying of cancer. I had however been a fan for over twenty years before I met him, and had seen his play, *An Evening Party for the Sake of 5 June*, in Damascus in 1971. I wrote his obituary for *The Guardian*. This was published on 19 May 1997. But I wrote this more personal and expansive piece for the first number of *Banipal*. This appeared in February 1998.

Sa'dallah Wannus, one of the Arab world's greatest playwrights, died in Damascus at the age of fifty-six after a long illness on 15 May 1997.

Sa'dallah was born in the village of Husain al-Bahr near Tartus to an Alawite family and was educated in Cairo and Paris. Like others of his generation, raised in the shadow of Gamal Abdul Nasser, the June 1967 war with Israel was a shattering and disorienting blow. Behind much of his work lies the idea of betrayal by corrupt and complacent rulers of the compliant ruled.

He worked in Damascus as a journalist, editor and theatre director, and was writing stories and plays, but mostly plays, from the early sixties. Plays from the 1960s were often based on folk tales but in the work of his middle and later years his dramas were set specifically in time. He was revolutionary both in the structure of his plays, breaking down the barrier between actors and audience, and in his message, always applicable to the contemporary situation.

In 1992 he became ill. Cancer was diagnosed and for the rest of his life, his health declined, and he was battered and weakened by the relentless devastation of the disease. Yet these last years were the most productive of his life. 'I have so much still to say,' he said to his secretary as he went into hospital to die. His personality changed with the illness. No longer somewhat morose and bitter, the fight against cancer made him appreciate life and laughter. He became congenial in a way he had not been before.

During the first half of 1997, there were four different productions of Sa'dallah's work in Syria and Lebanon. At the beginning of the year, Dr Ajaj Salim directed *Yawm min Zamānnā* (A Day in our Times), written in 1993. The play has a contemporary setting. An earnest young teacher, Fārūq, is distressed that girls from his school are frequenting the house of Madame Fadwa, who has the reputation of being the madame of a brothel.

His headmaster, on hearing his complaint, is much more concerned about political slogans that have appeared on the walls of the students' lavatories.

Fārūq takes his complaint to the sheikh of the mosque. The sheikh is giving a long and elaborate speech to a radio reporter about the canonically prescribed procedure for cleaning private parts after going to the lavatory. When Fārūq makes his complaint he explains that he teaches at the school. The sheikh denounces the state schools as centres of secularism that do nothing to prepare pupils for the afterlife. When the name of Madame Fadwa is mentioned, the sheikh becomes animated. 'How dare you calumniate somebody? Do you realise that calumny is a graver offence than thirty acts of adultery?'

It then emerges that Madame Fadwa has contributed to the redecoration of the mosque. 'How can such a virtuous person,' asks the sheikh, 'be guilty of evil acts?' Fārūq is similarly humiliated by the mayor, who adds that Fārūq's own wife is often at the house of Madame Fadwa. Fārūq calls on the Madame herself who tells him the story of her life, before acknowledging that Fārūq's wife, excellent woman, has indeed been at her house. Fārūq goes home. His wife miserably admits what she has done. She did it to earn money so as to purchase things for the house. There is no future for either of them and the play ends with both in a suicide pact.

In January 1997 at the Madina Theatre in Beirut, Nidal al-Ashqar directed a sumptuous production of *Tuqūs al-Ishārāt wa'l-Tahawwulāt* (Ritual for a Metamorphosis) written in 1994. The story takes place in late Ottoman times and revolves around a conspiracy among an urban elite to cover up a scandal. A wronged wife embarks on a voyage of self-discovery and moves into a brothel. Nidal al-Ashqar's set was superb and the production imaginative.

Liberties, however, were taken with the text in deference to Lebanese censors. A character, the mufti, is given a name, Wasim al-Mufti, to avoid, shall we say, calumniating the holder of a senior Muslim office. Wannus's play stresses the theme of upper class arrogance and contempt for the people, but the production brought out the secondary theme of feminine consciousness.

What is of interest in this is that the production of a play has to be far more circumspect in Beirut than in Damascus. Only two lines from the text, lines that required a mocking reading of the Holy Koran, had to be dropped from the production of *Yawm min Zamānnā*. Otherwise the scathing satire on educational, religious and civil authorities passed the eye of the Syrian censors.

Sa'dallah's work is not (yet) well known in Europe or the United State. Two plays have so far been published in French, one in English. But the first English language production of one of his plays took place in Damascus in April 1997, just three weeks before Sa'dallah died. *Al-Fīl ya Malik al-Zamān* (The Elephant,

O Lord of Ages), a short play written in the late sixties, was performed by students of the British Council under the direction of a gifted teacher, Andy Williams. I was the translator and worked with director and cast. Non-Syrians who saw the play were surprised at its outspokenness, a thinly veiled, allegorical attack on the callous brutality of a ruler towards his own subjects.

Finally in June 1997, as a kind of celebration of the fortieth day after Sa'dallah's death, the Higher Institute for Dramatic Arts in Damascus presented *Munamnamāt Tārikhiya* (Historical Miniatures), written in 1993. Naila al-Atrash was the producer. The play tells the story of Tamberlaine's siege of Damascus in 1402. Citizens and the authorities debate whether to confront, to make accommodation or to flee.

The play was a majestic tribute to the memory of the playwright and was put on in the citadel of Damascus, the actual location of some of the play's scenes. One of Syria's best known actors, Jamal Sulaiman, played the part both of the chronicler/chorus and of Ibn Khaldun. The Tunisian historian in Sa'dallah's play is presented as a dispassionate academic, interested in the nature of tyranny and unmoved by the passionate issues of national struggle or survival.

All four productions demonstrated Sa'dallah's variety and creativity, especially of his last years. But these last years also showed up a nobility of character. In 1995 the poet Adonis was expelled from the Syrian Union of Writers for entertaining ideas of dialogue with Israelis. Sa'dallah resigned from the Union, not because he agreed with Adonis, but because he insisted on Adonis's right to express a view.

And in 1996 Sa'dallah made one of his last public appearances and gave a message for World Theatre Day. Wearing a woollen cap to conceal the baldness brought on by the chemotherapy treatment, he stood up and made an eloquent protestation of the importance of freedom of speech, and of the value of the individual and his/her creativity. Sa'dallah was the first Arab writer to be invited to give this annual message, joining a distinguished company that has included Jean Cocteau and Peter Brook. It was a moving occasion to hear this implicit challenge to an authoritarian regime. Many of those present were in tears.

Far from attempting to silence Sa'dallah, the Syrian authorities co-opted him. President Hafez al-Assad paid for the cost of expensive medical bills. His death dominated national television news and when his body left the Shami Hospital hundreds stood around to pay a final tribute as the hearse started its journey to the cemetery back in the village in the hills above Tartus.

Mahmoud Darwish

I never met Mahmoud Darwish, but I was first familiar with his work in the late 1960s, and followed his work and his career ever since. I first wrote this obituary in 1998 when he had a heart attack. It was revised and updated the day he died. It was published in The Guardian of 11 August 2008.

> They fettered his mouth with chains,
> And tied his hands to the rock of the dead.
> They said: You're a murderer.
> They took his food, his clothes and his banners,
> And threw him into the well of the dead.
> They said: You're a thief.
> They threw him out of every port,
> And took away his young beloved.
> And then they said: You're a refugee.

With poems from the 1960s such as this, Mahmoud Darwish, who has died aged sixty seven in a Texas hospital of complications following open-heart surgery, did as much as anyone to forge Palestinian national consciousness, and especially after the Six Day War of June 1967. His poems have been taught in schools throughout the Arab world and set to music; some of his lines have become part of the fabric of modern Arabic culture.

Darwish was born in the village of Birwa, east of Acre. His parents were from middle-ranking peasant families. Both were preoccupied with work on their land and Mahmoud was effectively brought up by his grandfather. When he was six, Israeli armed forces assaulted the village and Mahmoud fled with his family to Lebanon, living first in Jezzin and then in Damour.

When, the following year, the family returned to their occupied homeland, their village had been obliterated: two settlements had been erected on the land, and they settled in Deir al-Asad in Galilee. There were no books in Darwish's own home and his first exposure to poetry was through listening to an itinerant singer on the run from the Israeli army. He was encouraged to write poetry by an elder brother.

Israeli Arabs lived under military rule from 1948 to 1966. They were curbed in their movements and in any political activity. As a child, Darwish grew up aware that as far as those in control were concerned he, his family and his fellow Palestinians were second-class citizens. Yet they were still expected to join in Israeli state celebrations. While at school, he wrote a poem for an anniversary of the foundation of the state. The poem was an outcry from an Arab boy to a Jewish boy. 'I don't remember the poem,' he recalled many years later, 'but I remember the idea of it; you can play in the sun as you please, and have your toys, but I can't. You have a house, and I have none. Why can't we play together?' He recalls being summoned to see the military governor, who threatened him: 'If you go on writing such poetry, I'll stop your father working in the quarry.'

But relations with individual Jews varied. Some he liked, including at least one of his teachers; some he loathed. Relationships with Jewish girls were easier than with girls from the more conservative Arab families.

At his school, contemporaries remember him being very good in Hebrew. Israeli Palestinian culture was cut off from mainstream Arab developments. Arab poets who did impress him were the Iraqis Abd al-Wahhab al-Bayati and Badr Shakir al-Sayyab. Exciting innovators such as the Beirut group that clustered round the magazine *al-Shi'r* and the prosodic and thematic innovations of the Syrian poets Adonis (Ali Ahmad Said Asbar) and Nizar Kabbani did not reach the beleaguered Palestinians directly. Instead, much of Darwish's early reading of the poetry of the world outside Palestine was through the medium of Hebrew. Through Hebrew translations he got to know the work of Federico Garcia Lorca and Pablo Neruda. He also became influenced by Hebrew literature from the Torah to the modern poet Yehuda Amichai.

His first poetry symbolised Palestinian resistance to Israeli rule. His first volumes, *Leaves of the Olive Tree* (1964), *A Lover from Palestine* (1966) and *End of the Night* (1967), were published in Israel. During this time Darwish was a member of the Israeli Communist Party, Rakah, and edited the Arabic edition of the party's newspaper, *al-Ittihad*. Israeli Palestinians were restricted in any expression of nationalist feeling. Darwish went to prison several times and was frequently under house arrest.

His earliest poetry followed classical forms, but, from the mid-1960s, it became populist and direct. He used imagery that he could relate intimately to Palestinian villagers. He wrote of olive groves and orchards, the rocks and plants, basil and thyme. These early poems have a staccato effect, like verbal hand-grenades. In spite of an apparent simplicity, his first poems have several levels of meaning. There is a sense of anger, outrage and injustice, notably in the celebrated 'Identity Card', in the voice of an Arab man giving his identity number:

174

Write down at the top of the first page:
I do not hate people.
I steal from no one.
However
If I am hungry
I will eat the flesh of my usurper.
Beware beware of my hunger
And of my anger.

But his poetry also contained irony and a universal humanity. For Darwish the issue of Palestine became a prism for an internationalist feeling. The land and history of Palestine was a summation of millennia, with influences from Canaanites, Hebrews, Greeks, Romans, Ottoman Turks and British. Throughout all this, a core identity of Palestine has survived. He was able to see the Israeli soldier as a victim of circumstances like himself. He expresses the bureaucratic absurdities of an oppressive military occupation.

Darwish left Israel in 1971, to the disappointment of many Palestinians, and studied at Moscow University. After a brief period in Cairo he went to Beirut and held a number of jobs with the Palestine Research Centre. He remained in Beirut during the first part of the civil war and left with Yasir Arafat and the PLO in 1982. He moved on to Tunis and Paris and became editor-in-chief of the influential literary review, *al-Karmel*. Although he became a member of the PLO executive committee in 1987 and helped to draft the Palestinian Declaration of Statehood, he tried to keep away from factionalism. 'I am a poet with a particular perspective on reality,' he said.

His literary work was changing. He wrote short stories and he developed a style of writing poems that was a mixture of observation, humanity and irony. He argued that poetry was easier to write than prose. But the poetry continued, inspired by incidents or relationships. There is often an optimism against all the odds in his works of the 1980s:

Streets encircle us
As we walk among the bombs.
Are you used to death?
I'm used to life and to endless desire.
Do you know the dead?
I know the ones in love.

During his Paris years, Darwish wrote *Memory for Forgetfulness*, a memoir of Beirut under the saturation bombing of 1982, which has been translated into English. A poem in prose, it is a medley of wit and rage, with reflections on violence and exile. His later work became more mystical and less particularly concerned with Palestine. Often it was preoccupied with human mortality. He was careless of his own health and suffered heart attacks in 1984 and in early 1998.

Darwish resigned from the PLO Executive Committee over the 1993 Oslo Agreements between Israel and the PLO, which he saw as a 'risky accord'. He was able to return to Israel to see his aged mother in 1995. The Israeli authorities also gave him permission for an unlimited stay in the self-ruling parts of the Palestinian West Bank, and he spent his last years in Ramallah and Amman, the capital of Jordan.

In 2000 the Israeli Ministry of Education proposed to introduce his works into the Israeli curriculum, but met strong opposition from rightwing protesters. The then Prime Minister, Ehud Barak, said the country was not ready.

Darwish's work has been translated into Hebrew and, in July 2007, Darwish returned to Israel and gave a reading of his poetry to 2,000 people in Haifa. He deplored the Hamas victory in Gaza the previous month. 'We have triumphed,' he observed with grim irony. 'Gaza has won its independence from the West Bank. One people now has two states, two prisons who don't greet each other. We are dressed in executioners' clothes.'

Over the years, Darwish received many honours. He was given the Soviet Union's Lotus Prize in 1969 and the Lenin Peace Prize in 1983. He was President of the Union of Palestinian Writers. Married and divorced twice, he had no children; his first wife was the Syrian writer, Rana Kabbani, who elegantly translated some of his poetry into English.

Mamdouh Udwan

Mamdouh Udwan was a Syrian friend who died before his time. This obituary appeared in *The Guardian* on 25 January 2005.

Mamdouh Udwan, who has died of cancer aged sixty-three, was one of Syria's best-known writers. He distinguished himself as poet, novelist, dramatist, critic and translator. A rebel and a champion of liberty, he was uneasily respected by the Syrian establishment.

Mamdouh was born in Qayrun, near Masyaf in central Syria. He studied English at the University of Damascus and became one of a group of bright young men and women who came from rural and often Alawite backgrounds and challenged the presumptions of the generation that preceded them. They were the cultural but not uncritical allies of the Ba'athist regimes that have controlled Syria since the 1960s.

Mamdouh started his career as a journalist before working for the Translation Department of the Ministry of Information. He continued to be a contributor to the Arab press for the rest of his life. His first collection of poems, *The Green Shadow* (1967), was the first of twenty-seven small volumes. Three years later, he published his first – of twenty-four – plays, *The Man Who Did Not Fight*. He went on to publish two novels and translated twenty-three works from English, introducing new writers to the Arab reader, such as the Cameroonian Ferdinand Oyono and the Chilean Antonio Skarmeta. In his major novel, *My Enemies*, he writes of Syria in the last days of Ottoman rule, castigating the repression of the Turkish governor, Jamal Pasha.

Mamdouh's work combines humour and tragedy. He was ferocious in his denunciation of corruption and despotism. He broke away from stereotyping Jews. In *My Enemies*, they laugh and weep rather than threaten and fight. In this historical novel there is always a message for the present. His language was simple and direct and he was an enemy of official cant, 'cruel dreams coupled with cruel bread', as he put it in one of his poems. His plays present the dilemmas of contemporary citizens. One play, *The Mask*, has been performed in English, and explores the situation of a thirty-something Damascus career girl living alone.

Friends found his prolific output a mystery, for he was a lover of life, with a gift for friendship and conversation – his contributions accompanied by a wry chuckle. He always had time for other people, and encouraged young talent, especially when it came from those from his own rural background. In 1994, he was a visiting scholar at the Woodrow Wilson International Centre in Washington DC, and in 1997 won the Jordanian Arar Prize for poetry.

He is survived by his wife Ilham and three children.

Sargon Boulus

Sargon Boulus was a pillar of the magazine *Banipal*. He was a charismatic figure, and I met him on one of his visits to London. The obituary appeared in *The Guardian* on 18 January 2008.

In 1967 a penniless twenty-three-year-old Iraqi, with no documentation, applied to the American Embassy in Beirut for a visa to enter the United States. A writer, he claimed an intimate knowledge of American poetry. He was called to meet the Ambassador, who asked him about poetry. He started with Walt Whitman and referred to many contemporary Beat poets, of whom the Ambassador had not heard. But he was impressed. 'Enough!' he said, 'you've got it.' The young man went to New York, and on to San Francisco, which became his home for the next forty years. The young man was Sargon Boulus, who has died in Berlin aged sixty-three, after some months of poor health.

Sargon was born in al-Habbaniyah, on the Euphrates in Iraq, to an Assyrian family. The Assyrians were an ancient but threatened Christian sect, speaking its own Semitic language, and the British had provided them with a safe haven near their military base. His family moved to Kirkuk, where Sargon had his secondary education. He started writing poetry at the age of twelve. His first published poem came a year or two later since when, as he wrote, 'I haven't stopped. It just grabbed me, this magic of words, of music.'

It was an exciting time for Arabic poetry, with a rejection of classical forms that had held sway for a millennium and more. Beirut was the centre of experimental poetry, especially the magazine *Shi'r* (Poetry), edited by Yusuf al-Khal. When he was seventeen, Sargon sent some poems to Yusuf al-Khal that were immediately published. He was encouraged to go to Beirut and made the journey from Baghdad with no identification papers, avoiding public transport and official border posts. He was warmly welcomed by the innovative poets based in Beirut and lived a hand-to-mouth existence, gathering at the Horseshoe Cafe with other writers, and writing for the press. He was picked up by police as an illegal immigrant and jailed. Friends intervened and he applied, successfully, for entry to the United States.

In San Francisco, he became part of the Beat generation. Sargon lived on the edge, running a Middle Eastern restaurant, writing and translating, demonstrating for native American rights and against the Vietnam war. He introduced Arab readers to Allen Ginsberg, Carl Snyder and Lawrence

Ferlinghetti. He became intoxicated by the classical English poets and translated Shakespeare's sonnets, as well as Shelley, Ezra Pound, Ted Hughes and Sylvia Plath. At his death, he left uncompleted a major study and translation of the writings of WH Auden.

He wrote his own poetry, feeling savage about the limitations of Arabic and the upholders of formal classical traditions. He talked about 'linguistic fundamentalists'. Arabic, thought Sargon, 'is always too full of decoration, unnecessary words and fat – linguistic fat. I'm cutting it like a butcher and I'm trying to show the bones behind the flesh and I think that's something worth doing.' He wrote poetry in Assyrian, Arabic and English.

He spent time in Athens and Germany, where Iraqi publisher Khalid al-Maaly helped promote his work. He was also a journalist, and translated romantic novels into Arabic. From 1998 he was a Consultant Editor of *Banipal*, a London-based magazine of Arab literature, and a prolific contributor, translating a range of contemporary Arab poetry into clear and concise English.

Sargon worked hard, played hard and travelled hard. His last years were dogged by ill-health, but he was working and writing to the end. He is survived by his partner of several decades; she shares a name with film star Elke Sommer.

Literature

I was lucky enough at the age of sixteen to fail English Literature at the Ordinary Level of the General certificate of Education. I did not feel lucky at the time, but it did mean that I did not study English in the sixth form or at university. As a result, my approach to literature has been unschooled, indeed unsophisticated. I have always been a voracious reader. My academic training was as a historian and, perhaps in consequence, I have a preference for novels that light up a historical period or disclose social or political ideas.

The experiences of other visitors to the Middle East have intrigued me. I have also sought out novels with a Middle East background, written either by people of the region, or by foreigners. One writer whose work I found totally absorbing – and instructive – was Marmaduke Pickthall. So absorbing was he that I wrote a whole book about him in the 1980s.

Marmaduke Pickthall and Saïd the Fisherman

I first read Marmaduke Pickthall's novel *Saïd the Fisherman* in 1977 and was bowled over by it. I then found in second hand bookshops more of his Middle Eastern novels – *Children of the Nile* and *The Valley of the Kings* – and his fictionalised memoirs of his travels in Syria and Palestine in the 1890s, *Oriental Encounters*. I found out what I could about the man. There was one biography, *Loyal Enemy* by Anne Fremantle, published in 1939. I did not think it adequately conveyed the Middle Eastern and Islamic aspects of this extraordinary man, so I wrote my own book, *Marmaduke Pickthall British Muslim*, published by Quartet Books, London, in 1986 – on the fiftieth anniversary of Pickthall's death. When I look at the book now, I would have eased up the prose. It reflects the style of what I had most been used to writing – a PhD thesis and public service minutes.

Quartet Books also reissued Pickthall's best novel and I wrote an introduction to it: it can stand as an introduction to Pickthall's life and work.

Saïd the Fisherman was published by Methuen, London, in July 1903 and went on sale to the public for six shillings a copy. Its author was a twenty-eight-year-old man who lived at Holton near Halesworth, Suffolk. He had no profession and lived a life of straitened gentility. It was Marmaduke Pickthall's second novel. *All Fools* had been published in 1900, a far-fetched story of some dashing blades and a fair young maid – *Saïd the Fisherman* was quite different in style, theme and purpose. Critics at once recognised it as such.

The *Athenaeum* thought it 'a triumph of the story-teller's art'. The reviewer compared it to James Morier's *Hajji Baba of Isfahan*. 'It belongs to a little exploited school of fiction, and is one of the best of its select school that we have come across,' he wrote. James Barrie sent a letter of congratulation. H G Wells wrote to Pickthall, wishing he could feel as certain of his own work 'as I do of yours, that it will be alive and interesting to people fifty years from now.' *Saïd the Fisherman* went through fourteen British editions in the following quarter of a century, but since then has been remembered only by a handful of discriminating critics.

Saïd the Fisherman was one of nine novels with Near Eastern backgrounds written by Pickthall. E M Forster reckoned in 1923 that Pickthall was 'the only contemporary English novelist who understands the nearer East'. Pickthall is best remembered today as Muhammad Marmaduke Pickthall, translator of the Koran, a translation that is widely known among Anglophone Muslims and that has been reprinted in the 1980s in the United Kingdom, Libya and the

United Arab Emirates. Many who are familiar with the translation do not know that Pickthall was also a novelist.

Marmaduke Pickthall was born in 1875, the son of a Suffolk clergyman with deep roots in traditional English rural society. He had a conventional upper middle class childhood, dominated by a widowed mother and private education. He spent two years at Harrow School where one of his contemporaries was Winston Churchill. He attempted to enter Woolwich Academy, the training establishment for the Royal Engineers, but failed his examination because of weakness in mathematics. More surprisingly, he failed to gain admission to the Levant Consular Service.

At this crisis in his life he chose to travel. A relation was a friend of the chaplain of the Bishop of Jerusalem. Introductions were furnished and in 1894 Pickthall, not yet nineteen years of age, set off to Marseilles, paused awhile in Egypt, crossed over to Jaffa and fell in with a couple of resourceful adventurers, Suleyman and Rashid. For the next two years he wandered around Syria and Palestine, learned Arabic thoroughly, became familiar with the legends, beliefs and attitudes of the unexalted Syrian Muslim Arab and occasionally surfaced to pass time with his fellow countrymen. Pickthall was not at ease on these occasions and preferred to chat in colloquial Arabic with the servants. But one British contact made a strong impression: the Reverend J E Hanauer, a fluent Arabist, who collected Palestinian folktales, legends of the Islamic conquest in the seventh century and tales of magicians and saints.

In 1896 Pickthall nearly entered the Levant Consular Service by the back door by being offered the post of British Vice-Consul of Haifa. The offer was withdrawn on account of his extreme youth. He returned to England, married and settled down in cheap, rented houses as a country gentleman with private means. He was however a compulsive writer. He published short stories in 1898 and 1899 and was simultaneously writing *All Fools* and *Saïd the Fisherman*, perhaps the worst and the best of his novels.

In the years after 1903 Pickthall published a novel a year, either on the Near East or on a British (usually Suffolk) theme. He prepared for publication the material Hanauer had collected, wrote an introduction and provided footnotes. Pickthall's novel, *The Children of the Nile* (1908), written after a visit to Egypt, has as a background the Urabi Pasha revolt of 1882 and traces the fortunes and misfortunes of a mixed-up young soldier from a Delta village. *The Valley of the Kings* (1909) deals with the identity crisis of a Palestinian Christian torn between his Orthodox Arab roots and the allurements of English visitors to the land. *Veiled Women* (1913) is an ambitious attempt to explain the world of Egyptian women and includes a description of the therapeutic ritual of the *zar*.

In 1913 Pickthall spent a few months in Turkey and became a partisan of the Young Turks. He wrote passionate articles in *The New Age* and elsewhere on the Turkish point of view and on the reforms undertaken by the revolutionary Turks. The outbreak of hostilities between Britain and the Ottoman Empire in November 1914 shattered him and he became an active propagandist for a separate peace with Turkey. As such he was seen as a 'rabid Turcophil' and a security risk by the British authorities. A job he might have taken up with the Arab Bureau in Cairo went instead to T E Lawrence.

Pickthall was appalled at the outburst of hatred released by the war, especially the ideological venom directed towards the Ottoman Empire and Islam. He announced his own conversion to Islam in 1917 and at once became a leader of British Muslims. The British Muslim movement included many visiting Indians and a handful of British converts. Pickthall's beautiful rendering of Arabic, his social and literary contacts, his energy and his dedication qualified him to be Acting Imam of the London mosque (then in Notting Hill) and editor of the *Islamic Quarterly*, the British Muslims' journal which combined the characteristics of a parish magazine and a heavy intellectual Victorian review.

After the war, his new Indian contacts offered Pickthall employment in India. He was for four years editor of the nationalist *Bombay Chronicle* and became a close ally for a year or two of Gandhi when the latter was trying to forge links between Muslims and Hindus through the Khilafat movement. For a while Pickthall lived at the Bombay School of Art in the house in which Rudyard Kipling was born. He later became the headmaster of a large school in the State of Hyderabad and entered the service of the Nizam of Hyderabad, at that time one of the richest men in the world and a great patron of Islamic studies. Pickthall edited a quarterly journal, *Islamic Culture*, for ten years and spent several years in touch with scholars all over the world. The climax of his life's work was the publication of *The Meaning of the Glorious Koran* in 1930.

He returned to England in 1935 and died the following year at the age of sixty-one, and is buried at Brookwood Cemetery, Surrey.

Saïd, the central character of the novel, is a fisherman who pursues his livelihood on the Palestinian coast outside Haifa. He is an unscrupulous opportunist who decides to seek his fortune in Damascus. He lies and poses to all whom he meets and arrives in Damascus in the summer of 1860 at a time of growing tension between Christians on the one hand and Muslims and Druze on the other. The tension leads to riots and a massacre of Christians. During these riots Saïd abducts the daughter of a Christian merchant and becomes a prosperous carpet seller. Prosperity leads to overconfidence. He is betrayed and robbed by the Christian girl, now his wife, loses his friends and becomes an outcast, and escapes from Beirut on a boat bound for London. In London, helpless, penniless and friendless, he becomes crazed and is rescued by a Christian missionary who has him taken to Egypt. There he is succoured as a holy madman until 1882 when, intoxicated by the riots against foreigners and Christians, he meets his death, imagining he is upholding the honour of the religion of the Prophet.

Saïd the Fisherman is carefully written. Pickthall develops a style that he maintains throughout the book, a style that is formal and archaic. In doing this he is creating a world that is not at once familiar to his readers. The world of Damascus and Palestine is presented through the eyes of Damascenes and Palestinians. Had he used the customary language of Edwardian English fiction we might have seen Syria either as if we were visiting expatriates or in a totally unengaged way. The technique of a special language is similarly used by Doughty in *Arabia Deserta* and by Thomas Hardy in his Wessex novels. It establishes a distance between the reader and the subject of the novel and demands a little effort. But the archaic formality also, paradoxically, gives the prose a timelessness and durability. Nothing is more transient than a contemporary fashion or style.

Sir Walter Scott used to make the characters in his medieval novels speak the language of his great grandparents. Authenticity would have been incomprehensible. Contemporary English would have been unrealistic. The language of three generations back was not remote enough to be misunderstood, not contemporary enough to fall flat. Pickthall resolves the difficulty by getting his Syrians to use an English that is a direct translation of expressions used in Syrian Arabic: 'My house is thy house.' 'May Allah increase thy wealth.' 'The right is with him.' Such language and such dialogue make the subject matter of the novel take over the reader and sweep him away. As soon as we open 'his cheerful pages', as E M Forster wrote, 'the western world vanishes without a malediction, like night at the opening of day. We sell carpets at Damascus or visit Tantah fair with no sense of strangeness; it seems our natural life, and when our compatriots do stray across the scene they seem quaint and remote.'

Pickthall was enchanted by the Near East. He accepted it all without qualification. He had a very personal theory of fiction. Fiction was, in his view, a most fitting vehicle for presenting truth. Fiction, he wrote in 1918, 'drives home truths of real importance.' Facts could be presented, challenged or modified. But a fictional record of clothes, behaviour, expressions, reading matter and thoughts has a veracity that is impregnable. And his presentation of the world of Syria as he saw it and loved it rings true and resembles old photographs of the period. Pickthall does not remove the disagreeable. That was sentimentality and Pickthall deplored sentimentality. Things are clearly black or white – or even black *and* white. Only a fictional record could depict Damascus as Pickthall does: 'Sweet, languorous odours, wafted from the shop of a vendor of perfumes, a whiff of musk from the shroud of some passing woman, the fragrance of tobacco, a dewy breath of the gardens from a mule's panniers crammed with vegetables – little puffs of sweetness were alternate in Saïd's nostrils with the reek of dirty garments and ever-perspiring humanity, with vile stenches from dark entries, where all that is foulest of death and decay was flung to glut the scavenger dogs that slept, full-gorged, by dozens in every archway and along every wall. Saïd inhaled sweet and foul alike with a relish as part of the city's enchantment.'

And Saïd, the central character of the novel, is also drawn without sentimentality. He is an amoral rogue, a hypocrite, capable of extremes of cruelty and callousness. He abandons his wife, cheats whomever he meets, steals what he can and yet conscientiously observes the obligations of his religion. In spite of ourselves, we sympathise with him. His exuberant vitality is engaging and we are forever wondering what he will be up to next. There is something Falstaffian about his irrepressibility. Saïd seems to lack any moral restraints. He is also without restraints of kin. We know nothing of his mother or father, whether he has brothers or sisters, uncles or aunts. We know that in 1860 he is about twenty-three years of age and married seven years earlier. But in the course of the novel he develops a filial relationship, first with an old beggar, Mustafa, who makes Saïd the heir of his carefully garnered savings, and then with Nur, formerly a whore, now a marriage broker, who helps Saïd by coaxing the abducted Christian girl into accepting Saïd as her husband. Thus Saïd's prosperity is based on help from a couple of outcasts. When, in his pride, he repudiates Nur, she uses her influence to undermine his standing. Nemesis exacts her due.

Saïd also builds up an intimate relationship with Selim, who seeks and accepts the junior role in the partnership. Selim is a good Muslim, 'pious and devout both in practice and at heart. Had he been born to wealth and eminence he would have been revered of all men for a saint.' He acts as Saïd's conscience. Whenever Saïd disregards Selim's advice, which he often does, disaster follows. Yet even this relationship has been sealed by the fruit of iniquity. On his way to Damascus, Saïd burgles the house of a Frankish missionary and steals the dressing-gown. He gives this to Selim – possibly the only act of generosity on Saïd's part in the whole book – and Selim is forever grateful. It is doubly appropriate that Saïd meets his death in the riots against Christians, wearing the dressing-gown that he has now stolen from Selim.

We get a picture of Ottoman Syria from *Saïd the Fisherman*. It is a picture where the government is remote from the concerns of most people. Government means taxes or soldiers who may be quartered on your village. Islamic solidarity resents the influence European Consuls have with the Ottoman government and the consequent elevation of the status of Arab Christian communities. Within Damascus there is a most elaborate hierarchy, a complex of deference and patronage. Human relationships are based on inequality.

E M Forster in 1923 thought that Pickthall was 'a writer of much merit who has not yet come into his own.' But Pickthall's reputation as a novelist has been in eclipse since then. D H Lawrence wrote an essay on *Saïd the Fisherman* in 1928 but otherwise next to nothing has been written on Pickthall as an author. The reasons for the slump in his reputation are instructive. Pickthall was a loner all his life. Hanauer apart, he had no mentor. He had no disciples. After the First World War, his time in India was tantamount to self-exile from Britain. He was unable to salvage his 'unpatriotic' reputation with his right-thinking fellow-countrymen. He was a conservative, a monarchist and a traditionalist and so had nothing in common with the body of left-wing opinion that had opposed the war. The causes he supported soon became lost, unfashionable or dead. After the First World War nobody – not even in Turkey – wished to champion the Young Turks. Pickthall had been hostile to the Arab Revolt and had no sympathy for the Arab states that emerged after the war. He was critical of British imperialism in India but supported it in Egypt. He regretted the passing of the Caliphate, a cause that soon died. He had no sympathy for the massacred Armenians, and in India his enthusiasm for monarchy and the world of the Nizam of Hyderabad seems quixotic and anachronistic today.

But what Pickthall did appreciate was the popular strength of Islamic identity. In *Saïd the Fisherman* he depicts the humble unsung Muslims of Syria. Islamic faith and practice – even with its corruptions which Muslims are the first to condemn – had a greater reality and were far more pervasive than many other western visitors to the Near East cared to observe. Islam commanded more loyalty from more people than did the transient political institutions to which secular western observers could relate. Although *Saïd the Fisherman* was written fifteen or so years before Pickthall embraced Islam, the novel has much in common with the two novels of the Near East the Muslim Pickthall wrote – *Knights of Araby* (1917) and *The Early Hours* (1921). Although Saïd is an engaging hypocrite and a bad Muslim there are virtuous Muslims in the novel – Selim and the Algerian Abdul Cader, for example. But, alas for morality, vice is always more captivating than virtue.

The last ten years have seen a western bewilderment at the factor of Islam in the countries of the Near East. It had been assumed that economic development, a wider spread of education and prosperity would encourage a secular approach to the world. But the people of the Near East have not flatteringly copied the West in this respect. The western world has been let down. A reading of *Saïd the Fisherman* reminds us of the authority of Islam among ordinary people a century ago. Islam affected and affects the most private part of life, the parts not penetrated easily by outsiders. The licence of the novelist permits him to observe, record and describe this private world of Islam, this world that has changed least in the last century. If we wish to reappraise our perception of Islamic life and behaviour, we cannot do better than start with the writings of Marmaduke Pickthall. The time has now arrived when Pickthall can 'come into his own.'

Marmaduke Pickthall and his Yemen Novel

I started writing my book on Pickthall while I was in Yemen between 1980 and 1984. When I was there I gave a talk to the American Institute for Yemeni Studies in Sana'a about the novel Pickthall had written with a medieval Yemeni background. A version was published in the *Journal of English University of Sana'a* in their September 1984 number. This is a slightly revised version of that.

In 1917 Collins of London published *Knights of Araby* by Marmaduke Pickthall. The book was subtitled: 'A Story of the Yaman in the Fifth Islamic Century'. 1917, the year of the Russian Revolution and of the Battle of Passchendaele, was hardly a propitious year in which to transport novel readers to eleventh century Yemen. In his foreword the author explains that his novel is 'an attempt to quicken those dry bones of memory, and reinvest them with some comeliness of flesh and blood. Even if unsuccessful, it may have the merit of calling the attention of the English reader to the fact that Muslims, all those centuries ago, confronted the same problems which we face today.' *Knights of Araby* was one of nine novels Pickthall wrote with a Middle Eastern theme. Most are, in my view, quite unjustly neglected.

Marmaduke Pickthall is best remembered today as the author of *The Meaning of the Glorious Koran*, described as an explanatory translation, first published in 1930 and still in print. Pickthall embraced Islam in 1917. He was at one time Acting Imam of the Muslim congregation in London and was dissatisfied with the versions of the Koran in use. 'It seemed nonsense to the English people who came to my services. So I put it on one side and made my own translation of any passage which I wished to read out in English.' He thought previous translations did not treat the Koran as a sacred book, nor do justice to the Arabic:

Also certain words are left translated so as to give quite a wrong impression of the book. Thus the words 'Islam' and 'Muslim' are left untranslated, thus implying that they had at the time of revelation the technical meaning which they acquired afterwards. I translate those words, as any Arab hearing them understands them, as 'surrender' or 'submission', 'those who surrender' or 'submit' (ie to Allah). For example, the text which has always been translated 'the religion with Allah is Islam' in my translation reads 'religion with Allah consists in the surrender unto Him', which besides being the accurate rendering, is a statement of a universal truth instead of a sectarian assertion.

I have said enough to indicate that Pickthall merits closer examination. His knowledge of Arabic and Islam gave him a standpoint, unusual among British or western novelists, from which to observe the Middle East. In the first thirty years of this century, the period of his productive output, other images of the Arab East prevailed that inhibited the English reading world from appreciating his informed sensitivity.

In addition to the nine Middle Eastern novels, Pickthall also wrote twenty-eight short stories on Arab themes. They have been published in three collections of short stories – the collections include tales of Europe and England. The Middle Eastern stories stand out for their detail, insight and humour. Pickthall's fiction attempted to portray the perspectives of the Turk, the Arab Muslim and the Arab Christian for English readers. With the exception of *Knights of Araby* they all take place in Greater Syria, Egypt or Turkey in the sixty years before the First World War.

In the nineteenth and early twentieth centuries, the European penetration of the Islamic world produced an extensive literature. European networks of communication built up a picture of the Islamic world that was at best (in the works of Edward Lane, Richard Burton and C M Doughty) uncomprehending, at worst hostile. Many wrote reports full of accurate detail. Some explored the world of Islam for deeply personal reasons. Most saw what they wanted to see. If you read the travel literature of the nineteenth century you learn more about the perceiver than the perceived. There was a romantic yearning for the desert where you were 'free'. The concept of the 'true' Bedu was an ideological descendant of the Noble Savage of the Age of Reason. Travellers idealised the true Bedu with their code of honour and hospitality to strangers, even though these same travellers may have been stripped and robbed by these same Bedu and were lucky to escape with their lives.

Pickthall would have none of this. He saw the Bedu as urban Syrians saw them: potential predators. There is no sentimentality in Pickthall's novels. Yet there is great understanding. His central characters are ordinary, unexciting people, usually urban or urbanised. They read translations of European romantic novels, smoke cigarettes and travel on railways. Government and authority are monsters to avoid and to outwit. The inheritance of popular Islamic beliefs is confronted with importations – material, cultural, economic, political, individual – from western Europe. Such is the stuff of Pickthall's fiction. And Pickthall's contemporaries had limited interest in such matters. Hence the neglect of his work. But the vastly changed relationship between Europe and the Islamic world – increased personal contacts, exchange of people, the development of a shared culture in technology, films, music and reading – makes Pickthall's writings extremely relevant today.

In Pickthall's Middle Eastern novels, the central characters are allowed to behave according to the image they have of themselves. The reader after a few pages has to surrender to terms of reference that are not English or European. The environment is described with flawless accuracy. Practices and pretexts are presented with no special pleading. If a westerner is introduced, it is usually after we have accepted the Middle Eastern perspective. The westerner has to be explained in Middle Eastern terms. Westerners have red or pink faces, straw hair, strange hats and peculiar habits of laughing loudly and greeting each other indecorously.

For Pickthall the Arab East was an escape from the rigidities of a class system and from a prescribed code of behaviour. *Oriental Encounters* describes the exuberance of such an escape. A character in one of his English novels, *The Myopes*, published in 1907, sees in the Middle East 'the land where illusions grow not, where man accepts his destiny with praise to God.' But, like Pickthall, he enjoys the privilege of such escapism without abandoning his solid British base. Pickthall only escaped from his class system and the prescriptions of his background. He did not reject them. He was a conservative – indeed a reactionary – in politics, and a firm believer in hierarchy, deference, tradition and authority. In his personal life he was punctilious, formal and correct.

His personal inegalitarianism shows up in his perception of human relations in the Middle East. They are based on inequality. Within small tight-knit communities each person knows his place and his relationship to patron and client. Outside that community a man's place is as he wishes to present it. Status is a matter of assertion and presumption on the one hand, and acceptance of these claims on the other. The central character of one novel has days of prosperity in Damascus:

Many there were who louted to him in the way; he acknowledged their presence by the slightest scooping motion of the hand. But a notable of the city, riding by on a grey horse, heralded by an outrunner with cries of 'Oah', scattered the crowd to right and left. Saïd was foremost of all to bow his head and touch his lips and brow in token of reverence.

Pickthall has a great gift of conveying the colour, noise and bustle of ordinary people. I offer two examples. The first is from the same novel, *Saïd the Fisherman*. Saïd approaches Damascus:

At the foot of the hill, on the utmost fringe of the gardens, he could see a little village of flat-roofed houses. A string of camels was drawing near to it along the base of the steeps. The tinkle of their bells rippled the twilight cheerily. Of a sudden the noise of chanting arose – a wild, delicious song of piercing shrillness. It came from the high platform of the only minaret of the village. Somewhat mellowed by the distance, it reached Saïd's ears as heavenly music. The clangour of bells had ceased of a sudden. The camels had halted. Their drivers, obedient to the muezzin's call, were prostrate in prayer.

The second is from *Knights of Araby*, a description of a camp on the pilgrimage:

They strolled together through the camp where folk were busy packing up their arms and finery preparatory to assuming the rough garb of pilgrimage. Barbers were busy shaving heads each in a circle of expectant customers. Savoury smells of cooking floated on the air, together with the ceaseless chanting of the devotees, the groan of camels, bray of asses, and the shouts of people seeking friends amid the crowd. A lady in a palanquin set down upon the ground kept screaming: 'Ya Muhammad! Ya Huseyn!' after some child or servant who had strayed, forgetful that every mother's son in that assembly was named Muhammad or Huseyn.

As these passages show, Pickthall's language has at times a contrived archaic remoteness. This can be initially off-putting, but he is creating an idiom for a context with which the English reader is not necessarily familiar. In this he is following the example of two older contemporaries, Charles Montagu Doughty and Thomas Hardy. The archaism creates a gulf, linguistic and psychological. The reader must cross the gulf before he can appreciate the context. As with Doughty and Hardy, the shared assumptions of everyday speech are forsaken in order that the reader may the more easily absorb assumptions of a different world. As with Doughty, the reported speech of Pickthall's Arabs is direct translations of the Arabic. Pickthall's spoken Arabic was the Arabic of Palestine and Syria. He was familiar with Egyptian Arabic but not with Yemeni Arabic and on occasions in *Knights of Araby* he makes his Yemenis come out with English translations of Syrian expressions.

Knights of Araby takes place mainly in Zabid in the fifth century AH, the eleventh century AD, the time of Sulayhid dominance. The best known of the Sulayhid family is the lady known as Queen Arwa. Two generations of the Sulayhid family appear in the novel: Ali and his proud wife, Asma bint Shihab, and their easy going son, al-Mukarram Ahmad, and his wife, Arwa, but called by Pickthall and the sources he used, al-Sayyida (the Lady). The Sulayhids came from Manakha but held Sanaʻa as their capital before moving to Jibla. Their authority was upheld in the mountains by shifting alliances with other

193

princelings. From time to time they occupied the Tihama and its principal city, Zabid.

The central historical figures in the novel are, however, members of the Najahid family, originally Abyssinian freedmen, who ruled Zabid in alternation with the Sulayhids. The fortunes of two brothers over a decade are traced: Said and Jayyash. Said, the elder, is called al-Ahwal (the squinter) and is impetuous and ruthless. Jayyash is gentler, more scholarly, a lover of chess and the author of a history of Zabid.

The novel opens with the Najahids in exile on the Red Sea island of Dahlak. But Said and Jayyash recapture the city of Zabid, defeat a Sulayhid army at Mahjam, capturing the Sulayhid queen Asma. After two years, al-Mukarram Ahmad seizes Zabid, releases his mother and massacres many of its citizens. But the city is lost to Said again. Said is lured to an ambush near Jibla and is killed and Zabid falls to the Sulayhids again, but by the end of the novel the city is safe in the hands of the heroic Jayyash. Several authentic historical personages make their appearance. Al-Husain ibn Salama, builder of mosques throughout the Yemen (including one in Sana'a) appears – in a dream – as a worthy saint of the previous century. Among others whom Pickthall conjures to life are Khalf ibn Abu Tahir the Umayyad, Jayyash's minister and poet and state secretary, Husyan al-Kumm and his son Ali, and a pious sheikh, Muhammad ibn al-Ulayya.

Pickthall's source for the events of his novel was a collection of chronicles of medieval Yemeni history, published in London in English and Arabic in 1892. The major chronicle was that of Najm al-Din Umara al-Hakami (1135-73). His chronicle included fragments of Jayyash's own history of Zabid. Umara's chronicle with its picturesque tales was the material for analysis by Ibn Khaldun. This analysis also appears in the 1892 volume that was edited and translated by Henry Cassels Kay.

Pickthall used the dry bones of the chronicle and turned them into a living yarn. Pickthall was an accomplished Arabist and it is clear that he worked on the Arabic rather than on Kay's translation. For example, before al-Mukarram Ahmad takes Zabid on the first occasion in the novel, he addresses his troops and quotes a line of the poet, al-Mutanabbi. Kay translates this as:

Grasping my death-dealing sword, I will go down among my foes
A field whence only they return who deal effective blows

Pickthall makes no attempt to put this into verse. His rendering is both simpler and more accurate:

> I go down, with my sword in hand, to waters
> Whence none return save by force of arms.

To illustrate the novelist's technique I will quote one passage from the novel and then the passage from the chronicle of Umara that Pickthall used. I could choose twenty or thirty similar examples. Al-Mukarram Ahmad has now taken Zabid in AH 475 (c 1078 AD):

A knight in armour rode full tilt across the palace square and at the street-end reined his horse and looked about him; then he proceeded slowly to the mansion of the severed heads. Two other horsemen followed at full gallop, overtaking him as he drew up beneath the lattice from which the Lady Asma leaned intent.

He cried: 'May God perpetuate your honour, sovereign lady!'

His two companions proffered the same greeting each in turn.

She replied in each case: 'Welcome, noble Arab!' She then inquired of the first rider: 'What is thy name?'

'My name', he said, 'is Ahmad son of Ali son of Muhammad.'

'Among the Arabs there are many Ahmads sons of Ali. Have the goodness to disclose thy face to me.'

The knight pushed up his visor.

She exclaimed with pride: 'Welcome to thee, O our sovereign lord Mukarram! Who are thy companions?'

'This, upon my right, is Al Karam the Yamite, and this, upon my left, is Aamir Ez-Zawahi.'

'Upon Al Karam I bestow the revenues from Aden for the present year; to Aamir I assign the fortresses of Kaukaban and Jauban, with jurisdiction over all their territories. The grants are near of equal value, as I think.'

Now that little bit of drama is from Umara which Kay has translated thus:

The first warrior to reach the spot where the two heads were set up, and to stand below the casement of Asma, daughter of Shihab, was her son, al-Mukarram Ahmad. He said unto her, and she did not recognize him, 'May God safeguard and perpetuate thy renown, O our lady.'

'Welcome,' she replied, 'O noble Arab!'

Al-Mukarram's two companions saluted her in the same words as his.

She asked him who he was, to which he answered his name was Ahmad, son of 'Aly son of Muhammad.

'Verily the name Ahmad son of 'Aly,' she answered, 'is borne by many Arabs. Uncover thy face that I may know thee.'

He raised his helmet, whereupon she exclaimed, 'Welcome, our Lord al-Mukarram!'

At that moment he was struck by the wind, a shudder passed over him, and his face was contracted by a spasm. He lived many years thereafter, but continued subject to involuntary movements of the head and spasms in his face.

She then asked who were his two companions, and he named them. Upon one she conferred a grant of Kaukaban and Hauban (?), together with their territories, the assessments upon which are not inferior to the revenues of Aden.

The differences between the Umara text and the Pickthall novel are revealing. Pickthall does not disclose the identity of the soldier who first greets the captive queen. We learn with Asma. Pickthall has no authority for naming the two companions who, we learn from an earlier paragraph of Umara, were with al-Mukarram Ahmad in this campaign. But naming them gives a smack of authenticity. The twitches and spasms al-Mukarram has are given a novelistic twist by Pickthall. Al-Mukarram Ahmad had waited for nearly two years before getting round to rescuing his mother. He was shaken out of his lethargy by a letter Asma smuggled to him (in a loaf of bread) saying that she was pregnant by Said the Squinter. 'Come and rescue me,' she begged. The letter with its contents was a deceptive ruse. In *Knights of Araby* al-Mukarram's spasms occur only after he learns how his mother has deceived him. He is mortified, massacres half the population of Zabid in abstracted fury and hardly ever speaks to his mother again.

It must not be thought that rival royal households are the exclusive stuff of Pickthall's novel. There is in Zabid a gallery of personalities – some based on historic people, others completely invented. We have the pedantic but honourable historian, Abdul Halim. We have the jester, Abu Dad, who becomes, accidentally and reluctantly, a favoured courtier of both households. He longs to retire to a remote village and give up having to make jokes. There is the sinister Shaykh Salama, a dealer in girls and poisons, based on a person Umara talks about in the following century. We have the holy men, the learned men, the showmen, the marriage-makers, the cameleers.

Pickthall never visited Yemen but he had obviously read the available travel books. There is at least one echo of Ibn Battutah. One of Pickthall's closest friends, Aubrey Herbert, went to Yemen in 1905. Pickthall was also well-versed in Yemeni history as his word-picture of Zabid indicates:

The city of Zabid in those days was a seat of learning, to which students came from all parts of Arabia and East Africa. History, geography, astrology, literature, medicine, besides, and in conjunction with, religious law, were deeply studied in its mosques and colleges by men whose names were known throughout the Muslim world.

The doctors of Zabid were Sunnite to a man; indeed the city was a tower of orthodoxy; yet the heretics consulted them on points of doctrine, and sent their children to be educated in their schools. And now that the Shi'a had obtained political supremacy, and a Shi'ite governor was in the royal palace, they half-scornfully and half-indulgently admitted men of loose opinions to preach on Friday in the greater mosques, since it was decreed that in the introduction to the sermon prayerful mention should be made of one whom they accounted an imposter. Thus, without the least guilt of apostacy, they were able to conform to the existing order, and receive the gifts of the heretical Ali es-Suleyhi, as they had received those of Najah the orthodox. The poets, when they wished to earn a trifle, wrote in praise of the Suleyhi or his governor, and one of them remarked in public, with a shrug and a smile, that it was a blessing they were men possessed of some good qualities, since they must be eulogized.

The fact was that the Learned of Zabid – a term including half the population, for education in the public schools was free to all – considered all the children of ambition and their works as utterly unworthy the attention of a serious person.

'What are they in the sight of Allah?' said a great professor, when a student asked him wherefore, in his history of a certain country, he made no mention of its kings and famous warriors. 'They come and go. It is of infinitely more importance to record the sayings of the learned, the achievements of the poets and the men of letters, the example of the pious and the growth of mosques and schools, which long endure.'

This reflected the attitude of Pickthall when he was writing this novel. For it was the first novel he wrote after he had embraced Islam and during a war which he abominated and which alienated him from most of his countrymen. Pickthall both in his personal life and in the novel stressed the quietistic aspects of Islam, the scholarly withdrawal from temporal and transitory concerns. This point of view echoed the remarks of one of the characters of *Veiled Women*, published in 1913. In this novel the character contrasts European and Muslim attitudes: 'They spread life's agitation over a vast surface and account it progress; we value depth and stillness.'

War is deplored as the selfish activity of rulers, chiefs, great ones. As one sheikh of Zabid puts it:

Ye know the saying of the Prophet (may God bless and save him): 'Vengeance for blood is forbidden from henceforward, and the feud of blood practised in the days of the ignorance is abolished.' All men know that vengeance for blood is unlawful, yet look at all the country of the Arabs. The chiefs both great and small are all at feud. It is among the learned and common people that the precepts of our faith have taken root and flourished. I say, those great ones, self-exalted, and their doings, are of small importance. They are lauded only by their slaves and their paid flatterers. The people as a whole endure them, while the learned hold them in contempt.

At another council of the Zabid ulama, Shaikh Muhammad ibn Ulayya makes the same point:

The more that are indifferent to change of rulers, so only that each ruler be a Muslim, the better for Islam and the world at large; since fanatical attachment to one chieftain or one spot of ground, and hatred of another, is the cause of half the evils which afflict mankind. The quiet folk are brothers in all lands. What part have they in the contentions of the proud?

Pickthall's novel, based on Umara, is about the doings of great ones. But the great ones cause all the trouble. However Pickthall's hero is a quiet, great one, the scholarly Jayyash. (Pickthall transliterates the name as 'Jeyyash') When Jayyash, as king, has taken Zabid finally and definitively, he tells his commanders:

'My command is that of the Prophet, as he entered Mecca. Let there be no bloodshed!' said Jeyyash to Khalf and other leaders ere the work began. The order was at once communicated to the soldiers, who all received it with immense enthusiasm.

'No bloodshed! A white victory! Jeyyash! Jeyyash!' they shouted in a cadence as they marched along; and, at the cry 'Jeyyash,' the quiet folk poured out of all the houses, till the streets were full – men, women, children, howling praise to Allah and blessings on Jeyyash, the righteous king.

In such passages we are at the core of the novel. Here we have a novelist who is very much in a British tradition of novel writing, an art form in which the British (with the French and the Russians) have done very well. Pickthall's Middle Eastern novels in general and *Knights of Araby* in particular have the circumstantiality of Sir Walter Scott, the exuberance of Charles Dickens, the moral strength of George Eliot, the compassionate tragedy of Thomas Hardy and the universality of E M Forster. I am not suggesting that Pickthall is as great as any of these but that his writings are recognisably influenced by the literary heritage to which these others have contributed. But what makes *Knights of Araby* unique is that we have an accomplished practitioner novelist writing a Muslim novel. As in none of his other novels, all the characters in *Knights of Araby* are Muslims. Their terms of reference are exclusively Islamic. There is no problem of adjustment to the values and patterns of life of others. This is in contrast to his other Middle Eastern novels which directly or (more often) indirectly touch on the challenges caused by the cultural, economic and political penetration by western Europe of the Middle East in the nineteenth and early twentieth centuries.

As in his translation of the Koran Pickthall is expounding the ideals of Islam to an English reading world. He is not overtly evangelical. Pickthall was however aware of unfavourable western interpretations of Islamic practices and attitudes, for example, to the role of women. He had written a novel on the subject and on three separate occasions in *Knights of Araby* he goes out of his way to explain. This is one example:

Outside the polity of El Islam women were despised and badly treated. In the hands of the slave dealers, also, they were liable to blows and insults. Once incorporated in the Muslim world by purchase, women had rights secured to them by law, and were respected.

And before the battle in which Said is killed, Said comforts his wife:

O beloved, art thou not a Muslimah, and truly pious, so my brother tells me? Say, does Allah make distinction between men and women. Is not each quite independent in His sight? – I mean, as regards the next world and the way which leads to it? Surely His mercy will be on thee, when I die, and thou wilt not despair like a weak, faithless soul. I do not speak of such things well or readily. Jeyyash, my brother, is a better preacher. But I know that this world passes. Then will come the day of meeting with the Lord, the day of reckoning, when thou and I shall stand or fall by our own doings, separately. And then, if God so wills it, I will ask for thee in paradise.

Pickthall said of himself, 'I call myself a Sunni Muslim of the Hanafi school.' He accepted totally the authority of tradition and saw Islam within this tradition, as peaceful, tolerant and progressive. He came to be regarded as an outstanding Islamic scholar in his lifetime.

I will conclude this paper with the final words of *Knights of Araby*. The pacific warrior and the passionate scholar King Jayyash goes on the pilgrimage. Pickthall himself never performed the obligation of the pilgrimage. He was planning to do so in 1931 with the son of the Nizam of Hyderabad but the plan was abandoned, because of an epidemic in the Hijaz arising from the outbreak of plague in the Yemen. There is thus a tragic irony in the serene and intense words describing Jayyash's first sight of Mecca:

Lines from the ancient Arab poets thronged his memory like voices half awake before the dawn – the dawn of El Islam, of truth and light. The day was breaking. Far away across a land whose dust was hallowed by the persecuted footsteps of God's messenger, he saw the cruel, the beloved city in a glow. It was the blessing, and had been the curse, of El Islam – this city which contained no relic save its ancient memories of cruel persecution and idolatry; no beauty to seduce man's thoughts from God. And, as he pondered on the glory of the Unity, and how the folk of old obscured its light with vain imaginings, he praised the wisdom which had made men pilgrims to an empty house.

Pickthall's Busy Year 1931-32

In 1998 I was approached by a young Turkish-Indian with a remarkable photograph. The young man was Husain, a grandson of Princess Durrushehvar, daughter of the last Ottoman Caliph, Abdulmecit. I wrote an article on the background of the photograph which appeared in *Islamic Culture*, the journal of which Marmaduke Pickthall had been founding editor and which was still being issued from Hyderabad in October 1999. I never had the opportunity of meeting Husain's grandmother who lived on in London until 2006.

Marmaduke Pickthall's translation of the Koran was published by Alfred Knopf of New York on 2 December 1931. It was the greatest achievement in the life of the novelist, polemicist and convert to Islam, who had begun his acquaintance with the Islamic world in Ottoman Syria in the early 1890s, and ended it in Hyderabad (Deccan) in the 1920s and 1930s. If there were two strands in the life of Marmaduke Pickthall, they were his love of Turkey and the Islamic world, and his devotion to a life of letters. He had spent two years full-time working on his translation under the patronage of the Nizam of Hyderabad, Mir Osman Ali Khan. In the spring of 1931, he learned that it had been the subject of debate and some criticism in Egypt. The Rector of al-Azhar, Shaikh Muhammad Ahmad al-Ghamrawi – who knew no English – had questioned its validity, arguing that the translation should be translated back into Arabic and submitted to the judgment of the professors of al-Azhar. Pickthall thought this was absurd. Ideally he wanted his translation to appear with English on one page and the Arabic text opposite. This was finally achieved when the Government of Hyderabad Press published such an edition in 1938, unfortunately two years after Pickthall's death.

During 1931, Pickthall was Director of the Information Bureau in the Hyderabad Government. He was also the founding editor of *Islamic Culture*, and wrote prolifically for each number. He wrote an article about the events in Egypt, which was published in the July issue of that year. In the winter that followed the last rains of 1931, he was a member of the wedding party accompanying the Nizam's two sons, Azam Jah, the Prince of Berar, and a younger son, Muazzam Jah, to Nice where they were to marry respectively Durrushehvar Sultan, daughter of Abdulmecit, the last Ottoman Caliph, and Nilufer Hanim Sultan, daughter of Adile Sultan. The wedding ceremony took place on 12 November 1931, and after the wedding, the Prince and new Princess of Berar spent a week or so in Nice, with Marmaduke Pickthall and his wife, Muriel, in discreet attendance, where they called on the film studios of Rex Ingram, the Irish film director.

Ingram was one of the masters of the silent cinema who had directed Rudolf Valentino in his first great film, *The Four Horsemen of the Apocalypse*, in 1921, and Ramon Navarro, the Mexican heartthrob, in *Scaramouche*, in 1923. Ingram moved from Hollywood to Nice in the mid-1920s with his actress wife, Alice Terry, who had played opposite both Valentino and Navarro. It was the custom for distinguished visitors to the south of France to call on the studios. The Duke of Connaught, George Bernard Shaw, John Galsworthy and Charlie Chaplin all visited the Ingram Studios. Ingram's name was originally Reginald Ingram Montgomery Hitchcock, but he changed his name from Hitchcock for professional purposes. 'You'll never get anywhere with a name like that!' he advised a younger film director called Alfred Hitchcock.

There was a particular interest in the young royal couple and the Pickthalls calling on Rex Ingram. Ingram was very interested in the Islamic and Arab world and Morocco in particular, and went out of his way to employ actors from Syria and Tunisia. Indeed, like Pickthall, he had embraced Islam, having made his declaration of faith in the presence of Caliph Abdulmecit, the bride's father.

Pickthall and the newlyweds were hoping to journey back to India by way of the Hijaz. But a plague in the Yemen made them change their minds and they returned directly to India on the liner, Pilsna. One of the other passengers was Mahatma Gandhi, returning home after the second Round Table Conference in London. Pickthall had known Gandhi briefly in Bombay in the early 1920s, when they had worked together in the Khilafat movement that aimed to restore the Caliphate. Gandhi was interested in meeting the daughter of the last Caliph, and so Pickthall arranged a meeting in the Second Class – since the Princess was travelling in First Class, and Gandhi was in Steerage, this seemed the most appropriate compromise.

By 1931-32 Pickthall had achieved the completion of perhaps his life's greatest work, and had re-acquainted himself with the world he probably felt he had left behind with the coming of the First World War. The article he wrote for *Islamic Culture*, 'Arabs and non-Arabs and the Question of Translating the Qur'an', and the photograph of Pickthall, the Prince and Princess, and the Irish Muslim film director, bring together the intermingling strands that made up Pickthall's life.

In July 1932 Pickthall was asked to present himself to the Nizam to discuss the Egyptian criticisms about which Pickthall had written in his article for *Islamic Culture*. Pickthall's position was clear, and there was no question of the withdrawal of any support from the Nizam. Pickthall stayed on in Hyderabad until January 1935, when he returned through Europe to Britain, only to die in Cornwall at the age of sixty-one in May 1936.

Marginal Literatures of the Middle East

I gathered together a lot of my thoughts about the multiculturalism of the Middle East in a paper I gave at a conference at the University of Edinburgh in July 2000 on Literature and Nation in the Middle East. The article was published – with the carapace of academic footnotes – in *Literature and Nation in the Middle East*, edited by Yasir Suleiman and Ibrahim Muhawi and published by Edinburgh University Press, 2006.

In the last hundred years the Arab world has been given a unity that has been more ideological than real. Most Arabs both within the Arab world and beyond acknowledge to some extent some idea of cultural unity. The idea is reinforced by the existence of the Arab League and other regional organisations and has, by and large, been accepted by all Arab governments. Other Arab countries are *shaqīq* 'brother' rather than *sadīq* 'friend'. Modern Standard Arabic, Arab Clubs among students in British, mainland European and American universities, tapes of Umm Kulthum, the novels of Naguib Mahfouz, the poetry of Nizar Kabbani and the issue of Palestine all contribute towards this cultural unity. Arab newspapers treat news of other Arab countries as of greater relevance than news of Europe, the Far East or the United States.

It is easy to see this successful idea, with its emphasis on the territory of the Arab world, as somehow deep-rooted and everlasting. The Arabic language, as the language of Islamic revelation, suggests an unchanging nature of *'urūba*, Arabness. Its status is within the realm of sacred geography, and cannot be subject to academic examination or scientific analysis like secular languages. Study of the colloquial Arabic is seen as divisive. Even the study of local history can open old wounds and conflicts to the detriment of Arab unity.

Yet this victorious ideology is, we must remind ourselves, very new. If we look at the Arab world a century ago, we can discern three different cultural worlds that transcended the convergence of territory and language. Each had its distinctive characteristics. Each overlapped with others. I refer to the Ottoman world, the Mediterranean world and the world of the Indian Ocean.

The Ottoman Empire was probably the most successful Islamic political institution in history. It occupied major areas of the Arab world for up to four centuries. Greater Syria, Egypt, and North Africa up to but excluding Morocco were all deeply affected by the nominal political unity of the Ottoman world. Islamic legitimacy was reinforced by political suzerainty of the Holy Places of the Hijaz. One of the titles of the Ottoman Sultan, Servant of the Two Sacred

Places, is now adopted by the Kings of Saudi Arabia. Elites in the Ottoman Empire, political, religious and educated, were mobile. The colloquial Arabic of each country has Turkish words – *belki* 'perhaps' in Damascus, *kūbrī* 'bridge' in Egypt, *hastahāne* 'hospital' in Iraq, *yalek* 'waistcoat' in Yemen or *mekteb* 'school' in Tunis. In the first generation of Arab independence an education at the Istanbul Law School or service in the Ottoman army provided a unity of common experience for many Arab politicians. The first Hashemite rulers of Iraq and Transjordan had grown to adulthood in Istanbul. Their families were linked by marriage to the Ottoman aristocracy. I remember in 1970 when President Suney of Turkey, an elderly soldier, made a state visit to Jordan. One evening was spent with aging Palestinians and Jordanians, including senior members of the ruling family. All had memories of the First World War and, I was told, the evening ended with the singing of old Ottoman army songs.

Contemporary Arabs are often ambivalent in their attitudes towards Turkey and the Turks. In the University of Damascus the Turkish language is taught only in the Department of History. There is a political repudiation of the Ottoman Empire from whose occupation Arab countries liberated themselves. On the other hand Turkish architecture and interior decoration is admired, and it is rather chic to have a Turkish grandmother. There is still a branch of the Syrian Azm family in Istanbul.

The Mediterranean world overlapped with the Ottoman. But the major ports of the Mediterranean, from Barcelona to Haifa, all had features in common. They all had international communities and a perspective that looked away from the territory. Until the nineteenth century transport was always easier and cheaper by sea than over land. For two millennia Alexandria had large Jewish and Greek populations. Istanbul had Jews, Greeks, Italians and Armenians. Beirut and Haifa had strong European and American communities. Salonica had its Jewish and Dönme community. Palermo has a church still with an old Byzantine rite. Pisa, Venice, Naples, Marseilles and Barcelona have flourished as a result of trade with the Ottoman and Arab worlds. Tunis had a quarter known as La Petite Sicilie. The cosmopolitanism of the ports contrasted with the nationalism of the inner cities – Cairo, Ankara, Damascus. The idea of *omerta* in Southern Italy is identical with ideas of family honour in many Arab societies.

The Ottoman and Mediterranean worlds also overlapped linguistically. A number of commercial words, such as *sigorta* 'insurance', entered Turkish and colloquial Arabic. There were even hybrid words, such as the Syrian colloquial *gommaji* 'puncture repairer' that uses the Italian for rubber with the Turkish agent suffix.

The Indian Ocean also had an economic and cultural homogeneity. There was a generic similarity in its ports on the north west shores from Karachi to Mombassa via Kuwait and Aden. Arabia, the Gulf and to some extent Iraq were part of this cultural world. Until 1970 the countries operated with one unit of currency – the Indian rupee. Those who were educated into the modern world received their education in India. Bahrain and Bombay were the great commercial transit centres for the pearl trade. The British government of India had a foreign policy that was almost separate from that of imperial government in London. The Colony of Aden was run from India. British consuls and agents in Arabia, Iraq and Iran were appointed from the Indian military and civilian services. Just as Maltese could be found in every Mediterranean port, so Somalis were ubiquitous on the northern and western shores of the Indian Ocean.

The ideologies of Arab nationalism have denied these rich heritages. The twentieth century has seen the triumph of the territorial nationalism of the cities of the interior. The kaleidoscopic mix of communities that were in all the cities and ports has yielded to a more monochrome uniformity. The Ottoman Empire was a multi-ethnic polity. The successor states have worked towards a unified culture. Those who have had a country to return to – Greeks, Maltese, Italians – have gone home. Those Armenians who survived early twentieth century Anatolia have contributed to forming the largest non-Arab communities in cities like Beirut and Aleppo. Others have moved to Armenia that for seventy years was under Moscow's influence. Ottoman Kurds and Jews have had contrasting fortunes. So many Jews of the former Empire have moved to Palestine, at the expense of the indigenous Palestinians, that it could be argued that the State of Israel is a succession state of the Ottoman Empire. From outside the Arab world, people of South Asia – Indians, Pakistanis, Bangladeshis and Sri Lankans – have however increased in numbers in Arabia and the Gulf, albeit on sufferance.

Most countries of the area achieved independence only in the twentieth century. A major target of the elites of each country was to establish their own legitimacy. This legitimacy has been based on a mono-ethnic identity. Other foci of loyalty – national or linguistic – have been discouraged. The national ideologies of Israel and Turkey have been similar. Even the more internationalist ideology of the constitution of the Islamic Republic of Iran enshrines Iranian nationality as a condition for full citizenship. In all these countries illiteracy has been effectively eliminated with an emphasis on a *national* language. Marginal languages – Armenian, the Circassian languages, Nubian, Coptic, Berber, the languages of Southern Arabia or Southern Sudan – are not taught in government schools, though English and French are. An official mainstream culture has been promoted through schools, universities and the official media, and backed by the resources of the state, through censorship and ultimately force.

There is nothing exceptional in the Middle East about this. Countries have been following the practices of most European countries in identifying a national identity with territory and language. In nineteenth century Italy and France only a small minority spoke standard Italian or French. In the Arab world perhaps an even smaller minority speak the prescribed taught formal Arabic.

The teaching of literature in schools and universities has been similarly nationalistic. Most literature is taught according to the language in which it is written – English, French, Spanish, Arabic, Turkish, Hebrew etc. The student and common reader have usually to discover world literature, usually in translation, on his or her own. But when we look at writers who have an impact and an influence, we find they often defy the concurrence of language and territory. Arabs of North Africa have long expressed themselves in French. The French educational and cultural influence from the 1930s onwards in Tunisia, Algeria and Morocco was overwhelming.

A nationalist writer, such as Kateb Yacine, thought the French 'wanted to destroy our nationalism … Thus, whoever wanted an education had to attend French schools, so much so that intellectuals cannot express themselves in French.' Algerian literature, written in French, argued Yacine, was 'independent of the language it uses, and has no emotional or racial relationship.'

Yacine wrote initially in French in order to address the French directly, showing them what was wrong with the colonial system, rather than telling his people about a situation they knew in a language they did not read. Some North Africans who wrote in French, such as the Moroccans Tahar bin Jelloun and Driss Chraieb, have won French literary prizes. The Egyptian Albert Cossery has written from the 1930s to the 1990s in French. Others, such as the Algerian Rachid Boujedra, switched to Arabic in the 1980s and 1990s. Kateb Yacine's later work was in the Algerian Arabic and Berber dialects. But is their work only Arabic if it is written in Arabic? Is their French work part of Arabic or French literature? In the last ten years we have witnessed a growing literature of Arab consciousness expressed in English. The Sudanese Jamal Mahjoub, the Jordanian Fadia Faqir and, above all, the Egyptian Ahdaf Soueif have all received critical acclaim for their English novels.

We must get this in proportion. The British are today insular and are singularly fortunate in having English as a global language. But most people in the world have a choice of languages in which to express themselves. Seventy per cent of the world's population operate in two languages, forty per cent in three. Early in the twentieth century, the Pole Joseph Conrad and the Russian Vladimir Nabokov mastered the English language to the extent that their works have entered the canon of English literature. In earlier centuries even the British had a choice of languages in which to express themselves. In the eighteenth century the first published work of that master of English prose, Edward Gibbon, was in French. In the seventeenth century, John Milton wrote poetry in Latin. In the centuries before that writers from Britain were part of a Latin writing European civilisation.

Again throughout the twentieth century there have been Arabs writing in English. There is a library of academic writing by Arabs in English. Eighty years ago, Khalil Gibran Khalil and Amin al-Rihani adopted an American English to express their Arab consciousness. In the 1940s, another Lebanese, Edward Atiyah, wrote novels about Lebanon and Sudan in English. The Palestinian Jabra Ibrahim Jabra wrote novels equally in Arabic and English. The Egyptian Waguih Ghali's *Beer in the Snooker Room*, published in the 1950s, has recently been reprinted. These writers have all come from the older Ottoman and Mediterranean cultural worlds, but use of a European language was not restricted to these. The Bahraini poet, Ibrahim al-Urayyid, was born in Bombay in 1908. His father was a Bahraini pearl-merchant, his mother from Iraq. His first education was in Urdu and English and he went to Bahrain for the first time in his teens. But he became a distinguished poet in Arabic, arguably his third language. He represents too an Indian Ocean culture, having written poetry also in English and Urdu, and having translated *Umar Khayyam*.

The number of Arab writers of quality who are writing in English today has become a critical mass. This is a distinctive phenomenon requiring an explanation. The phenomenon reflects aspects of the contemporary culture of the Arab world. Individuals have not complied with the orthodoxies prescribed by different Arab regimes. The monopoly of truth assumed by Ministries of

Information and Education, and backed by Ministries of the Interior and security systems is challenged by the availability of alternative sources of information, from satellite television to the internet. Millions of Arabs have in the last thirty years migrated as never before, either within the Arab world to oil richer states or to Britain, mainland Europe or the Americas. Tens of thousands have gone outside the Arab world – to east and west Europe and North America – for higher education. Students return. Families reunite. Experiences are exchanged. The authority of the propaganda from the home country crumbles, if it does not collapse. This weakening of the authority of the domestic education and information apparatus has coincided with the emergence of English as a global language. English has become the commercial language of Arabia and the Gulf. Commercial contracts between Japanese and Arabs are drafted in English. It is the language of numerous international professions. It is the language of the major international news agencies. Most Arab countries have English television channels and English language daily newspapers. *Al-Ahram* has an English edition. It is not surprising, therefore, that English has become a language of creative expression for many Arabs. Some Arabs find a formality in modern standard Arabic that inhibits freedom and also style of expression. A Syrian journalist and academic who writes with equal fluency and distinction in Arabic and English has said that she has a sense of humour when she writes in English, but not when she writes in Arabic.

This emerging critical mass of Arab writers writing on Arab themes in English has some similarity to those North Africans who have written in French. Although most are subject to anglophone cultural influences by living outside the Arab world, they do not have to write in English. The Syrian Zakaria Tamir, the Sudanese al-Tayyib Salih, the Jordanian Amjad Nasir and the Lebanese Hanan al-Shaykh have long lived in Britain but continue to write in Arabic. With four daily newspapers that circulate widely throughout the Arab world London has become a centre of Arab journalism. But we are seeing an Arab literature in English that is parallel to Indian or Caribbean literature in English. Jabra Ibrahim Jabra probably spoke for them all when he wrote, in an essay entitled 'Why Write in English?'

> … my work could only be, in the final analysis, Arabic in the profoundest sense. Cultures have always interacted, but never to the detriment of a nation conscious of its own vital sources, of the complexity of its own identity.

The contemporary writers I have mentioned have all been writers of fiction, and their work has first been published in Britain. There have been no first rank English medium poets in Britain from the Arab world. This is in contrast to the United States that has produced an Arab consciousness expressed through poetry. I may mention here the Libyan Khalid Mutawwa', the Iraqi Sargon Boulus and the Palestinians Naomi Shihab Nye, and Suheir Hammad whose Palestinian consciousness has been grafted on to a tradition of American black poetry.

I have so far been talking of Arab writing in French and English. But a century ago Middle Eastern cities were multilingual. Members of the British Levant Consular Service were expected to be familiar with Latin, French, Greek, Turkish, Arabic and Persian. Italian, German and Spanish were optional. Today most British diplomats serving in the Middle East do not even have Arabic.

I have mentioned how Alexandria had a huge Greek population. There was an Alexandrian Greek literature. The work of Constantine Cavafy is well known. His life and work are intimately connected with the city. Greeks were in most cities and towns of Egypt and the Sudan in the early years of the twentieth century. I would like to pause and consider the interesting case of Stratis Tsirkas. Born Iannis Hadjiandreas in Cairo in 1911, the son of a second generation Greek barber, he worked in industry in Upper Egypt, and started publishing poetry in the 1930s, and was active in the Egyptian Communist Party until the 1960s. He was no part of the Greek plutocracy and his feelings for Egypt could have been expressed by any Egyptian nationalist:

> And I sing of Egypt
> because she shelters and nourishes me like a mother,
> because she hurts, like a mother
> and because she hopes, like a mother.

His novella, *Nourredin Bomba*, was published in 1957. It is about the Egyptian revolt against the British in 1918 and was written in honour of the revolution of 1952. But his major work was a trilogy that has been translated into English as *Drifting Cities*. Although the main themes are based on the Egyptian Greek community, there is a portrait of a multi-racial, multi-ethnic city neighbourhood with a shared humanity. In one scene, the muezzin has called for the sunset prayers, an announcement to all that it is the end of the day:

Arab women came out on their doorsteps and called their children in singsong tones. 'Tolbah, Hassan, Felfel, where are you hiding?' From the balconies, other voices called: 'Marco, Nicola, Virginia, come home now.'

The trilogy is unquestionably an Egyptian novel, part of Middle Eastern literature. Tsirkas migrated from Egypt and settled in Greece in 1966, dying in 1980. His work is an example of what I call marginal literature. Today the Greek community of Egypt is a shadow of a shadow, yet, up to fifty years ago, Greeks were a vital element at all levels of society. To overlook their literature is to overlook an essential ingredient of twentieth century literary Egypt.

I would like to turn to another fictional work that even more defies easy categorisation. *Mohammed Cohen* by Claude Kayat was published in Paris in 1981. The author was a Jew from Sfax in Tunisia. He migrated to France and became a teacher of French and English. The novel, written in French, tells the story of the child of the union of a Sfax Jewish barber and his Bedu wife. Having swallowed the improbability (but not impossibility) of that union, we follow the narrative of the Sfaxian childhood and youth of Mohammed who lives to the full on the margins of Tunisian nationalism. He has three passions in life: French literature, Arab music and Jewish cuisine. The boy is involved in Tunisian Zionist camps and he migrates with his family to Israel. He resists pressure to change his name from Mohammed to something more Hebraic. Mohammed experiences the difficulties of a Tunisian Jew in Israel and becomes disillusioned with Zionism. He gets a scholarship to Sweden, stays on, takes Swedish nationality and marries a Swedish girl. He has problems explaining that he is an ex-Israeli Tunisian half-Jew. When he tries to explain his attachment to his Arab heritage, someone says to him:

> - *Alors, tu te sens à moitié juif et à moitié arabe?*
> - *Non. Cent pour cent juif et cent pour cent arabe.*

He and his Swedish wife take a holiday in Tunisia and pay what is for Mohammed a sentimental visit to Sfax. Just as they identify the flat where Mohammed was born, the wife has labour pains and, of course, gives birth in that flat: a satisfying completion of the circle. The novel is a great read, but also an intriguing and revealing account of Tunisian provincial life, of the dilemmas of a disillusioned Zionist and of the issue of multiple identities. Is it a Tunisian novel? A Jewish or an Israeli novel? A French novel? Should such pigeon-holing matter?

A real writer who, like the fictional Mohammed Cohen, may also see himself as one hundred percent Jewish and one hundred percent Arab, is Samir Naqqash, now living in Petah Tikvah in Israel. Naqqash was born in Baghdad in 1936 and has written plays, novels and short stories, often using the Baghdad Jewish Arabic of his childhood. He migrated to Israel as a teenager but has resisted submission to Israeli Hebrew culture. He sees himself as part of the Arabic cultural world and has expressed the wish to live in an Arab country. He looks back to Iraq with a certain nostalgia. In his Baghdad childhood he had access to the literature of the world. Coming to Israel meant a narrowing of horizons and a submission to a dominant European Jewish culture. His works have limited print runs and, inevitably, the number of readers who will understand the Baghdad Jewish dialect of the 1940s must be declining annually. Fortunately his works often have a detailed glossary. Nevertheless his work has received critical acclaim, not least among Arab critics. He is happiest when he visits Egypt and meets Egyptian writers, and keeps in touch with trends in contemporary Arab literature. He keeps abreast of Palestinian literature but finds it too focussed on one political issue touching the chords of dispossession, nostalgia, loss and grievance. Take that away, he argues, and not a lot is left. Literature should be either personal or universal, uncommitted to any political issue. Is his work part of Arab literature? Israeli literature? Does it matter?

Samir Naqqash is one of a group of Israelis of Iraqi origin who have written in Arabic. Yizhak Bar-Moshe and Shimon Ballas long continued to write in Arabic – 'It is the language in which we lived', said the former – but, like North Africans in the 1970s and 1980s, they have for national reasons switched to Hebrew after twenty or thirty years. Iraqis who migrated to Israel often did so to escape political persecution in Iraq, rather than from any messianic Zionism. Jews such as Murad Mikha'il and Ya'qub Bilbul were pioneers of the Iraqi novel and short story. There is often a sentimentality, perhaps best represented in Sami Mikha'il's novel, *Victoria*, for a mythic Baghdad that may never have existed. Nissim Rejwan, in his memoirs, recalls working in al-Rabita bookshop Baghdad, which became a meeting place for intellectuals and bookworms, and adjourning to the Café Suisse with Buland al-Haydari and other Iraqi writers.

If the number of Israeli Jews writing in Arabic is declining, the number of Palestinian Israelis writing in Hebrew is increasing. The success in 1986 of the Hebrew novel, translated into English as *Arabesques*, by Anton Shammas, was an outstanding but not an isolated phenomenon. Atallah Mansur had published a Hebrew novel in 1966. Anton Shammas is one of a group of Palestinian writers – Na'im Araydi, Nazih Khayr, Siham Da'ud, Samih al-Qasim, Muhammad Hamza Ghana'im, Salman Masalha – who are translating between Arabic and Hebrew and writing poetry in Hebrew. All were born or grew to maturity after the foundation of the State of Israel. The revival of Hebrew was a pillar of twentieth century Zionist. The incoming Jewish migrants came speaking numerous languages. Just as a people needed an exclusive territory, so they needed an exclusive language. Other languages associated with Jews – Yiddish or Ladino – were seen as languages of the Diaspora. Hebrew would help to cement the new nation. Conversely many Arabs outside saw the adoption of Hebrew as a language of literary expression by Palestinians as a kind of cultural treason. But Palestinian Hebrew is not simply an attempt to challenge and undermine the Jewish monopoly of the Hebrew language. It is an example of an interaction between Arabic and Hebrew culture that is taking place in contemporary Israel, that defies mainstream Arab and Israeli ideologies. 'I do not know,' Na'im Araydi wrote, 'if I, who write in Hebrew, am writing Hebrew literature. But I do know that I am not writing Arab literature in Hebrew.'

Palestinians choose to write in Hebrew out of convenience rather than for ideological reasons. This should not come as a surprise. The Palestinians in Israel have, like Arabs in most other countries, enjoyed universal schooling in the last generation. In their case they have learned Hebrew from primary school. They live in a Hebrew-medium environment. All their dealings with police and officialdom are in Hebrew. They are exposed every day to radio and television in Hebrew. Palestinian lawyers, doctors, civil servants and academics have to work in Hebrew. In all this their situation resembles that of North Africans forty years ago. Hebrew for Palestinians, like French for North Africans, is the imperial language, the language of access to authority. The isolation of Palestinians from the rest of the Arab world has made Hebrew an inescapable option as a language of literary self-expression. The language has become internalised. Unlike most of the Israelis of Iraqi origin who have shifted from Arabic to Hebrew, the Palestinians are not writing exclusively in Hebrew or abandoning the use of Arabic. But do we define the novels and poetry produced by Israeli Palestinians Arabic literature? Israeli literature? Hebrew literature?

Enough has now been said to indicate that there is a huge amount of what I call marginal literature emanating from the contemporary Middle East. It may also be defined as the literature of exile, of *ghurba*, of *ightirāb*. This may include Arabs expressing themselves in French, English or Hebrew – or, like the Syrian, Rafik Schami, in German. It may be the literary expression of minorities who have been eclipsed. It may be Israelis and Palestinians indulging in linguistic cross-dressing. Is it valid to group these disparate writings under one label? Perhaps not, but they all represent different aspects of a common Middle Eastern experience and narrative. And I think they do reflect other cultural developments in the Middle East.

The experience of many people from the Middle East in the twentieth century was one of dramatic change, of upheaval, dislocation, exile.

I have referred to the fact that most Middle Eastern states are creations of the twentieth century and, from the early part of the century, had to assert their own legitimacy in repudiation of either long Ottoman centuries or the overwhelming international, economic and technical power of the British and French Empires. The infancy of the new states coincided with developments in effective techniques of state control and of propaganda. Within most Middle Eastern states, freedom of expression is often severely curtailed. There are of course nuances from state to state, and the situation is neither monolithic nor unchanging. But imprisonment, unemployment or exile have been common experiences for most writers in the Arab world. Some writers have found hospitality in other Arab countries: Jabra Ibrahim Jabra in Iraq, Abd al-Rahman Munif in Syria. Nizar Kabbani and Adonis were for many years based in Lebanon. Very few Palestinian writers have avoided imprisonment, expulsion or exile.

Physical and cultural dislocation has been a fact of life and not just for writers. Among the thousands who have been educated outside the Middle East many have taken spouses from abroad. Their offspring composes a generation that is growing up belonging to more than one culture. Multiculturalism is not a matter of public policy, but of personal experience, an experience that is constantly being reinforced by the information revolution. The assumptions of nationalism – the convergence of state, territory, people and language – that nourished mainstream literature have broken down. But the aspects of a Middle Eastern cosmopolitanism of a century ago have reasserted themselves in these marginal literatures. It is these literatures that touch on universal themes of change, identity, dislocation and adjustment. The marginal should be mainstream and the mainstream should be marginalised.

Agatha Christie and the Arab World

I was invited to write this as a contribution to a volume that never saw light. It was written in 1999 but has not been published before. It was written before the exhibition, Agatha Christie and Archaeology, at the British Museum, 2001. The exhibition and the companion volume, *Agatha Christie and Archaeology*, edited by Charlotte Trumpler, published by the British Museum Press, touched on similar themes but from different angles.

A great wave of happiness surges over me, and I realize how much I love this country, and how complete and satisfying this life is.   *Agatha Christie on Syria, 1946*

Agatha Christie (1890-1976) was one of the most successful writers of the twentieth century. Although she was quintessentially English her style, her plots and her characters such as Miss Marple and Hercule Poirot are internationally known, thanks to films and translations. In 1959, UNESCO announced that the Bible had been translated into 107 languages, Agatha Christie's writings into 103 and Shakespeare's into ninety. Agatha Christie enjoyed travelling and was familiar with Europe. But the part of the world where she had a close and sustained acquaintance was the Arab world, which she visited and lived in at various times for over half a century. She visited Egypt and Morocco but best knew Syria and Iraq, thanks to the archaeological work of her second husband, Max Mallowan, fourteen years younger.

In this essay I wish to trace her connections with the Arab world, her degree of involvement, and to consider how Arabs and the Arab world came into her work. A number of novels had the Arab world as background, most notably *Murder in Mesopotamia* (1936) and *Death on the Nile* (1937). I will examine one novel, *Destination Unknown* (1954), the location of which is Morocco, and examine the translation into Arabic, considering the balance of loss and gain. This leads to some observations on the challenges of translating Agatha Christie's work into modern literary Arabic.

In 1910 when Agatha Christie was twenty, her mother was unwell. As a rest cure, mother and daughter went to Cairo for the winter. With regiments of handsome British soldiers, polo at the Gezira Club, dances five times a week, Cairo possessed a cultural veneer of an imperial British upper middle class. Cairo was the extension of a London season. The young Agatha Christie enjoyed it all. Her mother tried to interest her in the antiquities of Egypt but with limited success. Egyptians were never encountered socially except as attendants and servants. Agatha Christie had already spent some months in

France, and this was her second period of prolonged overseas residence.

The Egyptian winter had little obvious direct impact on Agatha Christie, although, as her principal biographer Janet Morgan has written, 'it was certainly a happy visit, her first association of the East with feelings of comfort, amusement and success.' Moreover when a year or two later she started writing seriously, her first unsuccessful and unpublished novel, *Snow upon the Desert*, was set in a Cairo hotel.

She was not to return to the Arab world for eighteen years. In 1928 she had published several detective stories and was building up a reputation and a following. After the collapse of her first marriage and her mysterious disappearance, she wanted to get right away from Britain and booked a ticket to the West Indies. Two days before she was due to set off she had dinner with a young naval couple who had been in Baghdad and the Gulf. The more they talked about Baghdad the more she became enthusiastic. Her enthusiasm was doubled when she learned that it was possible to get there by train. 'Next morning,' Agatha Christie wrote in her autobiography, 'I rushed round to Cook's, cancelled my tickets for the West Indies, and instead got tickets and reservations for a journey on the Simplon-Orient Express to Stamboul; from Stamboul to Damascus; and from Damascus to Baghdad across the desert. I was wildly excited.'

Five days later she set off alone. She stayed for several days in Damascus, exploring and sight-seeing, was enchanted by the place, and was determined to return. Another single British woman was in Damascus that year – Freya Stark, whose *Letters from Syria* record her impressions. Freya Stark was more politically sensitive – Syria was recovering from armed revolt against the French Mandatory government that had led to an aerial bombardment of the city. Agatha Christie in her autobiography makes no mention of the tense political background that dominates Freya Stark's letters. From Damascus, Agatha Christie took the Nairn bus that crossed the desert to Baghdad. An overpowering hospitable British lady took her over on this last stage of the journey and in Baghdad Agatha Christie found herself part of a colony of British expatriates in the British suburb of Alawiyya. She felt reluctantly that she was becoming a memsahib instead of a tourist. But she was delighted with Baghdad: 'You could turn off Rashid Street and wander down the narrow little alleyways, and so into different *suqs*: the copper *suq*, with the copper-smiths beating and hammering; or the piled up spices of all kinds in the spice *suq*.'

Memories of Cairo and reading about Leonard Woolley's excavations impelled her to pay a visit to Ur. Woolley's work, which seemed to authenticate Noah's Flood and the background of the Patriarch Abraham, had captured popular imagination. Woolley did not encourage visitors to the dig, but his temperamental wife, Katharine, had read with enthusiasm Agatha Christie's successful novel, *The Murder of Roger Ackroyd* (1926), and immediately took to her. She was pressed to extend her stay and invited to return. She was enchanted by Ur,

... with its beauty in the evenings, the ziggurrat standing up, faintly shadowed, and that wide sea of sand with its lovely pale colours of apricot, rose, blue and mauve changing every minute. I enjoyed the workmen, the foremen, the little basket-boys, the pickmen – the whole technique and life. The lure of the past came up to grab me ... The carefulness of lifting pots and objects from the soil filled me with a longing to be an archaeologist myself. How unfortunate it was, I thought, that I had led such a frivolous life.

She recalled with shame her lack of interest in the past glories of Egypt, her preference for dancing with young men.

Friendship with the Woolleys was sustained; in the summer of 1929 they stayed in a London house belonging to Agatha Christie. Family crises detained her in Britain but she was able to return to Iraq in early 1930. She stayed with the Woolleys whose team now contained a young archaeologist, Max Mallowan, fifteen years younger than Agatha Christie. During the spring, at Katharine Woolley's request, Mallowan and Agatha Christie travelled together looking at the local sites such as the Shi'ite pilgrimage cities of Najaf – 'a wonderful place' and Karbala on the way to Baghdad. In Karbala they stayed at a police post. One policeman spoke to them in hesitant English and then burst into a recitation of poem by Shelley. 'I should never have envisaged myself,' she recalled thirty years later, 'coming all the way to Iraq so as to have Shelley's 'Ode to a Skylark' recited to me by an Iraqi policeman in an Eastern garden at midnight.' Such shared experiences with Max Mallowan led to a deep friendship, love, and marriage by the end of the year.

Agatha Christie seemed utterly English even though her father was American. Mallowan was cosmopolitan by contrast. His father was Austrian, his mother French. He had an English public school and Oxford education, and had a career as archaeologist, digging pre-classical sites in Iraq and Syria. He was to become a Professor, Fellow of All Souls Oxford, Fellow of the British Academy and end up as Sir Max.

Through marriage with Max Mallowan, Agatha Christie became a regular visitor to the Near East – apart from the years of the Second World War –

almost annually for thirty years until 1960. In 1931 she was with Mallowan and the Woolleys for the final season at Ur. That year also saw them visiting Nineveh outside Mosul. Mallowan led a team at Arpachiyah near Nineveh in 1933. Agatha Christie accompanied him as a working member of the team. She kept a written record of the work and helped to arrange and reassemble pottery fragments. She took and developed photographs, repaired ivories and involved herself in the administration of the expedition, in matters such as the pay of the workmen. But in 1934, she also wrote *Murder on the Orient Express* (which opens on the railway station at Aleppo) and dedicated it to Mallowan.

The following year they embarked on archaeological work in Syria. In late 1934 they surveyed the Khabur Valley that runs from the Turkish frontier to the Euphrates below Deir ez-Zor. They returned to Syria each year until 1938, digging at Chagar Bazar near Qamishli in 1935, 1936 and 1937, and at Tel Barak between Qamishli and Hassake in 1937 and 1938. There were also visits to obtain provisions to Beirut, Damascus (staying at the Orient Palace Hotel) and Aleppo (staying at the Hotel Baron). And trips to other parts of the Arab Near East – to Petra in Transjordan (Jordan after 1948) and to Egypt.

War interrupted archaeological work. Mallowan's knowledge of Arabic was helpful to the war effort and he was posted to Cairo and Libya while Agatha Christie remained in Britain. Agatha Christie missed Syria during the war and in 1944 wrote her Syria memoirs, *Come, Tell Me How You Live* (1946). Writing it was 'not a task, but a labour of love,' she said. She loved 'that gentle fertile country and its simple people, who know how to laugh and how to enjoy life: who are idle and gay, and who have dignity, good manners, and a great sense of humour, and to whom death is not terrible.'

After the war, in 1947, they both spent five months living in Baghdad, first at a hotel and then in a rented house overlooking the river Tigris, and from 1949 to 1960 spent each season at Nimrud, the major Assyrian site on the junction of the Tigris and the Greater Zab half way between Mosul and Baghdad. The season was usually from January to March. Life on the archaeological dig was often austere, with nights sleeping under canvas. By the 1950s, travel to Baghdad was by a direct flight instead of the more leisurely and interesting overland route. But it was also an insular life. The team would take Stilton cheese and air mail editions of *The Times* would be flown in. Life could be formal, everybody being expected to change for dinner. But life on a dig provided Agatha Christie with material for her novels. Such insulated life was similar to the isolated country house or long distance railway train, with a limited number of middle-class Europeans socially interacting. In addition to assisting with the archaeological work, Agatha Christie wrote several of her stories and novels in Iraq, including *A Pocket Full of Rye* (1953) and *Destination Unknown* (1954). The royalties of the former went to the British School of Archaeology in Iraq. The straw hat, worn by Agatha Christie at Nimrud, was for many years on display at the Baghdad headquarters of the British School.

The Arab world features in several of Agatha Christie's novels and stories, published from the 1920s to the 1970s. Five novels have most of the action taking place in Arab countries. One of her perennial creations, Tommy Tuppence, appears in her second published novel, *The Secret Adversary* (1922). He had seen active war service in Egypt and Mesopotamia.

Hercule Poirot first appeared in *The Murder on the Links* (1923). The following year a collection of Poirot stories, *Poirot Investigates* (1924), included a story, 'The Adventure of the Egyptian Tomb', in which Poirot investigates the deaths of people involved in the opening up of the tomb of King Men-her-Ra. Agatha Christie was clearly interested in archaeology before she met her second husband. Ten years later, in *Parker Pyne Investigates* (1934), one story, 'The Pearl of Price', is located in Petra. Another story is located in Baghdad. In *Death in the Clouds* (1935), alternatively known as *Death in the Air*, some of the characters have been staying at a small hotel in Syria.

The late 1930s saw the publication of three of her best known novels dealing with the Arab Near East. *Murder in Mesopotamia* (1936) takes place on an archaeological dig in Northern Iraq, and has characters based on the colleagues of Max Mallowan. The victim, the wife of the leader of the expedition, is based on Katharine Woolley. *Death on the Nile* (1937) takes place on a Nile boat trip. (The film of the novel, with Peter Ustinov as Poirot, is widely known. It was also a play, and in 1956 was due to be presented in Canterbury. It was cancelled because of sensitivity to deaths on the Nile following Britain's invasion of Egypt three months after Egypt's nationalisation of the Suez Canal.) The victim and suspects are all isolated on the boat, just as in *Murder in Mesopotamia* victim and suspects are restricted to the archaeological team, cut off from the rest of society. *Appointment with Death* (1938) takes place in Jerusalem and Petra. Victim and suspects are on an expedition to Petra. Poirot fortuitously turns up in each novel to resolve the disputes in Iraq, Egypt and Transjordan.

During these prolific years Agatha Christie also wrote one of her first plays,

Akhnaton (written in 1937, but not published until 1973). This is based on the ancient reforming Pharoah.

The Regatta Mystery (1939) is a collection of stories starring Miss Marple and Hercule Poirot. One story, 'The Mystery of the Baghdad Chest', is of such marginal relevance to the city Agatha Christie loved that later editions have retitled it 'The Mystery of the Spanish Chest'. But another story, 'Problem at Sea', is located on a ship berthed at Alexandria.

In order to escape being seen as an exclusive writer of detective stories and thrillers Agatha Christie wrote six novels under the pseudonym of Mary Westmacott. *Absent in the Spring* (1944) takes place on the Turkish-Iraqi border. A middle-aged woman is visiting her daughter married to a man working in the Iraqi Public Works Department. Because of floods she is stranded on the border and reviews her own life and marriage.

Christie went back to an ancient Egyptian theme with *Death Comes at an End* (1945), written as a challenge made by Professor Stephen Glanville, Egyptologist friend of Mallowan. Agatha Christie had at first hesitated, but then accepted the challenge on the grounds that people 'are the same whatever they live, or where.'

The events of two postwar novels take place in Arab countries. *They Came to Baghdad* (1951) takes place in Iraq, in Baghdad and Basra as well as on an archaeological dig. *Destination Unknown* (1954), alternatively known as *Many Steps to Death*, is located in Fez and in the southern deserts of Morocco. Both novels are thrillers with young women as central characters, who become caught up in a fight against sinister all-powerful international conspiracies run by conscienceless megalomaniacs. In this respect they pre-echo the James Bond novels of Ian Fleming. In *Destination Unknown* the master villain, as in some of the Bond stories, has an elaborate laboratory in a remote and inaccessible location where top scientists plot fiendishly to take over the world.

The Poirot novel, *Cat among the Pigeons* (1959), has a reference to a small but rich revolutionary Middle East state called Ramat.

Miss Marple did not travel as Poirot did. However in one of the stories in the collection, *Double Sin* (1961), the cat in the vicarage at Miss Marple's village, Chipping Cleghorn, has the name, Tiglath Pileser, the name of an ancient Assyrian king.

The last novel Agatha Christie wrote featured an ageing Tommy Tuppence. The only allusion to the Arab world is the title, *Postern of Fate* (1973), which alludes to the poem, 'Gates of Damascus', by James Elroy Flecker:

Four great gates has the city of Damascus …
Postern of Fate, the Desert Gate, Disaster's Cavern, Fort of Fear.

Although the Arab world provided a background for many of Agatha Christie's writings, they are no more than that: background. She reflected the values of her generation and class in having a Eurocentric, even an Anglocentric, view of the world. Foreigners are foreigners and natives are natives. She was conscientious in providing detail, but no Arab plays a significant role. They are servants or workers, expected to be loyal and cheerful but offering no complexities or nuances of personality beyond that. Victims and suspects are British or Europeans (or American), who are catapulted into an Arab environment. 'Natives' may be auxiliaries to a crime, but Agatha Christie's 'racialism' – though the use of such a term seems morally anachronistic – does not permit them to have the sophistication of a motivation for murder or the significance of being a murder victim. This is of course part of the rules of the detective story. Her Near Eastern stories avoid involvement in the tensions and conflicts of Near Eastern society. That would also mean complications with local legal values and systems. Agatha Christie knew her limitations.

Her novels are like those orientalist paintings with European travellers in the foreground. She was not a scholar of Arabic or of Islam. Her writings flowed from a fertile imagination that had been nourished from childhood by stories and legends including *The Arabian Nights*. She was a deeply conservative person, with a quiet Christian faith, and an acceptance of a patriarchal society. She was uninterested in politics, though curious about other people's religious beliefs. She was a kindly lady, usually sympathetic to but occasionally caustic towards those she met, acutely observant of people, habits and things. She saw people as individuals not as generalisations. For an idea of her own perceptions we have to turn to the account of her years in Syria, *Come, Tell me How You Live* (1946), and her posthumously published *An Autobiography* (1977). (My 1990 Fontana paperback edition of the former work has a map of Syria and Mesopotamia with the names of the rivers Tigris and Euphrates switched. The town of Deir ez-Zor in the centre of Syria is consequently placed in deepest Turkish Kurdistan. Agatha Christie would have been shocked at this inattention to detail.)

In both these autobiographical writings her love of Iraq and Syria stand out. To some extent these countries were a background to her life, but they were cherished none the less. In her approach to the society and civilisation of the

Arab Near East she was similar to her almost exact contemporary, Freya Stark. Both were very feminine women, accepting uncomplainingly that they were operating in a world where men made the decisions. Freya Stark was not painfully shy as Agatha Christie was. The Englishness of both was deceptive, for just as Agatha Christie's father was American so Freya Stark had strong mainland European family connections. Both, when in Britain, were comfortable in the world of country houses and the professional upper middle class. They both had an eye for the significant detail. Both started their affair with the Arab Near East, first with Syria and then with Baghdad. Both came to the area, having read widely in the history and archaeology of the land.

In addition to *The Arabian Nights*, Agatha Christie's perception of the Arab world was filtered through the Bible. She was impressed by an Arab social etiquette that combined politeness and delicacy. But she was a privileged visitor, usually isolated from the turmoil and passion of the cities.

The people encountered and employed on the archaeological digs reflected the communal hotchpotch of the Near East in the first half of the twentieth century. Kurds, Armenians, Yezidis, Indians, Turkomans and Arabs form the human background. One of the few people from the area who stands out is the archaeological expeditions' foreman, Hammoudi, who was first recruited by Woolley before the First World War when he worked with T E Lawrence at Carchemish – present-day Jerablus – where the Aleppo to Baghdad railway crosses the Euphrates. Hammoudi brought some of his Jerablus relations to Woolley's dig at Ur and to the Syrian digs of Max Mallowan.

Syria in the 1920s and 1930s was not only a melting pot of communities from the whole region, it was also on a historical cusp. Agatha Christie records how the workmen were paid in the old Ottoman currency, the *majidi*. The Syrian currency only achieved legitimacy when the French banished the older currency by law.

Agatha Christie, in dealing with the workmen on the digs, acquired some Arabic. She modestly denies any fluency, deferring in this to her husband. Mallowan was also modest. In his memoirs he recalls that he:

… was expected to learn Arabic and become reasonably proficient at the spoken language. I was never a good linguist, but by dint of keeping Van Ess's grammar in my pocket for several years on end I became tolerably competent in the speaking and understanding of it and at eliciting sense by a dialectic method of question and answer, which stood me in good stead during the war when better Arabists than I were often unable to put their Arabic across.

Yes, but Max Mallowan was brought up speaking English, French and German, studied classical languages at Oxford and acquired some professional familiarity with ancient Semitic languages. Agatha Christie uses a lot of appropriate Arabic in the novels located in Egypt, Iraq and Syria, and in *They Came to Baghdad* (1951) she transliterates not only the song of a Tigris boatman but also a line, with translation, of the tenth century poet, Mutanabbi. Such a quotation is not the small change of the language of an expatriate who uses Arabic only to deal with workers on an archaeological dig.

The writings of Agatha Christie are widely read in the Arab world. It is difficult to establish the number of copies produced. Statistics are not very forthcoming. Airport bookshops are well-stocked with them. I would like to examine the translation of *Destination Unknown* (1954) by 'Umar 'Abd al-'Aziz Amin, who has been a teacher of English in Egypt and has translated several other of Agatha Christie's novels. Most of the novel is located in Morocco. It is published – as are many other of her novels – by al-Maktaba al-Thaqafiyya, Beirut, without a date, but presumably in the 1990s. The Arabic title is *al-Tā'ira al-Mafqūda*, which means literally 'The Missing Aeroplane'. The translation is extraordinary. There are omissions, major, including one whole chapter, and minor. There are grotesque mistranslations, distortions and sheer inventions. There are extraordinary mistakes in terminology and a surprising ignorance of the Arab world. Let me substantiate each of these charges.

One page of English is represented by well over a page of Arabic. But the English version – and I refer to the HarperCollins paperback of 1994 – has 214 pages, the Arabic 175 pages. The omissions are often of psychological subtleties or of circumstantial detail. For example, among the phrases and sentences dropped in the first chapter are:

There was about him an alert nervous energy. (English edition, p 7)
The man behind the desk sighed. (E, 7)
He was all set for a brilliant career over there. (E, 8)
He rubbed his nose. (E, 9)
He tapped thoughtfully on the table with his finger. (E, 10)
He sat staring into space. (E, 11)
He shook his head and said gently. (E, 11)
The man called Jessup said soothingly. (E, 11)
He answered quickly and reassuringly. (E, 18)
The voice at the other end coughed discreetly. (E, 19)
She fumbled in her bag. (E, 21)

Sometimes the omissions take the form of paraphrases. This is, it seems to me, legitimate but only when there is no distortion. But, the translator introduces his own notions and that is less acceptable. For example, one paragraph (E, 142) reads:

'Alcadi? Young, reasonably competent. No more. Badly paid.' He added the two last words with a slight pause in front of them.

In the Arabic version (A, 118) this reads:

al-kādī? innahu tayyār mughāmir marin al-damīr, wa lā yas'ā ilā warā' al-māl, wa lā yu'min bishai' min al-mu'taqadāt al-siyāsiya, bal lā shā'n lahu bi-l-siyāsa 'alā al-itlāq

This in English would translate as:

Alcadi? He's an adventurous pilot with a flexible conscience. He only goes after money, and has no belief in political issues, indeed he has absolutely nothing to do with politics.

(One may note here that Alcadi is an Arab family name, *al-qādī*, meaning judge. It is odd that the translator does not quote the name back into Arabic.)

When the British security police say that one character is not a communist (E, 13), the translator gratuitously adds (A, 14) that he was not a fascist either. An archaeological expedition in the English (E, 98) becomes an engineering expedition in the Arabic (A, 87).

Other distortions evade what may be excessively British, middle-class, cultural reference points. For example, the paragraph in English (E, 168):

'Must say, you know,' panted Murchison, as he capered perseveringly round the floor, 'they do you jolly well here. Said so to Bianca only the other day. Beats the Welfare State every time. No worries about money, or income tax – or repairs or upkeep. All the worrying done for you. Must be a wonderful life for a woman, I should say.'

This is translated thus in Arabic (A, 135):

innahum hunā yahsunūna mu'āmilatuna. kunt aqūl libiānka bi'l-ams inna kull shai' mutawāfir hunā ... al-ta'ām jayyid wāfir, wa'l-'ajr dakhim wa mujzin, wa lasna mutālibin bishai' min al-darā'ib, innanā fi'l-haqq na'īsh hunā hayā rā'i'a'

Translating that back into English, it becomes:

They are good here in their treatment of us. I was saying to Bianca yesterday that everything is available here. Food is good and plentiful, the pay is huge and abundant. We do not ask for any taxes. In actual fact we live here a superb life.

A fine example of creative translation.

Another example. The English reads (E, 177):

There is Turkish Delight beside you, Madame. And other sweetmeats if you prefer them.

The Arabic (A, 141):

ladayk qahwa turkiya rā'i'a, aw ghairhā min al-mashrūbāt in shi't.

Translating that back, it becomes:

You have some excellent Turkish coffee, or some other drinks [the Arabic word, *mashrūbāt*, usually implies alcoholic drinks] if you wish.

There are other mistranslations that indicate a sloppy reading of the English. For example, 'doing that' (E, 38) – and suicide is intended – becomes *intisār* (A, 38) meaning 'victory'. If the allusiveness is to be avoided it should really have been *intihār*, 'suicide'. A similar error occurs when 'beliefs' (E, 159) becomes *āmānī* (A, 136), 'wishes' instead of *īmān*.

The translator is also careless about places. Oslo (E, 11) becomes Warsaw (A, 10). A Dane (E, 84) becomes a *Hūlandī* (A, 76) (Hollander, Netherlander). A carelessness about Europe may be understandable if not excusable. But there is a similar carelessness, even ignorance, about the Arab world. Casablanca (E, 46 and elsewhere) is translated *Kazablanka* (A, 45 and elsewhere) instead of the more acceptable *al-Dār al-Baidā*. *Marākish* can be a translation of the city Marrakesh or, in an archaic sense, of the country Morocco. The more acceptable and official translation of Morocco is *al-Maghrib*. The translator uses *Marākish* for 'Morocco' throughout. (A, 32 and elsewhere, E, 21 and elsewhere). More seriously the city of Fez (E, 63 and elsewhere) is translated throughout (A, 60 and elsewhere) as *Fazzān*, 'Fezzan', the region of Libya. And the well-known hotel, Palais Djamai (E, 63 and elsewhere) is translated to *Qasr al-Jamāl* (A, 60 and elsewhere), 'Palace of Beauty' or 'Palace of the Camels'. A few minutes looking at an atlas or guide book to Morocco would have avoided such blunders. The task of translation goes beyond the text.

These omissions, distortions and mistranslations do no service to Agatha Christie or to her British and Lebanese publishers. One would hardly expect the translator to meet subtler challenges such as dialogue. One of Agatha

Christie's strengths as a writer is in her dialogue. She had an ear for appropriate phrase and expression, and in terms of social class, had perfect pitch.

In *Destination Unknown* she has conversation between intelligence agents, which is upper middle class, male, public school, slightly jokey. The style was perfected a generation before Agatha Christie in the thrillers of John Buchan, and continued into the James Bond novels of Ian Fleming. It is clipped with a special slang, full of allusion and understatement. Let us look at some examples. In the following, two agents are discussing a suspect (E, 26):

> 'Think he's been the contact to tip her off?'
> 'It could be. I don't know. He puzzles me.'
> 'Going to keep tabs on him?'

This becomes in Arabic (A, 27):

> *'a yakūn huwa alladhi haradhā 'alā al-safar?'*
> *'hadha muhtamal, inn kunt lā ' adri al-haqīqa.'*
> *'wa hal tanwī an tad'ahā taht al-murāqaba?'*

Which, translated back, comes over as:

> 'Is it he who provoked her to travel?'
> 'This is probable, but I don't know the truth.'
> 'And do you intend to keep her under surveillance?'

'Keeping tabs on' is informal English, a gentle understatement of mild police supervision. The Arabic *taht murāqaba* conjures up an idea of police surveillance that would convey something far more sinister to the Arab reader. The informal conversational register is lost in translation. This may be a limitation of the nature of modern standard Arabic, which is unable to absorb the varieties of informal English. We are reminded of the issue of dialogue in Arabic novels. Should it be the prescriptive, formal, modern standard Arabic, or should it reflect the kind of Arabic that was probably actually spoken? The range of responses in contemporary Arab authors has varied. The beggars and call girls of Naguib Mahfouz's novels speak in a register that is no different from that of a news broadcaster or an Islamic preacher. Other writers will use the appropriate colloquial, but this may restrict the readership to those who are familiar with that colloquial. There are academic pressures against the use of colloquials in writing: this is seen as perpetuating divisions in Arab culture. In translating a popular novel from English to Arabic academic pressure is added to the challenge of translating the appropriate conversational register. But in this translation of *Destination Unknown* much is lost in the translation of dialogue into Arabic. How could the translator overcome the problem? By assuming the patterns of speech of the Arab social or professional counterparts? By a literal translation of the dialogue? Each translator will have to resolve the issue in his or her own way. Unfortunately 'Umar 'Abd al-Aziz Amin has been as unthinkingly sloppy in this issue as in other matters.

In spite of the inaccuracy and unprofessionalism of this translator's work, Agatha Christie's writings are widely read in Arabic translation. The features that appeal are the conspiratorial background of many plots and the tight action. Moreover her qualities of providing intellectual riddles, contrasting – almost stereotypical – characterisation, circumstantial detail and a pacey plot offset the limitations of the translations. The subtlety of social observation of the British middle classes, with their linguistic nuances, their meaningful gestures and slight change of physiognomic features is cultural baggage that gives her work power with the Anglo-Saxon reader but may be irrelevant to the Arab reader. The power and genius of Agatha Christie survives a bad translation.

Translation and Responsibility

This is the text of a talk I gave at the Al Furqan Islamic Heritage Foundation Wimbledon in February 2004. It has not been published before.

In 1969 I was living and working in Jordan. Each day a cyclostyled newsletter arrived at the office that included notices of cultural events in the capital. One day I was intrigued to see that there was to be a film about dancing shown at the Russian Cultural Centre called 'Pelican Pond'. I was puzzled and made further enquiries, to discover that Pelican Pond was a translation of a translation, and that the original Russian was *Lebedinoye Ózera* better known in English as *Swan Lake*.

I illustrate this to show how straight (but bad) translation can get it totally wrong. Musical terms acquire a conventional acceptance, even when untranslated into English. Consider the contrast in the impact on your ear and understanding between *Der Fledermaus* and *The Bat*. A few years ago in Paris I saw an advertisement for an opera, *Le Chevalier de la Rose*. Was this a newly discovered Offenbach? It took me a minute or so to realise that it was not some light operetta but the French version of *Der Rosenkavalier*. And in Turkey I was at a concert performance of what the programme announced as Mozart's *Bir Küçük Gece Müsiği*. This sounds very different from the German original, *Eine Kleine Nachtmusik*, which we would not dare translate into English.

It is not only the sound of an otherwise honest and accurate translation that can give a misleading impression – and is therefore a bad translation – but there may be associations in words used that will ignite messages in the listener or reader that will be different from those sparked off in the original. For example, the late President Bourguiba of Tunisia was always referred to in the Tunisian Arab press as *al-Mujāhid al-Akbar*, meaning the supreme fighter. *Mujāhid* has clear Islamic echoes of a fighter for righteousness, the fight being *jihād*, often misleadingly translated as holy war: nonetheless the religious connotation is inescapable. *Jihād* in the Holy Qur'an is often coupled with the words, *jihād fī sabīl Allāh*, a fight for righteousness on the path of God. But the term *mujāhid*, plural *mujāhidīn*, was always used to add a divine authority to conflict and has more recently been taken over by Islamists the world over. So *mujāhid* was a strange term to apply to the very secular Bourguiba. But in the French press in Tunisia the epithet applied to the President in French was *Le*

Combattant Suprême, as if this was the equivalent of *al-Mujāhid al-Akbar*. We have no problems with *suprême* as the translation of *akbar*, but *combattant* has the whiff of grapeshot and the barricades of the French Third Republic, where Bourguiba received his political education in the 1920s. Indeed I suspect *combattant suprême* came first, and that *al-mujāhid al-akbar* was an attempted translation. An alternative version could have been *al-muhārib al-akbar*, but that in Arabic sounds like a job description: a *muhārib* could be a mercenary. *Mujāhid* has that touch of vocation, nobility, fighting the good fight, and in Arabic such aspirations receive full legitimacy only in association with the Islamic religion.

There is one other example of a translation that has acquired a life of its own, a term that is used daily and has shot off at a tangent from its original base. (Metaphors, like salads, should be well mixed.) The term, 'the third world', is a translation from the French *tiers-monde*. But *tiers* means a third, a fraction, not third, an ordinal. When the English term 'third world' became current in the 1950s and 1960s, a first world and a second world were posited. The first world was the United States, Europe and the developed countries of eastern Asia and Australasia. The second world was the Communist bloc and the third world the developing countries of Africa and Asia. The term in English spawned the fourth world, countries like Bangladesh and southern Sudan, that faced even more desperate problems than the developing world. And the term for the third world in Arabic is *al-'ālam al-thālith*, a translation of the English and not the French.

I have already said enough to emphasise the importance of getting a translation right. I do not wish to be too prescriptive about this, for there is no timelessly correct translation. In literary translation there can be many variants, depending on the translator, his or her background and baggage, style and skill. Let me give you an example from Japanese. The form of the Japanese haiku is well known. The poet Bashō wrote one haiku that has been much translated. It goes something like this:

> Breaking the silence
> Of an ancient pond,
> A frog jumped into water –
> A deep resonance.

Other translators rendered the idea differently. (These versions are taken from an essay, 'Translating "The Sound of Water": Different versions of a *Hokku* by

Basho,' by Nobuyuki Yuasi, in *The Translator's Art: Essays in Honour of Betty Radice*, edited by William Radice and Barbara Reynolds, Penguin Books, Harmondsworth, 1987, 231-40.)

> Old pond! The noise of the jumping frog.

Or

> Old pond – frogs jumping in – sound of water.

Or

> An old pond –
> A frog jumps in –
> A splash of water.

Or

> Old garden lake!
> The frog thy depth doth seek,
> And sleeping echoes wake.

Or

> Old pond –
> and a frog-jump-in
> water-sound.

Or

> The old pond –
> A frog jumps in –
> Plop!

I could go on. But who is to say which version is accurate? Each conveys the same idea with shifting nuances and styles. They are all variations on a theme. And it indicates that the task of translation is, or should be, creative. But not too creative. The eighteenth century poet, Alexander Pope, translated Homer's *Iliad*. The classical scholar, Richard Bentley, observed, 'It is a pretty poem, Mr Pope, but you must not call it Homer.'

My own career as a translator of contemporary Arabic started by accident. By training I am a historian but for over thirty years I worked for the British

Council, mostly in the Arab world. I was given a year off to learn Arabic in Lebanon and immediately consolidated that training by six years in Sudan. As part of getting familiar with the country, I read the local press and also books that Sudanese were reading. In 1972 a young historian published a big book on the Battle of Omdurman, presenting the perspective of the vanquished. All accessible accounts of that struggle were presented from the viewpoint of the victorious. This book should be available in English, I thought. So I translated it.

This apprentice work was not without traumas. I worked with the author, Ismat Hasan Zulfo, who had English. He was thoroughly familiar with the English sources, above all Winston Churchill's *The River War* and the newspaper reports of the 1890s. When he read my chapters he did not care for my style. I wrote short sentences, reflecting British journalism and other writing of the 1970s. He thought I was mocking the grandeur of the epic story. I said that to write in the style of Churchill or of the manner of the newspapers of 1898 would be anachronistic, would sound bombastic and ridiculous. We had arguments, frequently vehement, and the project of the translation all but collapsed. But I got my way and *Karari the Sudanese Account of the Battle of Omdurman* was published in 1980. But I quietly resolved never to publish anything by someone who was still alive: a resolution I kept for over ten years.

But like all bad resolutions I wisely abandoned it on temptation. In the late 1980s I was working in the United Arab Emirates and became entranced by the short stories of Muhammad al-Murr, a young writer in his early thirties. He had published eleven volumes of short stories during the 1980s, mostly about the life-crises of young Emiratis facing the temptations of oil wealth. Muhammad al-Murr's characters drank alcohol and had illicit affairs and, as I worked on the translation of the stories, I felt like an eavesdropper, listening into the private conversations of my hosts. Muhammad was happy to see his stories in English. I made a selection from over a hundred stories that had appeared in Arabic, and a dozen were published as *Dubai Tales* in 1991. When they came out, some Emiratis were unhappy. 'People will think we are all like that,' they said. I tried to argue that they were only stories and that a foreign reader of Agatha Christie's novels did not, I hoped, jump to the conclusion that the British middle class are all conspiring to murder each other.

A second collection of Muhammad's stories was translated by Jack Briggs and published in 1994 with the title of *The Wink of the Mona Lisa*. Now there has been criticism of translators for their selection of texts translated from

Arabic. There is a suspicion that texts are chosen to reinforce 'orientalist' prejudices. There may be a grain of truth in this. I chose a dozen or so stories from Muhammad's work. They were all about contemporary Dubai, and I chose them first because I liked them but also because they taught me something about the values and practices of the contemporary society I was living in. Jack Briggs made his selection and, unconsciously I think, based on what appealed to him. Now Jack is one of the most remarkable people I have ever known. He has three passions – police work, cycling and the Arabic language. He is nearly twenty years older than I am, left school at 14 and joined the police in Lancashire. During the Second World War he served in the Palestine Police and afterwards was in Qatar, building up the police there. He learned Arabic superbly, largely through interrogating prisoners. In 1965 he went to Dubai as head of police. He studied in his spare time, obtained 'O' levels and 'A' levels and then, with the encouragement of the late Professor Johnstone of SOAS whom he had helped in research on the dialects of the Gulf, worked for and obtained a degree in Arabic. When I got to know him in Dubai he was in his seventies and working on an MA on the short story in the Gulf. But he did not neglect his cycling and I remember seeing him, dressed up in a lycra suit and about to burn up fifty kilometres in two hours or less on the highway between Dubai and Abu Dhabi.

I divert. Jack had known the Gulf and Dubai for thirty or forty years. His selection of stories unconsciously reflected this. These were more about the Gulf of the past and the changes that had taken place. My selection was more about the dilemmas facing contemporary young people – those people who were my professional targets in my British Council tasks of promoting the English language and British culture.

Motivate Publishing will be publishing a new edition of *Dubai Tales*, which will include some of Jack Briggs' translations, later this year.

It will be noted that these two experiments in translation were completed while I was living and working in the countries of the authors whose work I was working on. This continued when I moved to Syria in 1992. I translated two novels by the doyenne of Syrian writers, Ulfat Idilbi, born in Ottoman Damascus in 1912, and still with us. In Syria I also became interested in the Arab theatre and in the work of Sa'dallah Wannus. In 1997 I assisted in the first English production of a translation of one of his plays, *The Elephant Oh Lord of Ages*, which was performed by the British Council in Damascus under the auspices of the Syrian Ministry of Culture a few days before Sa'dallah's death. Other Arab plays had been translated and published. Some of these had indeed been performed, but I realised that there are special demands made on the translator of drama, if it is for the stage rather than the page. If you are translating for production you are translating for a collective ear and not an individual eye. The reader of a book or magazine is in control about how much he or she reads and when. If the reader dozes he or she can always flip back and be reminded about what happened or the name of a character. This is not possible for the stage. Impact has to be immediate. The spectator cannot press the rewind button. Moreover the director and actors have to be happy that a translated text is workable. In the Wannus play I spent time with the actors during the rehearsals. At one point a character has to cry out 'Sensationalism!' in fortissimo outrage. The actor and director told me that this was theatrically difficult and much of the dramatic impact was lost in awkward declamation of the five syllable word. We had to find an alternative way of getting this across.

I have not lived in the Arab world since 1997 but have ventured to translate work from countries I have not known well. At one point I was asked by the Moroccan writer, Laila Abu Zaid, to translate one of her books. I started on it but gave up, painfully conscious that I lacked familiarity with the Moroccan background. I have translated work of the Tunisian, Hasuna Misbah, whose work is better known in Germany where he lives than in the United Kingdom or the United States. I have lived in Tunisia and this experience helped me avoid a howler committed by his German translator. In one story Hasuna writes of the girls of La Goulette and La Marsa, two chic outer suburbs of the capital lying on the coast. Now La Goulette is well known and the German translator had no problem with that. La Marsa is less well known. The word means port or, more precisely jetty, and the translator had rendered 'the girls of La Marsa' as *Hafenmädchen*, 'girls of the port', giving an entirely different idea from the Arabic. In novels of social realism it is most desirable for the translator to know the author's geographical reference points. I have usually tried to visit places written about in the original, or at least to study a map.

I have always felt a huge responsibility in translating a work. A translator has to be skilled in writing English (or the target language) as well as having competence in Arabic (or the source language) and, just as important, knowledge of the social and cultural environment of the author translated. There is the terrible danger of a bad translator transforming a first rate work in one language into a second or third rate work in the translated language.

Because of the unfamiliarity of contemporary Arabic literature, I feel we translators have to bring the text to the reader rather than expect the reader to come to the text. I accept the advice given three hundred years ago by the poet, John Dryden:

> A translator that would write with any force or spirit of an original must never dwell on the words of the author. He ought to possess himself entirely, and perfectly comprehend the genius and sense of his author, the nature of the subject, and the terms of the art or subject treated of; and then he will express himself as justly, and with as much life, as if he wrote an original; whereas he who copies word for word loses all the spirit in the tedious transfusion.

In short, I have the reader in my mind all the time. Very often the translator is trapped by the style or idiosyncrasies of the author. In my translations I usually ask my wife, whose knowledge of Arabic is limited, to read my early version, and point out where something makes no sense, or reads badly or sounds too like a dictionary translation. Her comments are a process of quality control. I am very happy if a reader says that what I have written does not read like a translation. I am in sharp disagreement with the words of Vladimir Nabokov who, in the introduction to his translation of Lermentov's *A Hero of our Time*, wrote:

> we must dismiss, once and for all, the conventional notion that a translation 'should read smoothly', and 'should not sound like a translation' (to quote the would-be compliments, addressed to vague versions, by genteel reviewers who never have and never will read the original texts).

The whole point is that the potential reader of Arabic literature in translation is unlikely to be able to read the original. That is the function of translation.

In the world of the twenty first century we translators have an extra responsibility in interpreting and explaining one marginalized, vulnerable and misrepresented part of the world to another. But the broader cultural literary scene is changing. There is no polarisation.

There have been other cultural developments in the last decade that offer hope. Publishing has become cheaper. It used to be said that Egyptians wrote books, Lebanese published them and Iraqis read them. Censorship can always be avoided by the publishing of books outside one's own country. But Arab consciousness is no longer exclusive to the Arab world, or even to the Arabic language. In the last thirty years, there has been a substantial out-migration from the Arab world. This has been partly for political, partly for economic reasons. A huge number from the Arab world study in the United Kingdom and Ireland, mainland Europe and the United States (though this number may be in decline). There are excellent Arab publishing houses in Cyprus, Germany and the United Kingdom. But you no longer need to publish to get your voice heard. Since the late nineties, Arab women have been diffusing their poetry through the internet. But there has also developed an Arab literature in other languages. This is not new. Nearly a century ago the Lebanese Khalil Jibran and Amin al-Rihani wrote in a very distinctive English.

I would like to consider the present state of translation of Arabic literature into English and end up with one or two practical suggestions. What is the present state of availability of contemporary Arabic literature in translation? Well, not too bad, really, and better than other European countries, though there is much room for improvement. Since the Second World War there have been two people who have made an outstanding contribution to this work. They are Denys Johnson-Davies and Salma Khadra Jayyusi.

Denys Johnson-Davies is now in his eighties, lives in Morocco and has translated twenty-eight volumes. He started in the 1940s with a volume of stories by the Egyptian Mahmud Taymour and has been a pioneer translator of Naguib Mahfouz and Tayib Salih. He was general editor in the 1970s of the Heinemann Arab Authors series that was aimed to follow the success of the Heinemann African Authors series. But it was not commercially viable. African authors have huge potential English readers in East and West Africa. Arabs will read their own literature in Arabic. The Heinemann project was abandoned but Denys has carried on regardless of fashion, translating novels, volumes of short stories plays and even a volume of the poetry of the Palestinian Mahmoud Darwish. Denys has also written his own novels and short stories.

Salma Khadra Jayyusi is now in her seventies, a Palestinian poet resident in the United States. In the early 1980s she set up the Project of Translating Arabic that aimed to produce in translation the best of contemporary Arabic. She has raised money from governments and mobilised an army of translators. Sometimes she raises money that cannot be transferred out of a particular country. I was commissioned by Salma to translate a volume of the work of the Palestinian Liana Badr while I was in Tunisia. She paid me in Tunisian carpets. She has produced several large anthologies – of poetry of the Arabian Peninsula, of Palestinian poetry, two of modern Arab theatre and most recently a volume of modern Arab fiction.

For a long time it was difficult to find publishers interested in Arab translations. (Translators of other languages assure me that other languages fare not much better.) Very little is taken up by mainstream publishers, and I can think of only four contemporary writers whose work is published by major publishers: Naguib Mahfouz and that only since he won the Nobel Prize for Literature in 1988; the late Abd al-Rahman Munif, originally Saudi; the Lebanese Hanan al-Shaykh; and the Sudanese Tayib Salih whose *Season of Migration to the North* has recently been the only contemporary Arab work to be published by Penguin Modern Classics. This is a most welcome development. Forty years ago, Betty Radice, the editor of Penguin Classics acknowledged that 'much is offered by the literature of China and Japan, India and the Middle East ... [but] Translations of this kind are not easy to sell.'

Translators have had to rely on minority niche publishers such as Quartet Books and Saqi Books in this country, and Interlink and the University of Texas at Austin in the United States. Niche publishers tend to have a niche readership. Arab literature in translation needs to escape from this and storm the citadels of the mainstream publishers. Risk for a mainstream publisher would be offset at a stroke if a publisher could be assured of a sale of five hundred copies of a translated novel on publication. For £5,000 an Arab Embassy would be achieving much for its own, and Arab, cultural relations.

In my view, this risk is more in perception than in reality. Publishers are competitive and do not want to take risks. There is a sense that somehow Arab culture and its artistic manifestations are alien. I find this puzzling. In Britain, stories of *The Arabian Nights* have been absorbed into British culture since the eighteenth century. Aladdin was first performed as a pantomime in London while Napoleon was still alive. No educated person in the west can afford to be unfamiliar with the teachings of Islam or of the Holy Qur'an. Words of Arabic have been entering English in the last half century or so. The British army brought back words like bint, and more recently words relating to cuisine (falafel, shawarma and so on) and religion (such as zakāt) have become part of the English language. Even colloquial Arab expressions are finding their way here, thanks to British who have worked in the Arab world. In his autobiography, Norman Tebbitt, of all people, uses the word ma'lesh without any explanation. The writings of Naguib Mahfouz in English translation have been a commercial success. Indeed more copies of his Cairo Trilogy have been sold in English than the whole of his work in Arabic. So there is nothing impossibly alien about the contemporary Arab world.

There are changes, and signs of improvement. The journal *Banipal* was launched in 1998 and has become a widely distributed outlet. *Banipal* comes out three times a year and has translations and articles about contemporary Arabic literature. It is newsy, with interviews with writers and reports of conferences and literary events. It has been brilliantly edited by Margaret Obank and covers the whole of the Arab world as well as Arab writers in exile. It has managed just about financially, thanks to grants, but it has upheld its independence.

But we translators need encouragement. You will recall that Dryden spoke of the translator as 'he'. Actually the majority of practising translators in Britain, I believe, are women. More women study languages at university than men. Translation is an activity that can be pursued at home: it is an underpaid domestic industry. As someone once said: 'Who ever saw a fat translator or a thin publisher?' Skilled translators can work as freelancers and earn £100 and more for translating a thousand words of a commercial document. Literary translation is an equally skilled craft, as skilled as precision engineering, and – at commercial rates – a translator should receive £5,000 or £6,000 for translating a novel of 50,000 or 60,000 words. A translator is lucky if she (or he) gets one tenth of that. In 2004 the occupation authorities in Iraq were recruiting students of Arabic to assist with the occupation at £200 a day.

There is an awareness that translation is an important factor in cultural interdependence. Both the British Council and UNESCO are showing interest. But there is resistance on the Arab side. I have often encountered a questioning of my motives in translating contemporary Arabic literature. Was I a spy? I spoke of the suspicion of the translator in the selection of work for translation. This attack on the integrity of translators appeared in one of the London Arab papers. The writer argued that Arab writers that were selected for translation were unrepresentative. They were from minorities (like Gamal Ghitani, the Egyptian Copt) or wrote about the desert such as the Libyan Ibrahim al-Kuni. Focussing on minorities helped to divide the Arab world – an old imperialist trick. Emphasising the desert meant that translators were trying to show that Arabs were backward Bedu. Twelve years ago I translated a long short story by Ibrahim al-Kuni: I think it was the first of his work translated into English. It is true that the location is Tuareg desert country in southern Libya. But the story is part-realism, part-fantasy and can be read at different levels. I came across the writings of Ibrahim al-Kuni through the recommendations of Arab readers not from Libya. I make this point

236

deliberately, for I have found that very few Arab writers have a pan-Arab appeal. Ibrahim al-Kuni is read by discriminating readers throughout the Arab world, not because he writes about the desert but because he is a great and profound writer. The best answer to this critic is to invite him to specify what should be translated. I am aware that there is a vast amount of quality literature waiting to be introduced to the rest of the world. But suspicions remain. The Arab world is sometimes a self-contained world, anxious about its reputation and wary of foreigners showing too much curiosity. In this it resembles nineteenth century China.

There are ways of allaying these suspicions. The American University of Cairo has a superb output in translated contemporary Arab literature. They have established foreign translators, such as Denys Johnson-Davies, and a number of translators, based in the region, who are translating works from their own Arabic language into English. This is to be encouraged, though the financial rewards for translators in the Arab world are even worse than in the United Kingdom.

For many European languages there is now an annual literary prize for translation into English. These have been funded by the overseas governments or by private initiative. From this year the Banipal Trust is offering a prize for translation of contemporary Arab literature into English. Funding is coming from the Arab world. The annual costs of such administering such a prize are, I have calculated, less than the cost to the occupation authorities in Iraq of employing three or four interpreters for one month.

Since this talk was delivered in 2004, there have been welcome and significant changes in the reception of Arab literature in translation. The magazine *Banipal* has helped. In 2007 the International Prize for Arabic Fiction was founded. It works in collaboration with and on the model of The Man Booker Prize and has so far been generously funded by the Emirates Foundation of Abu Dhabi. And of the fifteen translated novels in the long list of the 2010 Independent Foreign Fiction Prize, four are by Arab writers. One is a translation of a Syrian novel, written in German. Another is the translation of the first winner of the International Prize for Arabic Fiction.

Index

Abd al-Baqi Abd al-Wakil, 94
Abd al-Nur, Abeer, 32
Abd al-Nur, Ibrahim, 32
Abd al-Qadir Pasha Hilmi, 81
Abd al-Qadir al-Jaza'iri, 189
Abd al-Qadir Mahmud, 85
Abdel-Malek, Kemal, 9-11
Abdul Karim, Munshi, 129
Abdullah I, King of Jordan, 168
Abdullah II, King of Jordan, 154, 155
Abdullah bin Zayed Al Nahyan, Sheikh, 122
Abdulmecit, Caliph, 200, 201
Abu Anja, Hamdan, 80, 86
Abu Dhabi, 115, 121-122, 123, 166
Abu Hamad, 93
Abu Qirja, Muhammad Uthman, 84, 87
Abu Zaid, Laila, 232
Abu Zayd, Nasr Hamid, 48
Adam, Juliette, 53
Aden, 205
Adonis (Ali Ahmad Said Asbar), 213
Adowa, Battle of, 93
Ağaoğlu, Ahmet, 53-54
Ahmadani, Mahmud, 83
Ala al-Din Pasha Siddiq, 81, 84, 87
Aleppo, 7, 8, 36-37, 40, 157, 205, 217
Alexandria, 134
Ali, Abdullah Yusuf, 141

Ali wad Hilu, Khalifa, 87, 90, 96, 102
Amichai, Yehuda, 174
Amin, Umar Abd al-Aziz, 212, 222-226
Amit-Kochavi, Hannah, 5
Anavarza, 59, 65
Ansari, Humayun, 129-130
Arkell, A J, 150, 152
Arwa, Queen of Yemen, 193
Ashour, Radwa, 19
al-Ashqar, Nidal, 171
Araydi, Na'im, 11, 211, 212
Atatürk, Mustafa Kemal, 53
Atbara, 93, 94
Auden, W H, 180
Azam Jah, Prince of Berar, 200-201
al-Azem (al-Azm) family, 28, 204
al-Azem, Amat al-Latif, 29-30
al-Azem, Nazih, 29
al-Azem, Sara, 29
al-Azem, Yasir Mu'ayyid, 28-29

Badr, Liyana, 10
Baghdad, 70-71, 159, 211, 215, 219
Baghras, 61
Bahrain, 205, 207
Baker, Valentine, 105
Ballas, Shimon, 211
Ban Naga, Abd al-Rahman, 83,86
Baqa al-Gharbiyeh, 7-8
Bara, 79, 80
Barak, Ehud, 176

Barghouti, Mourid, 19-20
Bar-Moshe, Yizhak, 211
Bashō, 228-229
Bayati, Abd al-Wahhab, 174
Baybars, 63
Beckford, William, 162
Beddow, Tim, 41
Bentley, Richard, 229
Bergne, Paul, 166-167
Beshir, Mohamed Omer, 111-113
Berber, 93, 94, 103
Bevin, Ernest, 154
Bilbul, Ya'qub, 211
Blair, Tony, 166, 167
Birwa, 6-7, 173
Boase, T S R, 58
Boulus, Sargon, 179-180, 209
Bourguiba, Habib, 227-228
Boyajian, Zabelle, 61
Bradford, 134, 136
Bradley, Rebecca, 151-152
Brick Lane Mosque, London, 136
Bridges, Lord, 155
Briggs, Jack, 230-231
Brighton, 132, 135
Broadwood, Colonel Robert, 97, 100
Brook, Peter, 172
Brookwood, 185
Broumana High School, 28
Buchan, John, 225
Burbank, California, 33-34
Burges, William, 134
Burgess, Guy, 154
Burton, Richard, 191
Busati Bey Madani, 83, 87
Bute, Marquess of, 134

Cardiff Castle, 134, 135
Cardwell, Edward, 105-106
Carey, Roane, 13, 15-16
Cavafy, Constantine, 209
Cavanagh, James, 133
Chambers, W I, 134
Chambers, William, 133
Chaplin, Charlie, 201
Chesterton, G K, 146
Chraieb, Driss, 206
Christie, Agatha, 40, 214-226, 230
Churchill, Randolph, 154
Churchill, Winston, 90, 91, 97, 101, 105, 184, 230
Clark, J Desmond, 150
Cockerell, Sir Charles, 132
Cocteau, Jean, 172
Collinson, Colonel John, 98
Connaught, Duke of, 201
Conrad, Joseph, 207
Cossery, Albert, 206
Courbage, Youssef, 17-18
Crane, Charles, 29
Crawley, 136
Cromer, Earl of, 92, 109
Curzon, Robert, 119

Daghestani, Kazem, 148
Dalrymple, William, 119
Damascus, 26-31, 38-41, 42, 71-72, 134, 148, 170, 185-189, 192-193, 204, 215, 219-220
Daniell, Thomas, 132
Daniell, William, 132
Darmesteter, James, 53
Darwaza, Izzat, 72, 73

240

Darwish, Mahmoud, 6-7, 8, 10, 173-176, 234
Davidson, Christopher M, 119
Dawud (Da'ud), Siham, 11, 211
Deakin, William, 154
De Cardi, Beatrice, 150
Deir al-Asad, 173
D'Ibelin, Jean, 63
Dickens, Charles, 198
Dongola, 93, 103
Doughty, Charles Montagu, 119, 186, 191, 193
Douloughli, Gheorgis Demitrious, 83, 86
Dryden, John, 233, 236
al-Duaij, Ahmad, 3, 68, 70, 73, 115
Dubai, 115, 121-122, 230-231
Durrushehvar, Princess, 200-201

Edwards, Robert W, 57, 66
Elad-Bouskila, Ami, 11-12
Eliot, George, 198
Evans, Major Edward, 83

Fairouza, 32-34
Faqir, Fadia, 207
Fargues, Philippe, 17-18
Farquhar, Colonel Arthur, 83, 84
Farrah, Abd'Elkader, 130
Farson, Daniel, 40
Ferlinghetti, Lawrence, 179-180
Fez, 219, 224
Fleming, Ian, 219, 225
Forster, E M, 183, 186, 188, 198
Fuda, Faraj, 48
Fulton, Lord, 155

Galsworthy, John, 201
Gandhi, M K, 185, 201
Garrett, Sam, 38-39
Gatacre, General Sir William, 97
Ghali, Waguih, 207
Ghamrawi, Shaikh Muhammad Ahmad, 200
al-Ghana'im, Jamil, 7
al-Ghana'im, Muhammad Hamza, 7-8, 211
Ghitani, Gamal, 236
Gibberd, Sir Frederick, 136
Gibbon, Edward, 141-143, 207
Ginat, Joseph, 50-51
Ginsberg, Allen, 179
Gladstone, W E, 3, 68, 81, 106
Glanville, Stephen, 219
Glubb, Faris, 168-169
Glubb, Sir John Bagot, 168, 169
Gordon, Charles George, General, 77, 78, 87, 88, 91
Gordon, Violet, 144-145
Gotz von Seckendorff, Baron, 83
Greenlaw, Jean Pierre, 109-110
Grossman, David, 7, 15

Habash, George, 147
Habiby, Emile, 9, 11
Hackney, 135
Haider, Gulzar, 135
al-Hakami, Najm al-Din Umara, 194, 195-196
Hammad, Suhail, 12, 209
Hanania, Caroline
Hanania, Farid, 146-147
Hanania, Tony, 147
Hanauer, J E, 184, 188

Hardy, Thomas, 186, 193, 198
Hasan, Yusuf Fadl, 107-108
Hass, Amira, 15-16
Hastings, 135
Hastings, Warren, 132
al-Haydari, Buland, 211
Healey, Denis, 150
Henderson, Edward, 124
Henniker, Lord, 154-156
Heraclius, Emperor, 57
Herbert, Aubrey, 196
Herlth, Captain, 83
Hetum I, King of Armenia, 59-60, 62-63, 64, 65
Hetum of Korykus, 55-56
Hetumid family, 58-59
Hicks, William, General, 77-89, 91, 92, 95, 106
Hinnebusch, Raymond, 52
Hitchcock, Alfred, 201
Hodges, William, 132
Holman Hunt, Diana, 166
Homer, 229
Holt, P M, 105
Hourani, Albert, 34
Hourani, Cecil, 24-25
Hughes, Ted, 180
Husayn Pasha, 84
Hussain, Nasser, 130
Hussein, King, of Jordan, 21, 22-23
Hussein, Saddam, 165
Hyderabad, 185, 188, 199, 200-202

Ibn Battuta, 118-120
Ibn Khaldun, 172
Ibn Sina (Avicenna), 46

Ibn Rushd (Averroes), 46
Ibrahim al-Khalil, 96, 97, 99, 100, 102
al-Idilbi, Dr Hamdi, 148
Idilbi, Ulfat, 148, 231
Idilbi, Ziad, 149
al-Ijaija, 94
Ilyas, Umar, 84
Ingram, Rex, 201
Irving, Washington, 133
Inőnü, Ismet, 54
Isma'il Ayub, 105
Isma'il al-Manna, 80

al-Jabiri, Muhammad, 48
Jabr, Jabra Ibrahim, 208, 213
Jacobsen, David C, 9-11
ibn Jalloun, Tahar, 206
Jayyusi, Lina, 6-7
Jayyusi, Salma Khadra, 234
Jerusalem, 7, 64, 66, 134
Jibla, 193
Jinnah, Muhammad Ali, 130
Joffé, George, 21-22
Johnson-Davies, Denys, 234, 237
Jones, Owen, 133
Jones, Sir William, 162
Joris, Lieve, 38-39
Jubran, Salem, 6
Jumblatt, Nora, 41
Jumblat, Walid, 147

Kabbani, Nizar, 41, 162-165, 174, 203, 213
Kabbani, Rana, 176
Kanafani, Ghasan, 11, 169
Kay, Henry Cassels, 194, 195-196

Kayat, Claude, 210
Keenan, Brigid, 33, 40-41
Kew, 132
al-Khal, Yusuf, 179
al-Khalidi family, 30
al-Khalifa, Sirr al-Khatim, 111
al-Khalifa Abdullahi, 75, 85, 87, 88, 90-104, 105
al-Khalifa Abdullahi, Abd al-Salam, 75
al-Khalifa Abdullahi, Muhammad, 90
Khalil, Khalil Gibran, 207, 234
Khartoum, 75, 77-78, 79, 82, 88, 90, 91, 94
Khayr, Nazih, 211
Kilij Arslan II, 60
King, Henry, 29
Kinglake, A W, 119, 133
Kinross, Lord, 144
Kipling, Rudyard, 185
Kirwan, Sir Laurence, 152
Kitchener, H H, General, 75, 88, 92-104, 105
Kız Kalesi, 59, 60
Krak des Chevaliers, 27, 61
al-Kuni, Ibrahim, 236-237
Kuwait, 70, 115, 168, 205

Lampron, 58, 60, 65-66
Lane, Edward, 191
Lawrence, A W, 151
Lawrence, D H, 188
Lawrence, T E, 151, 185, 221
Leighton, Lord, 134
Leon I, King of Armenia, 59-62, 64, 65, 67

Leon V, King of Armenia, 55, 64
Lermentov, Mikhail, 233
Lewis, Colonel D F, 98, 102
Liverpool, 134
Lorca, Federico Garcia, 174
Lusignan, Guy de, 64
Lyttelton, Brigadier General Neville, 98, 106

al-Maaly, Khalid, 180
Mabro, Judy, 17-18
Macdonald, General Hector, 98, 101-102, 105
Mackintosh-Smith, Tim, 117
Maclean, Sir Fitzroy, 154
Mahbuba, Abd al-Hadi, 159
al-Mahdi, Muhammad Ahmad, 77, 79-89, 91-92
al-Mahdi, Sadiq, 75
Mahfouz, Naguib, 161, 203, 225, 234, 235
Mahjoub, Jamal, 207
Mahmoud, Fatma Moussa, 161-162
Mahmud wad Ahmad, 93, 94, 96, 103
al-Mala'ika, Nazik, 159-60
Malet, Sir Edward, 81, 82
Mallowan, Max, 40, 214, 216-217, 218, 221-222
Manakha, 193
Mansur, Atallah, 11, 211
Ma'oz, Moshe, 50-51
March, Fred, 112
Margaret of Soissons, 64
Marjayoun, 24
Martin, Colonel R G, 101

243

Masalha, Salman, 11, 12, 211
Matar, Nabil, 129
Maxwell, General Sir John, 98, 102
Maxwell-Hyslop, Rachel, 150
Mayhew, Henry, 130
Menem, Carlos, 34
Metemma, 93, 103
Mikha'il, Murad, 211
Mikha'il, Sami, 211
Milton, John, 207
Mirun, Yoram, 6-7
Mohaamed Sake Dean, 129
Mohamed, Rev James Kerriman, 129
Moore, Thomas, 133
Morgan, Janet, 215
Moss, Robert Tewdwr, 39-40
Muazzam Jah, 200-201
Muhammad Ali, Duse, 129
Muhammad bin Rashid Al Maktoum, 122
Muhammad Sharif, al-Khalifa, 96
Muna, Princess, of Jordan (Toni Gardiner), 154
Munif, Abd al-Rahman, 213, 235
Murdoch, Iris, 150, 151-152, 153
al-Murr, Muhammad, 230-231
Murray, Craig, 167
Musa'id Abd al-Halim, 84, 87
Musallim bin al-Kamam, 123-125
al-Mutanabbi, 194-195
Mutawwa', Khalid, 209

Nabokov, Vladimir, 207, 233
Naqqash, Samir, 5-6, 210-211
Nash, John, 133
Nasir, Amjad, 208

Navarro, Ramon, 201
Nehru, Jawaharlal, 147
Neillands, Robin, 105-106
Nerses, 60-61
Neruda, Pablo, 174
Netton, Ian Richard, 141
Nilufer Hanim, 200
Noor, Queen, of Jordan, 21, 22-23
Norwich, John Julius, 27, 147
wad al-Nujumi, Abd al-Rahman, 87, 92
Nuri Sha'lan family, 30
Nye, Naomi Shihab, 6-7, 12, 209

Obank, Margaret, 236
el Obeid, 77, 79-81, 83, 84, 87, 88, 89
Ockley, Simon, 142
O'Donovan, Edmund, 83
Ohrwalder, Father Joseph, 83, 93
Omdurman, Battle of, 90-104, 105
Oren, Assaf, 15
Osman (Uthman) Azraq, 97, 99, 100, 102
Osman (Uthman) Digna, 94, 96, 97, 99, 101, 102
Osman (Uthman) Shaikh al-Din, 96, 98, 99-100, 101, 102, 105
Oyono, Ferdinand, 177

Pappé, Ilan, 15
Perthes, Volker, 52
Philby, Kim, 147
Philby, H St John, 147
Pickthall, Marmaduke, 43, 44, 127, 141, 181, 183-202
Pickthall, Muriel, 201

Pipes, Daniel, 50-51
Plath, Sylvia, 180
Pococke, Edward, 142
Polo, Marco, 63
Pope, Alexander, 229
Porden, William, 133
Pound, Ezra, 180
Power, Frank, 106
Prideaux, Humphrey, 142

Qabbani, Abu'l-Khalil, 163
al-Qasim, Samih, 8, 11, 12, 211
Qinawi Bey, 86
Quilliam, Neil, 51
Qutb, Sayyid, 48
al-Quwwatli, Shukri, 30

Radice, Betty, 229, 235
Radice, William, 229
al-Raqqa, 157
Ras al-Khaimah, 121
Ra'uf Pasha, 105
Regent's Park Mosque, London, 136
Rejwan, Nissim, 211
Renan, Ernest, 53
Repton, Humphrey, 132
Reynolds, Barbara, 229
al-Rihani, Amin, 207, 234
Roberts, David, 133
Roden, Claudia, 25
Rosenberg, Betsy, 7
Roslin, Toros, 66
Rum Kalesi, 57, 66
Runciman, Sir Steven, 61
Rupenid family, 58-59, 65
Rushby, Kevin, 117-118

Al Sabah, Shaikha Hassa, 41
Sabaluka, 94, 103
Sa'd, Abdullah, 93-94
Said, Ilham, 69, 70, 73
Said, Wafic Rida, 41
St George's School, Jerusalem, 28
Sale, George, 142
Salih, al-Tayyib (Tayeb), 234, 235
Salim, Ajaj, 170
Salisbury, Marquess of, 106
Samuel, Sir Herbert, 146
San'a, 115, 117-120, 193
al-Sayyab, Badr Shakir, 174
Schami, Rafik, 212
Scott, Sir Walter, 186, 198
Seale, Patrick, 52
Segev, Tom, 15
Sempad, 63
Sezincote, 132
Shaaban, Bouthaina, 35
Shahbandar, Abdul Rahman, 29
Shahrur, Muhammad, 42-49
Shainin, Jonathan, 13, 15-16
Shalit, Yoram, 51-52
Shamma', Bushra, 71-72, 73
Shammas, Anton, 8, 11, 211
Sharif Pasha, 81
Shaw, George Bernard, 201
al-Shaykh, Hanan, 208
Shehada, Carmela, 6
Shehadi, Nadim, 34
Shemlan (Middle East Centre for Arab Studies), 68-69, 72, 166
Shendi, 93-94
Shibeika, Mekki, 88
Shinnie, Ama, 151, 152
Shinnie, Margaret, 151, 152

245

Shinnie, Peter, 109, 150-153
Shissler, A Holly, 53-54
Silifke, 60, 61
Simmons, Jack, 152
Sis (Kozan), 59, 61, 62, 64-65
Skarmeta, Antonio, 177
Slatin, Rudolf, 93
Smooha, Sammy, 10
Snyder, Carl, 179
Socotra, 117, 150, 152
Soueif, Ahdaf, 19-20, 162, 207
Stack, Sir Lee, 112
Stark, Freya, 26-31, 119, 215, 221
Steevens, G W, 90
Streatham, 134
Stubbs, William, Bishop, 62
Suakin, 78, 109-110
Sulaiman, Jamal, 172
Sulaiman Pasha Niyazi, 81, 82
Surkab (Surgham), 94, 98, 99, 100, 101
Sururab, 94
Sylhet, 130

Talbot Rice, David, 144
Tamir, Zakaria, 208
Tarsus, 59, 66
Taymur, Mahmud, 148, 234
Tebbitt, Norman, 235
Tel Barak, 217
Terry, Alice, 201
Thelwall, Robin, 151-152
Theobald, A B, 105
Thesiger, Wilfred, 119, 123-124
Thomas, Bertram, 123
Thubron, Colin, 119
Thumrait, 125

al-Tilib, Hamad, 83
Toynbee, Arnold, 147
Trollope, Anthony, 133
Tsirkas, Stratis, 209-210
Tunis, 204
Tuqan, Fadwa, 10
al-Turabi, Hasan, 90

Udwan, Mamduh, 177-178
al-Ujaili, Abd al-Salam, 157-158
Umm Dibaykarat, 90, 102
Umm Kulthum, 203
Urabi Pasha, 3, 68, 81, 82
al-Urayyid, Ibrahim, 207
Ustinov, Peter, 218

Vahka, 65
Valentino, Rudolph, 201
Van Dam, Nicolaos, 52
Verdi, Giuseppe, 86
Victoria, Queen, 129
Victoria College, Alexandria, 28
Vizetelly, Frank, 83
Vryonis, Spero, 56

Wadi Halfa, 93
Waghorne, Neil, 136
Wahba, Magdi, 161
Wannus, Sa'dallah, 72, 170-172, 231-232
Warner, Philip, 91
Watenpaugh, Heghmar Zeitlian, 36-37
Wauchope, Brigadier General Arthur, 98
Waugh, Evelyn, 154
Weissbrod, Lilly, 13-15

Wells, H G, 183
Wheeler, Sir Mortimer, 150
Whitty, Ken, 166
Wild, J W, 134
William IV, King, 132-133
Williams, Andy, 172
Wimbledon, 135
Winckler, Onn, 50
Wingate, Sir Reginald, 88, 91, 92,
    93, 97, 102
Woking Mosque, 134
Wolseley, General Sir Garnet, 105
Woolley, Katherine, 215, 218
Woolley, Sir Leonard, 150, 215,
    221
Wren, Sir Christopher, 132
Wright, Gail and David, 70
Wright, William, 132

Yabrud, 71
Yacine, Kateb, 206
Yakhlif, Yahya, 10
Ya'qub, 87, 96, 98, 102
Yeoman, Martin, 117-118
Yılan Kalesi, 66, 57
Yuasi, Nobuyuki, 228-229

Zabel, 62
Zabid, 193, 194, 195-197, 198
Zakaria, Benotto, 60
Zayed, Sheikh, 122
Ziegler, Philip, 91